FREE SCHOOLS, FREE PEOPLE

FREE SCHOOLS, FREE PEOPLE

Education and Democracy After the 1960s

RON MILLER

State University
of New York
Press

Published by
State University of New York Press, Albany

Printed in the United States of America

For information, address State University of New York Press,
90 State Street, Suite 700, Albany, NY 12207

Production by Susan Geraghty
Marketing by Michael Campochiaro

Library of Congress Cataloging-in-Publication Data

Miller, Ron, 1956–
Free schools, free people : education and democracy after the 1960s / by Ron Miller.
p. cm.
Includes bibliographical references and index.
ISBN 0-7914-5419-3 (alk. paper) — ISBN 0-7914-5420-7 (pbk. : alk. paper)
1. Education—Social aspects—United States—History—20th century. 2. Free schools—United States—History—20th century. 3. Holt, John Caldwell, 1923– I. Title.

LC191.4 .M55 2002
371.04′0973—dc21

2001049355

10 9 8 7 6 5 4 3 2 1

CONTENTS

PREFACE

Most scholarship on education in American culture focuses on public schooling. Historians, sociologists, and policy analysts have been primarily concerned with the social and political forces that shape public education. Researchers have concentrated on instructional techniques, decision-making practices, issues of behavior management, and school climate within the context of publicly funded, state-operated schools. This emphasis is understandable, given the massive resources committed to public education and the numerous political conflicts that surround the allocation of these resources. The vast majority of young people in the United States attend public, not private, schools. Moreover, since the time of Thomas Jefferson, the American experiment in democratic government has been linked in many people's minds to the success of public schooling.

However, a critical interpretive study of American culture has much to learn from dissenting educational movements in American history. Public schooling has reified particular notions of "education," "teaching," "learning," "knowledge," and other important domains of personal and social life at the expense of other possibilities. Public and professional discourse on education generally assumes that "education" means the transmission of a politically sanctioned "curriculum," requiring the efficient management of students' behavior and objective assessment of their academic achievement. These assumptions reflect a particular worldview, which might be termed "modernist" or (as in this study) "technocratic," and so long as the assumptions are taken for granted, the worldview is accepted tacitly and uncritically. Of course students should be separated into grade levels and ability groups; of course they should study clearly defined subjects and read officially approved textbooks; of course they should receive Ritalin if they cannot sit still or be retained if their test scores are inadequate—all these practices make perfect sense, from within a worldview that sees the natural world, and human abilities, as exploitable resources at the service of a vast economic enterprise. However, by viewing educational practices from the perspective of radical or "romantic" dissidents who reject the reified assumptions of public schooling, it is possible to step outside the modernist-technocratic worldview and explore other ways of understanding nature and human nature. It becomes possible to raise critical questions about the cultural matrix (what anthropologist Clifford Geertz called a "web of meaning") that ultimately gives rise to the economic, political, and educational systems of American society.

I am interested in the free school movement of the 1960s because it raised these questions so explicitly and so poignantly. For a few short years, American culture was shaken to its foundations, as wave after wave of protest and critique called into question previously sacrosanct assumptions about the nature of the good life in the modern world. The possibility of full-scale cultural transformation was greatly diminished by a popular and political backlash, and in the thirty years since the end of the 1960s the worldview of modernism has tightened its hold, not only on American culture but on an emerging global monoculture. This is dramatically evident in educational policy and practice, with a seemingly invincible movement toward state-mandated standards, rigorous testing, and a pervasive emphasis on management and control.

I am personally committed to a worldview that is more humanistic or holistic, a worldview that honors the spiritual, ecological, and existential dimensions of life and does not subsume human existence under a consuming economic materialism. My previous work, both scholarly and practical, has focused on the development of a holistic definition of education, and I have defined "holistic education" broadly, including not only the small number of "new age" or "new paradigm" thinkers of recent years who coined the term but also previous generations of educational dissidents who rejected the notion that education means solely the harnessing of human energies to the corporate economic system. The writers and teachers who conceived what I am here calling "free school ideology" did not often explicitly address spirituality, and their ideas have often been neglected in "new paradigm" versions of holistic education, which find mystics like Rudolf Steiner and Maria Montessori more congenial. Even in my own earlier work I was quick to portray educators like John Holt as more "libertarian" than "holistic" because of their apparent emphasis on an egoistic notion of freedom. But as I hope this study will make clear, neither Holt nor most of his colleagues were merely libertarians; their critique of authority and hierarchy aimed to reclaim the possibility of personal authenticity that lies at the heart of all holistic conceptions of education. Holistic educators do not all agree on what constitutes the "true self," but we do all agree that the competitive, materialistic, self-aggrandizing persona of the modern worker/consumer/voter is certainly not it! This, essentially, is what the free schoolers were trying to tell American society.

This study refers frequently to the "existential" quality of experience, particularly in contrast to "technocratic" definitions of human possibility. The opposition of these terms contains the core of my argument. Like the advocates of countercultural ideologies in the 1960s, I believe that human life is fulfilling and meaningful only when it embraces the embodied, emotional, moral, ecological, intellectual, and spiritual dimensions of experience that arise organically in our day-to-day lives. Human beings are multifaceted organisms, and our lives are whole and integrated only when all these dimensions are recognized and given some avenue of expression. By "existential" I refer to a conscious recognition and valuing of this organic experience—a deliberate search for meaning (purpose, identity, aspiration, a guiding set of ideals . . .). I am saying that meaning arises most fully from a person's conscious and active engagement with other people, with history and culture, and with the natural world. This quality of engagement is what the existentialist philosophers meant by *authenticity*. "Technocracy," on the other hand, is a conception of human possibilities that seeks to discipline and limit experience to make it conform to the routines of the assembly line, the bureaucracy, and procedures dictated by the machine and the clock. The individual is valued as a functional component of an impersonal, efficient system that is managed by experts and elites.

I think it is evident that modern educational practices serve technocracy, not existential authenticity. As Thoreau put it at the dawn of the modern industrial era, schooling "makes a straight cut ditch of a free meandering brook," a sentiment that other anarchist and romantic dissidents, especially the free schoolers of the 1960s, echoed through the years. This is an apt metaphor: the difference between a mechanically formed ditch and a naturally occurring brook precisely reflects the difference between technocracy's emphasis on control, technique, and abstraction, and a countercultural interest in existential freedom and organic wholeness. Technocracy's ditches are artificial—they are rationally planned, efficiently executed, and objectively evaluated—while the free-flowing waters of human life bubble and gush spontaneously, bringing aesthetic, emotional, and spiritual novelty to refresh and renew experience. Free school ideology sought to reclaim these life-giving waters.

The opening of several hundred free schools—educational sites completely independent of the public school system—represented a remarkable outburst of radical educational dissent. Between the mid-1960s and early 1970s thousands of young educators, parents, and students themselves explicitly rejected the assumptions, aims, and methods of conventional schooling and embarked on experimental attempts to reclaim authenticity, freedom, and wholeness. The literature of radical educational critique in the 1960s effectively deconstructed solidly entrenched assumptions about the nature of teaching, learning, and knowledge. Although the resurgence of mainstream cultural values rapidly banished this critique to obscurity, it remains potent and relevant to the educational challenges of an emerging postmodern culture.

Many of the transformative values of the 1960s, from gender and race relations to environmental consciousness to a heightened interest in spirituality, holistic medicine, and organic agriculture, are gradually working their way into the culture despite fierce resistance from conservative quarters. However, education lags far behind these developments, largely because federal and state governments and corporate interests have deliberately used educational institutions to promote a modernist discourse concerned with economic growth, global competition, and individual material success. The 1983 publication of *A Nation at Risk* by President Reagan's National Commission on Excellence in Education, followed by other widely publicized reports issued by influential agencies and foundations, strongly reinforced technocratic approaches to schooling at the expense of radical democratic alternatives. The religious Right, as well, has focused much of its cultural critique on perceived liberalization in education. Consequently, even as the medical profession, to take one example, began to accept acupuncture, biofeedback, and meditation, and books by holistic doctors, humanistic management gurus, and Buddhist meditation teachers have reached the best-seller list, educational policies retreated (perhaps one could say *recoiled*) from humanistic alternatives that emerged during the 1960s and 1970s. Authors who were respected and even fashionable for a brief historical moment (the subjects of this book) have been almost entirely forgotten, replaced by such traditionalists as E. D. Hirsch, William Bennett, and Chester Finn. Nevertheless, if there is an evolving cultural trend toward postmodern values, then education cannot indefinitely lag behind other social institutions. If the personalist, radical democratic critique expressed during the 1960s continues to inform protests against technocratic global capitalism, then sooner or later the free school literature will be rediscovered. This study is my modest contribution to that rediscovery.

I acknowledge from the start that I am sympathetic to the aims of the radical educators. This book is not intended to be a disinterested scholarly account but a provocative appeal to reconsider ideas that I believe are neglected. However, this is no mere polemic, either (as is much of the free school literature): I hope to provide a substantive historical and intellectual foundation for an educational ideology that for too long has simply been dismissed as "romantic." I have attempted to read the literature and original sources of the free school movement fairly and critically, and I deliberately bring in a broader perspective—Deweyan progressivism—to look at this ideology on terms other than its own. Still, my method is primarily phenomenological: I want to understand free school ideology as an expression of values, beliefs, and experiences that were *lived* by a particular group of people at a particular moment in history. Undoubtedly, this ideology was shaped in part by social and demographic factors such as socioeconomic class, age, ethnicity, and the like, but its content cannot be reduced to these causes. In this study I am not concerned so much with sociological facts as with the existential *meaning* of a radical educational vision that once moved thousands of people.

I have tried to achieve a workable balance between passion and scholarship, although I am aware that readers may or may not be satisfied with this balance according to their own perspectives on the issues involved. If my objectivity and critical analysis fall short of some readers' expectations, I hope they will bear in mind that my aim is not to dissect the subject matter but to rescue it from an undeserved obscurity. I wish to place it back on the table for public discourse, so that scholars might critique it seriously, educators might find inspiration for resisting the tide of standardization, and citizens might be informed that there are, indeed, alternative ways of conceiving the meanings of *education*, *teaching*, and *learning*. I am convinced that the moral idealism and democratic vision of those who promoted the free school movement can show us a way out of the sterile authoritarianism that permeates our educational policies today.

I would like to thank Dr. Bruce Schulman, director of the American and New England Studies Program at Boston University, and Dr. Richard Gibboney, professor emeritus of education at the University of Pennsylvania, for guiding me through this project. Dr. Schulman made it possible for me to complete my doctoral work in American Studies after a twelve-year hiatus during which my status was, as we say, "abd." I asked to return to BU after being encouraged by Dr. Polly Young-Eisendrath to complete this unfinished business in my life. I had quit the program when my original dissertation, written in 1986–87, was deemed unsuitable for academic purposes; interestingly, though, it has since become my most successful and influential book, *What Are Schools For? Holistic Education in American Culture*. Although this study, my second dissertation, did make the grade academically, I hope that enough of my passion has come through to make it an interesting and useful book as well.

The major collection of original free school materials is the New Schools Exchange papers in the Manuscripts and Archives department of the Sterling Memorial Library, Yale University. Tom Hyry arranged my visit there, and the entire staff was most helpful. Patrick Farenga and Susannah Sheffer, who have kept John Holt's vision and his organization,

Growing Without Schooling, thriving in the years since Holt's death, assisted my inquiry into his work and permitted me to quote from documents and publications in their care. Dr. Len Solo shared his extensive collection of documents from the Teacher Drop-Out Center, which he later donated to the progressive education collection at the University of Vermont library. I am grateful to Dr. Solo and to others who agreed to be interviewed for this study: Patrick Farenga, Susannah Sheffer, Jerry Mintz, Mary Leue, Jack Spicer, Allen Graubard, Madelin Colbert, and Bill Ayers. Don Glines and Joe Nathan provided useful insights through the mail. Tate Hausman, a student at Brown University, contacted me while writing his senior thesis on the free school movement, and shared many of his findings, including tapes of interviews he had conducted.

Last but not least, I am very grateful to my wife, Jennie, and to our sons Justin, Daniel, and Robin, for their encouragement and for understanding my need to burrow in the library and in my office for hours at a time. The questions and struggles discussed in this book have remained very much alive for Jennie and me as we've tried to provide our boys an authentic and nurturing education. I believe the questions are vital and the struggle is worth the effort.

ABOUT THE AUTHOR

Ron Miller has written or edited six previous books on the history and philosophy of educational alternatives, most recently *Caring for New Life: Essays on Holistic Education* (2000, Foundation for Educational Renewal). He has founded two journals, *Holistic Education Review* (now *Encounter: Education for Meaning and Social Justice*) and *Paths of Learning*, and was co-founder of the Bellwether School near Burlington, Vermont. He is on the faculty of the Off-campus Teacher Education Program at Goddard College.

CHAPTER 1

Cultural Context of the Free School Movement

American culture is not yet finished with the legacy of the 1960s. During the turbulent years within and surrounding that decade, an unprecedented uprising of popular discontent challenged many deeply established values and practices in American society, including racial segregation, the authority of government and academic institutions, and even the core values underlying industrial capitalism. Mass movements of African American citizens, university and high school students, and alienated young people, reinforced by the liberated voices of radical social critics, called for a greater social commitment to justice, freedom, and democracy in a modern world they saw becoming increasingly authoritarian, exploitative, and existentially sterile. They demonstrated in the streets, disrupted campuses, published underground newspapers, and developed an alternative lifestyle—a *counterculture*—involving Asian religious practices, communal living, hallucinogenic drugs, and rebellious, intoxicating styles of music. Although this outburst of protest and dissent failed to bring about the "revolution" that many envisioned, it left a complex legacy of cultural change that continues, to this day, to pose radical alternatives to the dominant economic, political, and social forces of the modern world.

Some elements of 1960s-era dissent have changed American culture significantly. The women's movement, an aggressive environmentalism, and new attitudes toward racial and cultural diversity and human rights were influenced by the ideals of protesters and visionaries of that time. "Postmodern" understandings in many fields of inquiry, a popular movement for "human potential" and spiritual renewal, and more fluid attitudes toward social and sexual mores have also entered modern culture as a result of the disruptions of the 1960s. To be sure, these cultural openings are not universally applauded: they are generally welcomed by those who identify themselves as "progressive," but they are stridently condemned by defenders of traditional values as a deplorable slide into immorality and anarchy, and the contention between these groups is described by some as a "culture war." Resistance to countercultural or postmodern values takes many forms, from well-funded conservative foundations and think tanks, to Bill Clinton's impeachment saga, to the juggernaut of corporate globalization. One arena in which the dominant culture has so far effectively suppressed radical change is the institution of schooling.

The protest movements of the 1960s included a vibrant, idealistic, and for a short time quite widely spread movement advocating a radical democratic vision of education, but this movement evaporated quickly and, outside of a small, marginal group of dedicated visionaries, its ideals have been abandoned. Ironically, the critique of public schooling helped provoke later developments, such as the homeschooling movement, voucher plans, and charter schools, which often reinforce traditional educational goals and beliefs even while seeking new forms for their expression, as well as a powerful backlash in the shape of the crusade for higher standards and stricter accountability. As I hope to show in this book, the radical democratic vision remains viable, awaiting rediscovery whenever cultural conditions become more favorable, but for the time being conservative forces hold the upper hand in the educational sector of the culture war.

Education is the social institution in which a culture makes its core values and vision of the future most explicit, and when there is significant cultural tension, there must inevitably be controversy over educational ideology and practice. Between the 1830s, when Horace Mann, Henry Barnard, William Seward, and other respected leaders organized state systems of common schools, and the dissent of the 1960s, Americans placed great faith in public education; despite frequent struggles over particular educational questions and regular crusades to reform school structures, Americans of all major political persuasions saw public education as a necessary and vital element of their democratic society. They supported, indeed celebrated, the existence of public schools—a system of education funded and controlled by the democratic state. The dissent of the 1960s dared to question this faith. The institutions of liberal democracy in general lost legitimacy and authority in the 1960s, and nowhere is this more evident than in the vital cultural function of education. Between 1960 and 1972, a dissenting *educational* ideology emerged from the countercultural movement and sparked a multifaceted reassessment of the practices as well as the effectiveness of public schooling.

Within a pervasive climate of alienation and protest, educators, high school students, and even parents took a closer and more critical look at their schools, and many of them were so disillusioned by what they found that they fled from public education entirely. Starting in the early 1960s, and increasingly after 1967, thousands of Americans became involved in "free schools"—small educational communities that were free from state control and the values of corporate capitalism, personalistic enclaves in which every child, and every teacher, was free to think, feel, dream, and engage in interactions according to their own authentic needs and passions. Free schools brought together small groups (generally around twenty to forty people) of families and idealistic young educators who, in the spirit of the time, believed that learning should be intimate, spontaneous, and joyful—specifically not controlled by textbooks, curricula, instructional methods, or rigid rules of behavior. Free schools had no use for grading, testing, or hierarchical authority, and they represented a shared desire to make learning relevant and responsive to the lively social and political issues of the day.

Since most of these experiments were ephemeral or reclusive (many were both), it is difficult to know for certain how many of these schools were begun; estimates range from 400 to well over 800. Nevertheless, the historical significance of the free school movement lies more in the nature of the phenomenon than in its precise scope. I am not attempting in this book to present solid sociological data, but to interpret the intellectual and cultural meaning of an educational ideology that moved thousands of Americans to abandon a long-established faith in democratic public schooling.

The free school movement should be distinguished from other alternative forms of education. Free school ideology was explicitly countercultural; that is, it sought to educate children and young adults according to a set of attitudes, values, and beliefs in direct opposition to those of the predominant culture. The people attracted to free schools consciously rejected the defining institutions and practices of American society—corporate capitalism and all that it entailed, from the traditional work ethic to competition to advertising; the authority of the state, especially as it was exercised in waging the war in Vietnam; and even, ultimately, the personality type that seemed to be valued by modern mass society, the rational, "well-adjusted" citizen and consumer. Free school ideology was utopian; participants in this movement believed that in their tiny enclaves they could escape the influence of modern culture and begin building a new society founded on values of love, joy, passion, freedom, and spontaneity. For them, education should not serve the interests of the state or the economic system, but should instead be entirely devoted to the happiness of the individuals who lived, loved, and played within each intimate community.

Radical educators had made similar claims in the past, particularly since the time of Rousseau and Pestalozzi in the latter part of the eighteenth century. A small number of schools were started by various romantic and anarchist educators in the United States between the early nineteenth and mid-twentieth centuries. But the ideals of freedom, authenticity, and joy had not sparked a significant educational movement until a group of writings published between 1960 and the mid-1970s sharply attacked the repressive practices of modern schooling and proclaimed that radical change was necessary. These writings constitute the core of what I am calling "free school ideology." The most influential of these works was A. S. Neill's *Summerhill: A Radical Approach to Child Rearing*, published in 1960. This account of a British libertarian school inspired the founding of the earliest endeavors of the free school movement in the United States; the Summerhill Society was the first network to give that generation of radical educators a forum for expressing and exchanging ideas. The writings of Paul Goodman, particularly *Growing Up Absurd* (1960) and *Compulsory Miseducation* (1964), argued that modern schooling offered a sterile, stultifying education and should be largely deinstitutionalized. In 1964, the appearance of *How Children Fail* established John Holt as a highly influential critic who went on to publish numerous articles in popular and professional magazines and books such as *How Children Learn* (1967), *The Underachieving School* (1969), *What Do I Do Monday?* (1970), *Freedom and Beyond* (1972), and *Instead of Education* (1976). Jonathan Kozol provided a more explicit political critique of schooling in *Death at an Early Age* (1967), *Free Schools* (1972), and *The Night is Dark and I am Far from Home* (1975). George Dennison's *The Lives of Children* (1969), Herbert Kohl's *36 Children* (1967), James Herndon's *The Way it Spozed to Be* (1969) and *How to Survive in Your Native Land* (1971), and Neil Postman and Charles Weingartner's *Teaching as a Subversive Activity* (1969) were other influential works.

After 1967, the passionate educational critique presented in these writings, coupled with the emergence of the youth counterculture, led to a rapid increase in the number of free schools being established across the United States. By 1969, people involved in these schools recognized that they were part of a significant grassroots movement. Conferences attracted hundreds of participants. Numerous newsletters and clearinghouses, both regional and national, were established; in particular, the *New Schools Exchange Newsletter* and the Teacher Drop-Out Center served as central sources of news, ideas, and information. Universities, foundations, and public school systems acknowledged the existence of a national educational crisis that demanded some form of drastic educational innovation, if not free schools; Holt and Goodman were even called to testify before an education subcommittee of the U.S. House of Representatives. Yet by 1972 the free school movement began to fade. The radical educators, like many young people in the larger counterculture, had spent most of their rebellious energy and found they had little patience for gradual social renewal. American society as a whole rebuffed the radical critique, using various strategies including police and military force, political opposition (such as the election and reelection of Richard Nixon), and sublimation of countercultural energies into more manageable forms (in the case of education, free schools gave way to public "alternative" schools).

Nevertheless, despite its short duration, the free school movement had a lasting impact on educational politics in the United States. The core of free school ideology was essentially antinomian and libertarian, and although this anti-authoritarian position was presented within the context of the New Left's romantic, utopian vision of participatory democracy, it proved to be highly compatible with the classical liberal doctrine of laissez-faire individualism, a doctrine which, in the hands of such theorists as John Stuart Mill, Herbert Spencer, Murray Rothbard, and Milton Friedman, fundamentally opposed state-sponsored education. Once the idea of educational alternatives and family choice entered popular discourse, libertarian notions such as vouchers and other forms of privatization gained popular support. Free schools largely disappeared, but in their place appeared the phenomenon of homeschooling, and although Ivan Illich and John Holt, the early champions of deschooling, were romantic, radical democrats, the homeschooling movement has primarily attracted extreme social and religious conservatives who reject the authority of the liberal state. It is ironic that the New Left and many free schoolers were influenced, at least indirectly, by the democratic theory of John Dewey, yet a major legacy of free school ideology is a significant social movement deliberately and strenuously opposed to Dewey's social vision.

Consequently, the free school movement marked the decline of the national consensus in support of public schooling. According to David Tyack and Elisabeth Hansot, until the mid-twentieth century the common school was treated as an "official agency for defining and creating citizenship"; public education was revered as "an almost sacred institution, the nearest equivalent in our constitutional order to an established church." Public school leaders could confidently assume that they represented universal American values because significant subcultures such as the Catholic community were effectively marginalized. But during the twentieth century, according to Joseph Kirschner, more severe social problems brought about "an increasingly frantic search for educational panaceas," and "by the end of the 1960s the idea of a national mission for public schooling had disappeared. . . . Gone was a belief that public schools could shape a virtuous citizenry." The result, wrote Tyack and Hansot, was that the "closed system of school governance" was shaken by divisive political forces. "From outside the system angry protest movements have arisen, as groups defined by basic social cleavages of race, sex, and class have become newly conscious of their separate interests, interests they no longer are willing to have the experts define." This marked "the end of an era when school leaders had hoped that education could remain above politics." No longer the equivalent to an established church, public education after the 1960s became a primary target for cultural dissent.[1]

Given the rich mixture of social, political, and educational forces that gave rise to the free school movement as well as its ambiguous legacy, it is remarkable that few scholars have studied it seriously. A few articles and chapters, by scholars such as Lawrence Cremin, Joseph Kirschner, Stuart Rosenfeld, and Henry J. Perkinson, are scattered in the professional literature, all published between 1973 and 1981, and provide only brief treatments of this complex topic. There is only one book on the movement as a whole, Allen Graubard's *Free the Children: Radical Reform and the Free School Movement* (1974), and although the author did offer an insightful and coherent analysis, he was an activist involved in free schools himself and did not provide the historical perspective that I am attempting here. The few other existing books on free schools took narrow views of the subject: sociologist Ann Swidler examined a handful of schools for her study of anti-authoritarian school policy, *Organization Without Authority: Dilemmas of Social Control in Free Schools* (1979), while philosopher Robin Barrow focused exclusively on the logical flaws of libertarian educational ideology in his *Radical Education: A Critique of Freeschooling and Deschooling* (1978). Most educational historians treat the free school movement as largely irrelevant to the major social and political controversies over public education in the twentieth century. For example, Diane Ravitch discusses it on a handful of pages in her 330-page *The Troubled Crusade: American Education 1945–1980* (1983), and suggests that the mass media overemphasized its importance. This neglect of the free school movement seems similar to the way that general American history texts, according to Bruce J. Schulman, have neglected or dismissed the importance of the New Left and counterculture as being a significant "alternative to liberal consensus."[2]

One might expect historians of political and cultural radicalism in the 1960s to be interested in the free school movement, but writers such as Todd Gitlin, Terry Anderson, and Doug Rossinow, whom I found especially valuable for interpreting the counterculture as a whole, mention free schools only in passing (Rossinow devotes exactly one page out of 345 in *The Politics of Authenticity* [1998] to the free school that was founded in the community he was studying intensively). It seems that nearly all historians of this era have overlooked the radical critique of education below the university level.

A number of educators and scholars concerned with alternative educational approaches in a more general sense have discussed the free school movement through the lenses of their own interests. For example, Terrence E. Deal and Robert R. Nolan edited a collection of writings on emerging alternatives in *public* education, and some of the authors reflected on the free school movement as one source of these alternatives (*Alternative Schools: Ideologies, Realities, Guidelines*, 1978). In contrast, educational historian Joel Spring described the philosophical roots of anarchist educational thought in the nineteenth and twentieth centuries and commented that the very term "free schools" was in use decades before the 1960s (*Wheels in the Head: Educational Philosophies of Authority, Freedom, and Culture from Socrates to Paulo Freire*, 1994). Similarly, in my own earlier work (*What Are Schools For? Holistic Education in American Culture*, 1990) I briefly reviewed the radical literature of the 1960s in order to demonstrate that it belonged to an ongoing countercultural tradition I identified as "holistic." These studies demonstrate that the components of free school ideology were not original or novel. As I will explain in Chapter Four, several radical educational experiments preceded the free school movement. As well, during the same period that free school ideology was developed, a number of innovative and nationally recognized educators with strong roots in Deweyan progressive education, including J. Lloyd Trump, John Goodlad, Don Glines, and Vito Perrone, were proposing and sometimes implementing radical changes in public schools. Glines later claimed that had their programs been widely adopted, there would have been little need for free schools.

However, as I hope to demonstrate here, free school ideology represented a distinctive educational movement that cannot simply be lumped with other expressions of pedagogical dissent. Within the unique context of the 1960s counterculture, the free school movement involved a cultural and political critique that recognized that mainstream public schooling would not and *could not* be radically transformed. No previous study has provided a thorough account of the cultural, social, and intellectual dimensions of the free school phenomenon. This book is an effort to provide just such an account, and by the end I aim to differentiate free school ideology quite clearly from other forms of alternative, progressive, or holistic education.

ORIGINS OF THE FREE SCHOOL MOVEMENT

The free school phenomenon rested on the perception, shared by many thousands of young people, that "America had run out of dreams. . . .

The great vision of opportunity and wealth for all, the magnificent ideal of freedom—these dreams could no longer hold America together. The romance was over; the lies behind the dreams were beginning to glare in the ever-present media floodlights."[3] This description, written not by a radical propagandist but by a journalist looking at urban public schools in the late 1960s, captures the sense of disillusionment that gave rise to the counterculture as a whole and to free schools in particular. The root causes of radical dissent in the 1960s were psychological and personal as much as cultural and political: many young people experienced dissatisfaction with the norms of American culture and embarked on a quest for personal meaning, social justice, and what they felt to be liberation from cultural repression. Often this quest was sparked by awareness of a particular issue, such as racial injustice or the escalation of the Vietnam War, but students and young people soon understood these issues in a larger context that raised deeply troubling questions about the very foundations of their society. Dissent in the 1960s was fueled by disillusionment with the very nature of modern political and social institutions; the young radicals were not calling for minor shifts of government policy, a redistribution of wealth, or special favors for particular interest groups, but for a drastic, holistic renewal of the culture itself.

The romance was over. The dreams, the ideology, the worldview that had sustained American culture for nearly 200 years were perceived by many people to be inadequate. It is no small matter for a culture to "run out of dreams," for this requires people to disown long-cherished values and assumptions, and imagine new ones to guide their lives. Sociologist Todd Gitlin, himself a leading activist in the 1960s, reflected in a later retrospective that the social movements of that time "forced upon us central issues for Western civilization—fundamental questions of value, fundamental divides of culture, fundamental debates about the nature of the good life." He argued that these vitally important central issues led students to begin questioning the legitimacy of established institutions and authority, and out of these "subversive questions" came a decade of "picket lines, sit-ins, a vast entangled web of organizations, collectives, publications, conferences, a great storm of nonnegotiable demands and radical caucuses and participatory democracy."[4] The free school movement occurred when it did, and in its own distinctive manner, as a result of these "fundamental questions of value."

Why did so many young people reach this point of political and cultural dissent in the 1960s? Why was their disillusionment so much more severe, widespread, demonstrative, and politically charged than the rebellious search for identity most generations experience upon coming of age? It is true, as some observers point out, that the young people of the 1960s had been raised in a more liberal, permissive atmosphere thanks to prosperity and new attitudes about child development; it is true as well that due to the postwar "baby boom," there were much larger masses of young people in the population, and when they gathered on university campuses they became conscious of their unique identity and power as a generation. These demographic factors no doubt contributed to the particular shape of the 1960s counterculture. However, they do not explain the nature of the cultural upheaval that occurred. The historical setting for radical protest was fashioned by a complex interaction of political, sociological, technological, and demographic factors that all converged at a particular moment in time.[5] The result of this convergence was a widespread perception that the core, defining myth of American culture—faith in the essential goodness and rightness of the American experiment in democracy—was inadequate for dealing with the troubling events that were taking place during the mid-twentieth century.

Observers such as Godfrey Hodgson and Richard N. Goodwin, who have taken a broad view of American society at this time, seem to agree that in the 1950s and early 1960s most Americans clung to an "illusion" (they both use this term) that the United States was uniquely able to develop into a near-utopian society due to its democratic ideals and its prowess in science, technology, and industry. There was a widely shared consensus about the virtue of corporate capitalism and the American system of government; liberalism was solidly connected to the political and economic establishment, and criticism from the Left, intellectually and politically active in the 1930s, was almost nonexistent. Nevertheless, this optimism and confidence were masks for layers of anxiety: despite unprecedented prosperity, Americans were still haunted by memories of the Great Depression, apparently interrupted only by wartime mobilization, and now they were haunted as well by the atomic bomb and the threat of nuclear annihilation, which loomed in the background of daily life during the cold war. By the 1960s illusion dramatically gave way to disillusionment.

Various historical accounts have suggested that during the years after World War II this lingering sense of anxiety, and efforts to avoid or overcome it such as the crusade against communist influences, produced cultural stagnation and conformity. A few astute observers of the time, particularly Paul Goodman, as well as later historians, have pointed to the existential discomfort of sensitive youths of the 1950s, who experienced this stagnation as oppressive and alienating and began a search for existential authenticity that contributed directly to the explosion of dissent in the 1960s. Goodwin recalled how the anxieties of the 1950s intruded into his own successful career. A top student at Harvard Law School, he dropped out in 1954 to join the Army as a protest "against a structure of rational expectations. . . . I had to get away. Some vacancy at the heart demanded response." Surely a certain number of romantic youths in any generation will experience this pull, but in retrospect Goodwin specifically interpreted his "vacancy at the heart" as an "augury" of "the sixties."[6]

The culture of the 1950s was particularly unsatisfying to those who sought a fuller, deeper sense of meaning than that which material prosperity alone could offer, and the anti-communist crusades in government and academia had a chilling effect on political and intellectual arenas where new meaning might be generated. Where liberals (including, we should note, progressive educators) in the years before the war had begun to address the failure of competitive individualism and corporate capitalism to achieve a just, equitable society, in the 1950s and early 1960s mainstream liberals found it wise to support the established system and seek only modest, technical means to improve it. Daniel Bell and other liberals identified the new consensus in support of American institutions as the "end of ideology," but as even they sometimes realized, when the creative conflict of social visions and political ideals is replaced by values of efficiency, rationality, standardization, and managerial expertise, then democracy has given way to *technocracy*—a social order that maintains stability and control by fitting human "resources" into appropriate, predefined institutional niches. The counterculture of the 1960s, including the free school movement, was essentially a rebellion against the triumph of technocracy over the ideals of democracy.

The rebellion against technocracy was not only a political movement, but an existential search to fill the "vacancy at the heart" caused by an overly complacent, materialist society. Exorcising the demons of the Great Depression, the nation celebrated economic growth in the 1950s by embracing values of materialism, consumerism, and conformity to the norms of corporate capitalism. Advertising and the increasingly ubiquitous media of radio and television promoted a "mass" society—a sweeping uniformity of ideas and an uncritical consumerism stimulated by mass production. Large institutions, in government, business, and education, grew even larger and more complex, threatening to erode self-reliance, local community, and small scale enterprise. As local enterprises increasingly gave way to national corporations manipulating a mass market, human relations became less personal and more functional, and even individual identity was shaped less by the need for self-reliance and more by opportunities to act in the role of consumer. As David Farber has suggested, this was a significant change.[7] Although the pursuit of economic goods appeared to satisfy most Americans, a number of artists and intellectuals (notably the Beat writers), and later inquisitive students, found these materialistic values inauthentic and stultifying. As we will see, observers such as Paul Goodman and Edgar Z. Friedenberg pointedly argued that young people could find no meaningful sense of self in a mass consumer culture.

Mass society represented a transformation from *organic* to *artificial* forms of community life. Bonnie Barrett Stretch, a journalist who described the free school movement in 1970, identified its roots precisely in this transformation. She pointed out that in earlier times, children were educated through continual contact with adults and the daily life of the community. "Today," she wrote, "the society has lost this organic unity. We live in times when children often see their fathers only on weekends. We live in a world that separates work from play, school from the 'real' world, childhood from personhood. The young are isolated from participation in the community. They seem to have no integral place in the culture." Stretch observed that schools had become "artificial environments created by adults for children."[8] The separation of education from the adult world—the "real" world—reflected the breakdown of a whole, integrated culture into functional parts. Where an organic culture supplies a rich sense of meaning to the new generation by involving young people in its activities, a fragmented and artificial culture isolates its youths, producing a sense of alienation.

In addition to Goodman and Friedenberg, other social critics of the late 1950s and early 1960s, such as Jules Henry, Herbert Marcuse, Erich Fromm, Lewis Mumford, C. Wright Mills, Theodore Roszak, Norman O. Brown, and others, decried the increasing fragmentation and artificiality of modern culture. They warned that an unprecedented centralization of economic power and intellectual influence was beginning to produce a technologically driven, conformist society hostile to individuality and the values of genuine democracy. They emphasized that the nature of work was being changed by "automation" (technological sophistication): there were fewer jobs for uneducated youths, so more of them remained in school (high school and college) than ever before—and as students they continued to be treated as dependent children, whereas in earlier generations most people their age would already have been earning independent livings and starting families. According to these critics, the end of ideology and rise of technocracy—what historian Terry H. Anderson has called the "cold war culture"—did in fact foster an existentially deadening conformity and a repressive intellectual and political discipline.

These trends were not new in the 1950s; industrialization, technology, and the rise of the United States as a global military power had been changing American culture since the beginning of the twentieth century. Early in the century intellectuals such as Herbert Croly, Walter Lippmann, and John Dewey were considering whether or not the ideals of

Jeffersonian democracy were still relevant in a complex technological society that more and more seemed to demand central management by specially trained professionals. However, after the end of the Second World War, the transformation of American life from the local, self-reliant, and largely egalitarian culture Tocqueville had described in the 1840s into a modern technocratic state became more dramatically clear. While many Americans saw a rationally managed bureaucratic society as a *solution* to the anxiety of the postwar years, a growing number of young people and intellectuals saw it as a dangerous cause of even greater alienation and anxiety. Most of those who became activists were not radical ideologues, writes historian Anderson, but pragmatists in the American grain, who simply believed that the concentration of political, economic, and intellectual authority was "inconsistent with the American ideal."

Reflecting on the alienation expressed by Beat poets, James Dean movies, and so-called juvenile delinquents, some of these critics began to see that the emerging hypermodern world offered young people no real opportunities to express their own innate personalities in meaningful roles in adult society, because they either had to conform to the technological system or drop out of it. In his influential 1960 book Paul Goodman argued that the young people of the time were *Growing Up Absurd* because serious ideals, meaningful work, and genuine feelings of patriotism had been usurped by cold war propaganda and sterile corporate and consumerist values. Several years later, after the youth movement had arisen to protest, he supported its claims by arguing again that the adult culture was characterized by "artificial complication in every sphere of life, general insecurity, competition heightened to the point of anxiety, and regimentation." He emphasized, as he did throughout his writings, that fundamental cultural issues were at stake. "It should be obvious by now," he wrote, "that the vital conflict today is not between one bloc and another bloc, nor between Left and Right, but between a world-wide dehumanized system of things and human decency and perhaps survival, yet only the young seem to recognize this."[9]

The critics of technocracy consistently emphasized this theme that modern life was dehumanizing. In a 1967 article in *Look* magazine, two of the more popular social critics of the time, Marshall McLuhan and George Leonard, portrayed the essentially inhuman nature of the emerging "mechanical age": "It was this civilization's genius to manipulate matter, energy and human life by breaking every useful process down into its functional parts, then producing any required number of each. Just as shaped pieces of metal became components of a locomotive, human specialists become components of the great social machine." Their fear was that human beings would no longer be treated as individuals with distinctive personalities, styles, needs, and personal destinies, but as objective, interchangeable parts in a rationally designed and hierarchically controlled system. Like many university and college students, and like educators and students who would be involved in the free school movement, the authors specifically noted that mass education was designed to serve this mechanistic worldview.[10]

Protest broke out on college campuses in the early and mid-1960s in response to various social issues, but beyond their specific criticisms young people were searching for a sense of existential *authenticity* and questioning the roles in adult society for which they were being prepared. They came to believe that educational institutions had allied with the increasingly mechanical system and disregarded or suppressed their search for meaning and critical questions about the nature of society. By the 1950s the intellectual resources of the United States were "mobilized in the nation's quest for world dominance," according to Andrew Jamison and Ron Eyerman. Knowledge became an industry, as universities increasingly came to serve military and corporate purposes and those with literary skills found more lucrative careers in public relations than in "critical reflection and social commentary." Scientific endeavors were sponsored by corporations, foundations, and the government and pressed into the service of a "blind faith [in] technocratic social engineering," while the social sciences carefully avoided engagement with political or social controversy. "What Marcuse would come to call technological rationality dominated the postwar universities, as moral or ethical issues were . . . discussed in splendid isolation from the real world of science and technology."[11] Students who began asking about civil rights and nuclear weapons and Vietnam rapidly became disenchanted by this technological rationality.

Contemporary accounts by sympathetic observers strongly testified to this state of affairs. In a 1968 letter to the *New York Times*, political scientist Benjamin Barber observed that "many students have grown weary of being admonished to respect democracy and academic sacrosanctity by the administrative officers of universities which are hierarchically structured, undemocratically governed, and increasingly subordinate to the intellectual tyranny of government and corporate research." Significantly, Paul Goodman argued in a 1967 essay in *Harvard Educational Review* that such government and corporate influence permeated the entire educational system, not only the universities. "Those who are intimately and humanly involved in the actual function" of education, he wrote, meaning students and teachers, "are not the source of [new] ideas; their needs are not expressed and taken into account. Decisions on education are made by a school establishment—whether superintendents, school boards, Harvard, or the National Science Foundation—that is allied in spirit with the corporations. Throughout, there is an emphasis on extrinsic motivation and social engineering for national goals that are, in my opinion, foreign to education or democracy or the decent future of mankind."[12] This evaluation, seconded by many young people, provided fertile soil for the rise of the free school movement.

While not entirely novel (earlier romantics and anarchists had raised similar objections) this perception of schooling was radically at odds with the reigning American attitude toward public education. Prior to the 1960s, educational theorists and historians by and large extolled American public education as the keystone of modern democracy. The writings of Ellwood P. Cubberley, a highly influential educational scholar of the early twentieth century, are frequently cited in this context. Sol Cohen has recently remarked that much educational history was written to bolster teacher education programs and was largely isolated from advances in historical scholarship; "the *only* historiographical tradition in the historiography of American education," he wrote, "was a story of the evolution and inevitable triumph of the public school idea, a story of the advance of educational progress on behalf of democracy, equality, and the realization of the American dream." Even if intellectually detached from the wider scholarship in American history, this tradition clearly echoes what Bruce J. Schulman has identified as a "smug, celebratory tone" in history texts suggesting "an ever-ascending trajectory of moral, social, and economic progress."[13]

However, alongside the awakening of cultural dissent there came a dramatic change in scholars' interpretations of American schooling that confirmed the students' critique. As early as 1962, Raymond E. Callahan's *Education and the Cult of Efficiency* demonstrated that business-derived values of efficiency, cost-effectiveness, and hierarchical management had virtually replaced pedagogical values in educational theory and practice during the early twentieth century. He considered it a tragedy "that educational questions were subordinated to business considerations; that administrators were produced who were not, in any true sense, educators; that a scientific label was put on some very unscientific and dubious methods and practices; and that an anti-intellectual climate, already prevalent, was strengthened." Given this mentality, which Callahan believed was still prevalent in the 1960s, schools were run "not as centers of learning but as enterprises which were functioning efficiently if the students went through without failing and received their diplomas on schedule and if the operation were handled economically."[14] Although Callahan did not use the term, he had provided historical evidence documenting the rise of "technological rationality" in American education.

Within the next few years, "revisionist" scholars such as Michael Katz, Clarence Karier, Paul Violas, Joel Spring, and others argued even more directly that schooling was organized and administered primarily to serve the interests of the corporate state and its ruling elite, by training young people to obediently fill their vocational and social roles. Even scholars like David Tyack, Carl Kaestle, and David Nasaw, who did not start with such radical premises, acknowledged that public education indeed reflected anti-democratic forces in American culture. Nasaw introduced his *Schooled to Order* (1979) by writing, "To understand why Americans have grown disillusioned with their public schools we must look beyond the immediate present to the larger history of the United States and its public schools," and in this history Nasaw emphasized "the primary tensions between the rhetoric of democracy and the reality of a class-divided society." David Tyack maintained that urbanization and industrialization of American society in the late nineteenth century replaced local, personal-scale community life with the "impersonal and codified roles" of the "corporate-bureaucratic model." He demonstrated that between the 1880s and 1920s school leaders recognized that "'modern civilization [was] rapidly tending to uniformity'" and they sought to organize school systems accordingly. "They tried to create new controls over pupils, teachers, principals, and other subordinate members of the school hierarchy. . . . Each person was to be accountable for specific duties as prescribed in detailed rules and regulations."[15]

Tyack argued that school reformers deliberately and openly advocated a social engineering model of education, believing that "obedience to bureaucratic norms" was an essential element of industrial development and hence social progress. Under the sway of a naïve faith in "scientific" management, they did not consider that such a machine-like society might produce alienation or depersonalization. Furthermore, they did little to challenge class and race inequities in American society, and believed that an efficient education should prepare young people for their "probable destinies" in the social order (to use the elitist phrase of Harvard president Charles W. Eliot). Writing in 1974, at the height of public school reform that had been stimulated by radical dissent, Tyack commented that the ferment of the 1960s seemed to represent a major turning point in American education, a widespread rejection of the corporate-bureaucratic model.

In *The Revisionists Revised* (1978) and *The Troubled Crusade* (1983), Diane Ravitch offered a counterpoint to the leftward drift in the writing of educational history; while her scholarship was as thorough and comprehensive as that of Callahan or Tyack, her interpretation rested on the premise that public education should concern itself with academic achievement as traditionally defined and should not become burdened by demands to solve intractable social problems. Following this premise, Ravitch saw the turmoil of the 1960s as a serious distraction from the pursuit of educational excellence rather than as a catalyst for educational reconstruction. She argued that American universities in the 1960s were essentially open and tolerant institutions that prized and guarded intellectual freedom, so it was ironic for radical students to make them "scapegoats for an unpopular war and for black grievances." If the police and national guard troops used violence against demonstrators, it was only fair to observe that they were taunted and pelted with debris. Finally, "with its contempt for rationality and its reverence for immediacy, the counterculture openly opposed the self-discipline, order, and respect for reason that educational institutions rely on."[16] Clearly, this view reflected the sentiment of the majority of Americans during the 1960s and in the years since. Ravitch, not Jonathan Kozol or Joel Spring, was called to serve in the U.S. Department of Education during the first Bush administration, and the wave of reform that led Tyack to pronounce the 1960s a turning point was soon dashed against the solid rock of the "conservative restoration," as critical theorists have referred to political life in the 1970s and 1980s.

Nevertheless, I maintain that in order to understand the free school movement phenomenologically—that is, as it was experienced by those who participated in it or were sympathetic to its ideology—it is not sufficient to dismiss its worldview as simply a "contempt for rationality." A significant number of people were alienated from traditional values and I seek to understand why. Ravitch, like other historians, recognized that "where once there had been a clear sense of purpose about educational goals, now there was uncertainty," but she implied that there could be certainty if only schools would remain faithful to their academic mission. In my view, education can never be concerned with academic excellence in a pure sense—in a cultural and political vacuum—because education is essentially concerned with the meaning of experience, and this is fundamentally contingent on a culture's ruling values and ideologies. If a culture is not providing a sustaining sense of meaning to some portion of its population, they are understandably going to experience disillusionment, alienation, and, in fact, contempt for that culture. What begins as an "existential" revolt provides grounds for an articulate cultural and ideological critique.

The free school movement, then, was a response to the existentially alienating character of the bureaucratic, machine-like system of schooling that had been deliberately organized earlier in the twentieth century. Like the dissidents who marched for civil rights, free speech, and peace, and the activists who started communes, co-operatives, and underground newspapers, alternative educators sought to reclaim social space for personal authenticity and self-expression. Herb Snitzer, who founded a Summerhill-inspired school in upstate New York in 1963, saw the free school idea as a deliberate effort to reestablish the value of human life. In a book about the school, he and co-author Doris Ransohoff very clearly articulated the cultural critique that lay at the heart of the free school movement. "In an increasingly technocratic, techtalitarian and monolithic society," Snitzer wrote,

> the desire for life diminishes. With the knowledge that man now has the power to destroy himself and all life around him, faith in the value of one's own life and in the ability of one's own life-force to sustain itself withers away. . . . It is the inhumanness of the society we live in and by and large accept that I am outraged by. . . . A number of people, particularly the young, no longer believe their personal wishes for self-fulfillment can be realized through democracy as it manifests itself in the American technological culture. . . . Today individual liberty as individual effort no longer makes sense. It is the team, the conglomerate, the institution, the system, that is all-powerful. Impersonal, even anonymous, no longer having anything to do with what you or I or the person next door wants.[17]

Like Snitzer, many other free school writers explicitly named *technocracy* as their enemy, or addressed specific facets of technocratic society. Neil Postman and Charles Weingartner, who were important interpreters of the radical school movement, pointed out that the education critics were responding to a cultural trend that since World War II had moved people "farther and farther away from control over their own institutions. . . . More than any other social institution, the American school mirrors what we want to think we are as a people. But when we approach it to ask, Are we not the fairest of all? it keeps replying, in the most irritating fashion, that we are not. . . . Our schools have been telling us that we are becoming dehumanized, empire-building technocrats, and that we care more for our missiles than for our children."[18]

This, then, was the historical soil in which the free school movement took root. A sensitive minority of the American population became profoundly alienated from the values and institutions of mainstream society and severed their allegiance to its authority. Thus set adrift, they attempted to build "counterinstitutions" (as Gitlin calls them) in which they might renew a Jeffersonian vision of personal autonomy and local, face-to-face democracy. This counterculture produced diverse expressions of dissent and social reformation, from the sober political agenda of the New Left to the Dionysian revelry of Haight-Ashbury, and although it is beyond the scope of this study to describe the various social movements of the 1960s in depth, one can fully understand free school ideology only by identifying the different themes of social and cultural critique that radical educators inherited from the larger counterculture. As Ann Swidler wrote, "Without the 1960s' peculiar constellation of the student movement, the counterculture, and a multitude of anti-authoritarian social experiments, [free schools] . . . would have been impossible."[19]

THE CIVIL RIGHTS MOVEMENT

Most historians agree that the protest movements of the 1960s owe a great debt to their pioneers, the African American people who rose up in the mid-1950s to end the injustice, bigotry, and violence of racial segregation in the United States. The rise of the civil rights movement was arguably the single most important factor in the transition from the self-satisfied cold war culture of the 1950s to the decade of disillusionment, dissent, and activism that followed. By shattering the nation's indifference to its most troubling and persistent moral problem—its deeply rooted racist attitudes and institutions—the civil rights movement created a rare opening for cultural self-examination and critical questioning of the values that constituted the "American way of life."[20]

Several streams of intellectual influence and activist struggle fed the civil rights movement. Considering this heritage as the historical background of radical protest in the 1960s, there is a good case for claiming that countercultural dissent was not merely a whimsical burst of rebellion by pampered college students but resulted from social, political, and intellectual tensions that had been brewing for a good part of the century. The free school movement, then, resulted from a serious, long-established body of social and cultural critique. Although a number of free schools arguably did little more than give vent to angry anti-authoritarian passion or Dionysian self-indulgence, the educational ideology behind the free school movement did rest on a coherent libertarian-democratic worldview. To a large extent, this worldview was legitimated by the intellectual and moral claims of the civil rights movement; therefore, a brief review of the African American struggle is necessary to a full understanding of free school ideology.

The National Association for the Advancement of Colored People (NAACP), founded in 1909, had been working tirelessly through the courts for legal victories over racial discrimination, and its challenge to school segregation led to the 1954 Supreme Court decision in *Brown v. the Board of Education* that overturned the legal sanction for racial separation in public schools. This was a crucial turning point that, by forcing segregationists into conflict with federal law, made civil rights an important national political issue during the next several years, dramatically illustrated by the sending of Army troops to Little Rock, Arkansas, in 1957 to enforce the integration of Central High School. There were other new pressures after the Second World War: for one, black veterans returning from wartime service were no longer willing to passively endure the denial of equal rights. Such an attitude infuriated segregationist whites in the South, who responded with violence, and the national conscience began to become aroused; both Presidents Truman and Eisenhower made cautious moves—against the opposition of powerful southern politicians—in support of civil rights legislation.

Meanwhile, African American leaders became familiar with new sources of critique and activism, including the spiritually rooted pacifism of Gandhi. In 1942, James Farmer and Bayard Rustin, working for the religious pacifist group Fellowship of Reconciliation, expanded their work for racial justice by organizing the Congress of Racial Equality (CORE) and leading what Farmer thought was "the first organized civil rights sit-in in American history" at a restaurant in Chicago.[21] In 1947 CORE sponsored desegregated rides on interstate buses, pioneering a tactic that would prove explosive fourteen years later. By the early 1950s, Gandhi's success in liberating India from colonial rule through nonviolent resistance attracted the interest of African American ministers such as James Lawson, who traveled to India to learn the principles of Gandhi's methods and returned to the United States to inspire a new generation of activists, including those who founded the Student Nonviolent Coordinating Committee (SNCC) in 1960. Many of his students would become leaders of the sit-ins and Freedom Rides of the early 1960s. Seeds of the civil rights movement were also planted at the Highlander Folk School in Tennessee, a racially integrated retreat center founded by Myles Horton that supported labor organizing and, through the work of Septima Clark, the political empowerment of African Americans throughout the South.[22]

The nationally acknowledged leader of the civil rights movement, Dr. Martin Luther King, Jr., soared to national and international prominence after his leadership of the Montgomery, Alabama, bus boycott between December 1955 and November 1956. In his stirring speech that helped launch the campaign, King served notice that African Americans would no longer passively accept the injustices of racism and segregation. "You know, my friends, there comes a time when people get tired of being trampled over by the iron feet of oppression." He linked his people's aspirations to the heart of America's ideals by saying that "the great glory of American democracy is the right to protest for right."[23] In the years that followed, thousands of people, young and old, black and white, staged sit-ins and demonstrations, rode on integrated buses, conducted voter registration campaigns and freedom schools, marched on Washington, and engaged in persistent political challenges to local officials, governors, and presidents. In many cases they were met with harassment, lawsuits, brutal violence, and determined actions by law enforcement officers to thwart their efforts. Nationally televised images of peaceful demonstrators being attacked by mobs, police dogs, and high pressure water hoses shocked the conscience of the nation.

The civil rights movement was profoundly important for at least two reasons. First, it expressed a deeply moral, indeed thoroughly religious and spiritual, vision of society guided by ideals of justice, brotherhood, and human dignity. Second, in the face of the conformist cold war culture the civil rights movement reintroduced the traditional American democratic practice of civil disobedience. Vincent Harding argues that the movement was "far more than a contest for legal rights"—it was "a Black-led, multiracial quest for democracy in America, for the healing of the nation, for the freeing of all our spirits." Harding recounts that religious people and young white seekers joined the movement because it spoke to a deeper part of their souls. "Their faith was renewed. Their love was set free. They gained a new sense of purpose, direction, and hope." By calling on people to face arrest, beatings, and even death for the sake of moral principles, the civil rights movement was a transformative experience for many of its participants. James Farmer recalled that "Not one of the men and women who shared the Freedom Ride could ever be the same. Nothing would ever again be routine. No more humdrum. A Promethean spark somehow had been infused into the soul of each of us."[24]

Participation in civil rights actions enabled white activists to stand outside the commonly accepted values and assumptions of their culture, including its racism, individualism, and consumerism. The major critics of mass society's treatment of young people pointed out that the moral integrity of the civil rights campaign gave alienated youths something to believe in, "something real" to live for, as Paul Goodman put it. Edgar Z. Friedenberg wrote that it offered a rare opportunity for "self-realization, . . . a focus for fidelity" in a culture that encouraged "infidelity, a disciplined expediency." Michael Rossman, a leading Berkeley activist and radical author who was involved as well in free schools, stated in blunt terms the psychological liberation he and other alienated young people obtained from the civil rights movement: "Touched off by a psychic contagion from the blacks, a broad process of deniggerization is spreading through America's white young, many of whom have been newly freed to develop personal and cultural identity." Another free schooler, who had been raised in an upper-middle-class family and sent to prep school and an Ivy League university in order to take his place among the elite, found "an alternative to the privileged life style" through his involvement in Freedom Summer (1964) in a segregated town in Florida. The black neighborhood in which he spent the summer "was probably the first real community I had ever lived in," and his experiences there "engaged dimensions of my personality that had lain dormant at college"—dimensions such as compassion and emotional wholeness.[25]

The civil rights movement also legitimated civil disobedience and gave the counterculture effective methods to express dissent: it taught young people that real social change could happen if they would act directly on behalf of their moral beliefs. The decade of protest began with sit-ins at segregated lunch counters in Greensboro, North Carolina, in February 1960, which soon spread to cities across the South. Within a few months, spontaneous demonstrations occurred in New York against a civil defense drill and in San Francisco against a hearing of the House Un-American Activities Committee (HUAC). (Surely it is ironic that a nation that celebrates the Boston tea party and Bunker Hill introduced an "Un-American Activities Committee" to stifle unauthorized views.) Many white youths were moved by the courage and principles of the black students and supported them by holding demonstrations in other parts of the country. In doing so, they rediscovered that a living democracy requires more than periodic voting for candidates—it demands active participation in the vital affairs of the community based on a commitment to principles. Learning this lesson, the "silent generation" of the 1950s became the activists of the 1960s. Michael Rossman recalled that his generation overcame the hypocrisy and fear of the cold war era in part through the inspiration of the civil rights movement. Demonstrations for racial justice "said what kind of action was possible, and that such action had for the first time a fighting chance for success."[26]

Jane Lichtman, a major advocate for the free university movement of the later 1960s, claimed that these alternative, anti-institutional forms of learning were made possible by the example of civil rights activism. "The sit-ins and freedom rides were unique because they were spontaneous outbursts by local people rather than massively organized political actions. [They] . . . were not run by the 'experts' but rather by locally affected people." Indeed, they were often run by *students,* and this fact galvanized white students, including those who would organize Students for a Democratic Society (SDS). Previously, the ideas of college students had rarely been taken seriously; Martin Luther King, Jr. himself told the Greensboro demonstrators in 1960 that "What is fresh, what is new in your fight is the fact that it was initiated, led, and sustained by students. What is new is that American students have come of age."[27]

The civil rights movement had a direct influence on the rise of free schools. Len Solo, co-founder of the Teacher Drop-out Center (TDOC), one of the central hubs of the free school network, attributes the outpouring of dissent among dissatisfied educators to the example of the movement for racial justice; the TDOC "received thousands and thousands of letters from people. It was really incredible. *The civil rights movement allowed people to get their voices.*" The movement blazed the trail for the free schools in a more specific sense as well. An important element of Freedom Summer (1964) in Mississippi was the organizing of dozens of "Freedom Schools" in which 200 volunteers (most of them white students from prestigious northern colleges) taught 2,500 African American people of all ages about their heritage and their rights as American citizens. The idea had its roots in community organizing by SNCC activists such as Charlie Cobb and Bob Moses in Mississippi, and in literacy and citizenship campaigns conducted in South Carolina and other states as early as 1957, as well as in mass boycotts of public schools in Boston, New York, Chicago, and other major cities by African American families in 1963 and 1964; organizers had set up one-day "freedom schools" for children who were being kept out of the public schools.[28]

The Freedom School phenomenon is significant here for at least two reasons. First, it showed that African American people themselves initiated a strong critique of their schooling, well before Kozol's *Death at an Early Age* alerted the nation at large to the endemic racism and even brutality of urban public education, and well before the literature of educational dissent was fully developed or widely known. The Freedom Schools were planned at a gathering in New York in March 1964 that included Bayard Rustin, Myles Horton, Septima Clark, Bob Moses, Paul Potter (a president of SDS), and pacifist historian Staughton Lynd, who would become the on-site coordinator of the program, among other civil rights activists; they devised a radical alternative to public education even as John Holt's first book (the jolting but politically neutral *How Children Fail*) made its appearance, and they seem to have owed little or no debt to A. S. Neill or Paul Goodman. Clearly, the civil rights movement gave the radical educational critique a powerful moral and political base without which the free school movement might not have been conceivable.

The Freedom Schools also provided a specific, coherent pedagogical approach that would be mirrored in the free schools. Although the organizers wrote a Citizenship Curriculum, they declared that "It is not our purpose to impose a particular set of conclusions. . . . Our purpose is to encourage the asking of questions, and the hope that society can be improved." Indeed, from the beginning, the intention of the Freedom Schools in Mississippi was to "'show people that they could question the situation, that they could take action about their situation,'" and to follow Horton's principle that "meaningful education . . . must always be rooted in immediate experience." In other words, the education practiced in these alternative schools would not seek to impose a culturally approved set of understandings and values, but would provide opportunity for self-understanding, self-expression, and engagement with other persons in an authentic community—with the process leading to liberation from social and political constraints. One volunteer teacher—a black minister's son, in fact—wrote that Freedom Schools were a "microcosm" in which "we begin to live a brotherhood we dream someday will expand into society. . . . We begin to have meaningful and revealing dialogue, we begin to formulate, together, new dimensions of ourselves and of society." These words could have been written five years later by any practitioner of the free school ideology; indeed, they virtually define the core of that ideology.[29]

The idea that education should serve human needs and individual interests rather than one dominant cultural agenda is the fundamental basis of libertarian educational thought and had been voiced by radical educators for nearly two centuries, but the civil rights movement created a climate in which this idea came to life as never before. Mario Fantini, a liberal (not radical) scholar and policymaker who advocated for public alternative education in the 1970s, explicitly recognized that "We can trace the roots of the current alternatives thrust in large measure to the civil rights movement of the 1960s. . . . For many blacks and whites alike, the freedom schools provided a glimpse of alternate programs tailored to their perceived needs." Daniel Hinman-Smith, who studied Freedom Summer extensively, argued that the young people who participated in these schools were deeply moved by this experiment in democratic education and went back to their campuses with their assumptions and expectations about education radically changed. They began to recognize that conventional education made them subservient to authority rather than preparing them to engage social problems critically. Many of them began to see academic learning, even in their elite universities, as sterile and lifeless, without genuine existential purpose.[30]

PARTICIPATORY DEMOCRACY: SDS AND THE FREE SPEECH MOVEMENT

It was not coincidental that Mississippi Freedom Summer was followed by a major outbreak of campus activism and dissent. Hundreds of students were radicalized by the experience of working for justice in a hostile and oppressive environment, and their participation led to a nationwide network of activists primed to address racial injustice, the Vietnam

War, and, significantly for our purpose here, the nature of American education. The student movement had deeper roots, however. In the late 1950s, small groups of liberal and leftist students met to discuss, and occasionally to protest, issues of the cold war culture, including the atomic bomb, racial segregation, and the narrow confines of political and intellectual life. A number of these young people were so-called red diaper babies—children of radicals who had been Socialists and even Communists during the Depression—and who had therefore inherited a measure of disillusionment with American society. Others began raising their own questions, especially after encountering the moral challenge of the civil rights movement. They found a few mentors in the adult generation: a handful of radical labor and socialist organizations remained from the 1930s, a small pacifist movement gathered around the journal *Liberation*, founded in 1956 by A. J. Muste, David Dellinger, and Bayard Rustin, and dissident intellectuals such as Hannah Arendt and C. Wright Mills were presenting critiques of modern society. At the University of Michigan, a group of activists led by Al Haber transformed the Student League for Industrial Democracy, a small network with roots in the socialist ideas of Upton Sinclair, Jack London, and Clarence Darrow around the turn of the century, into Students for a Democratic Society (SDS) in January 1960, and caught the attention of the campus newspaper editor, who would soon become one of the national leaders of the student movement—Tom Hayden.

In May 1960, this group sponsored a conference on "Human Rights in the North," which drew together civil rights, labor, and peace activists, and SDS began to rise as "the dynamic center of the decade," as Gitlin put it. In June 1962, the organization held a conference at a United Auto Workers retreat center in Port Huron, Michigan, and issued the defining manifesto of the student movement—the Port Huron Statement. Primarily authored by Hayden, who was steeped in the literature of social democracy and the radical sociology of C. Wright Mills, this document articulated the vision of the New Left. Rather than merely seeking political control of society's existing institutions, the young dissidents envisioned a participatory democracy that would attend to human needs, communal relationships, and local, face-to-face problem solving. They opposed hierarchy, authority lodged in impersonal institutions, and entrenched racial and economic inequality. Ultimately, their vision rested on a moral critique of modern society, which they believed did not allow people to develop the full possibilities of their humanness.

> We regard men as infinitely precious and possessed of unfulfilled capacities for reason, freedom, and love. In affirming these principles

> we are aware of countering perhaps the dominant conceptions of man in the twentieth century: that he is a thing to be manipulated, and that he is inherently incapable of directing his own affairs. . . . Men have unrealized potential for self-cultivation, self-direction, self-understanding, and creativity.[31]

The sexist language of this passage, so obvious to readers forty years later, reflected the fact that gender equality was not originally on the list of student demands; indeed, young women in SDS and other groups were often radicalized by the incongruity between the student movement's high ideals and the subservient role of women in most of their relationships to male students. Nevertheless, the emergence of these ideals did represent a significant step toward the feminist critique of patriarchal society; one later feminist scholar, for example, pointed out that the "climate of protest" of the 1960s enabled women as well as men to interrogate conventional sources of power in American society. Similarly, the ideals that emerged in nascent form in the Port Huron Statement would figure prominently in the humanistic psychology/human potential movement that began to take shape during these same years, and, if we substitute the word "children" for "men," this passage would fit comfortably anywhere in the free school literature. A few years later, Michael Rossman made a direct connection between the New Left movement and the goal of free schools when he wrote that "When freed from coercive authority, the young create a radical democracy, a non-coercive peer society which depends on mutual approval and trust, and whose native values are sharing, honesty, gentleness, and tolerance for the wide range of people's real natures. Such a Summerhillian society is now appearing wherever the free young practice their changes."[32] Although this statement is polemical and ignores the real difficulties of nonauthoritarian communal life, it accurately reflects the idealism of the counterculture.

The political activism of the 1960s was personalist and holistic rather than technocratic. It addressed existential and spiritual aspirations as much as material needs. Eric Foner comments that the Port Huron Statement "announced a new conception of politics"—a human scale conception that distinguished the New Left from previous progressive movements and mainstream liberalism. Many young activists rejected the manipulative, calculating politics practiced by the nation's leaders; although the election of John F. Kennedy in 1960 had given the Left "a sense of the possible" after a decade of conservatism, young activists were disillusioned by mainstream liberalism's continuing cold war mentality and allegiance to the military-industrial system, which Gitlin called "custodial or managerial liberalism." Richard Flacks, an

SDS organizer, saw the Kennedy administration's mode of operation as "the end of democracy, because the whole thrust was toward technocratic, top-down control." Civil rights activists found Kennedy to be slow to join their battle against segregation and racial violence (he approached civil rights, according to Allen Matusow, "as a matter of politics, not of morals"), and at the 1964 Democratic National Convention, mainstream politicians defeated the effort by the Mississippi Freedom Democratic Party to oust segregationist delegates. The student movement saw politics as usual, even liberal politics, as inadequate to the need for substantive social change. Even Richard Goodwin, a close advisor to Presidents Kennedy and Johnson, while portraying them as idealists who inspired "our belief in ourselves," became frustrated by "the triumphant ascendance of bureaucracy" and appreciated "the liberating forces outside government that were working to change America." As Rossman put it, the New Left was rooted in "simple, naïve, and stubborn" moral indignation directed against injustice: "This is wrong, it must stop!"[33]

This critique was political and ideological to be sure, but it went further by involving young people in self-transformation as well. Historian Doug Rossinow has amply documented the "existentialist politics" of the student movement; young people were rebelling against "massification" and conformity and searching for authenticity, community, and commitment to a moral vision. For the New Left, the alternative to technocracy was neither Marxist socialism nor liberal reform of corporate capitalism but a humanist, personalist culture in which feelings, relationships, and self-expression might thrive. As Rossinow points out, the civil rights movement demonstrated that moral and existential politics could produce effective social action; the search for meaning was not a private withdrawal from social issues but a catalyst for breaking out of social roles to build a collaborative, supportive community. This approach was quite foreign to the liberal establishment and so the student movement became increasingly disillusioned with mainstream political institutions. If young activists began the decade with a sense of optimism about the possibility of moral rejuvenation of American culture, by the end of the 1960s they began to realize how truly radical and alternative their vision was.

The civil rights movement inspired numerous demonstrations at the University of California at Berkeley during the 1950s and the early 1960s; students were concerned about racial injustice as well as nuclear disarmament and capital punishment, and hundreds of students were involved in civil rights demonstrations by 1963–64. When that academic year was over, students from around the nation, including about fifty from Berkeley—among them a young man named Mario Savio—

participated in the Freedom Summer campaign, and returned to their communities and campuses deeply inspired. The summer of 1964 also saw the divisive Democratic convention, which radicalized black activists, and the nomination of arch-conservative Barry Goldwater as the Republican presidential candidate. In August President Johnson persuaded Congress to pass the Gulf of Tonkin resolution, which plunged the United States more deeply into the Vietnam War. Meanwhile, students were reading Hannah Arendt's 1963 book *On Revolution*, which called explicitly for participatory democracy. (As in the case of the civil rights movement, the historical and intellectual roots of student dissent were deep; Arendt had been trained in existentialism by Jaspers, Husserl, and Heidegger.)[34]

When students, many of them now politically restless, returned to the Berkeley campus in the fall of 1964, the university administration attempted to ban students from promoting "off-campus" causes on a site they had previously used for this purpose. What happened next, according to Michael Rossman, was "an historical thunderbolt" that shook him and other dissidents loose from their "life within the old institutions." On October 1, police attempted to arrest civil rights activist Jack Weinberg for defying the new regulation, but students began to surround the police car, and by the next day 4,000 of them filled the central plaza on campus. Thus began the Free Speech Movement, which evolved into a massive, ongoing student movement for more democratic participation in their education. Paul Goodman, covering the Free Speech Movement for the journal *Dissent*, commented that students "who had taken their risks in Mississippi were not afraid to sit in against [UC President] Clark Kerr." Led by Mario Savio, the students continued to demonstrate and negotiate, and by the end of December had won back the right to express their views on campus. But they were not finished; their activism was now inflamed, and for the next several years students at Berkeley and around the nation actively confronted the problems and injustices they perceived in American society. Goodman observed that something new was emerging from the young generation. "The calm excitement and matter-of-fact democracy and human contact now prevalent on the Berkeley campus are in revolutionary contrast to our usual demented, inauthentic, overadministered American society."[35]

Indeed, the students themselves realized this. They saw connections between American militarism and other moral failures such as racism and poverty, and sought to expose the roots of the entire system. In one of his speeches, Savio proclaimed that "we have come up against what may emerge as the greatest problem of our nation—depersonalized, unresponsive bureaucracy." The radical students believed that an essentially technocratic system prevented the development of genuine democracy, and that the system as a whole needed to be transformed. This critique had definite implications for education. According to Rossinow, student activists explicitly sought "a place where people might be treated as human beings. They thought universities should not merely prepare students to become parts in a corporate machine." Berkeley graduate student Jeff Lustig wrote in 1969 that "where traditional [liberal] educational theory sought men who could criticize, [the present system] seeks men who will obey; where it wished to create men who could shape their society, this wants men who will agree to be shaped by others."[36]

The Free Speech Movement, writes Daniel Hinman-Smith, was "about the creation of public space in which students learned new roles for themselves and tested the limits of the possible. The Free Speech Movement became, in essence, a school," but a school in which top-down learning was replaced by more democratic models. The educational lessons learned during Freedom Summer were much in evidence at Berkeley, especially when students began organizing spontaneous classes to replace those they were boycotting and teach-ins on Vietnam; by the spring of 1966 they had organized the Free University of Berkeley. A few years later, a student activist reflected that the Free Speech Movement was "the decisive beginning of the educational revolution in the U.S. . . . the first time that students articulated a basic dissatisfaction with the forms and essence of our education. The phrase 'relevant education' was first used on campus by a mass based movement." This radical educational critique spread rapidly. Carl Davidson told the 1966 national convention of SDS that the system of "corporate liberalism" maintained its power by training people to perform their roles in the system beginning in elementary school; he called for the abolition of grading and suggested that schools of education should adopt the ideas of Paul Goodman and A. S. Neill. Here is significant evidence of the connection between the student movement—even in its most explicit political aspect—and free school ideology. Wherever we turn in the countercultural educational literature, we consistently find an underlying effort to challenge the economic, political, cultural, or psychological dimensions of "corporate liberalism" or technocracy. We consistently find a critique of "the logic of administration" (Lustig's phrase) or the social "machine" as being the enemy of genuine human relationship and authentic moral thought and action.[37]

Further evidence of the direct link between campus activism and the free school movement is found in the publication *Edcentric*, which was distributed by the Center for Educational Reform (CER), a project of the U.S. National Student Association in the late 1960s and early 1970s. *Edcentric* listed resources for student-initiated projects in higher education (including free universities) alongside networks and publications serving free schools for younger students, and promoted "communication around the country among groups working to restructure the whole idea of what education in this society should be." Although most of the writing in the magazine dealt with issues and politics on university campuses, some attention was given to radical educational reform at all levels. In the April 1970 issue, for example, CER Director Larry Magid reported on a New Schools Exchange conference, and lamented that most people there were more concerned with personal freedom than radical social change. Also in 1970, Barry Wood contributed an essay, "Free Schools and the Revolution," which argued that radical educational change was inherently political even if free schools seemed to act otherwise. Wood wrote that they were "not *just* rebelling from the boredom, coercion, stultification, and irrelevance of the American classroom," but were also questioning the values that are inculcated through schooling. He declared that "it has always been a myth to assume that a free school in the country could be an island of growth and joy in an ocean of repression. We can't escape the reality of Amerika [*sic*]1970. . . . It's impossible to be self-actualized in a repressive society." Jonathan Kozol would make the same argument in his 1972 book *Free Schools*; there was, in fact, a tension within the free school movement between those who primarily emphasized personal liberation and self-expression and those motivated by explicit political aims—a tension I address later in this book—but the important point is that activists did consider free schools to be a part of the larger Movement, and in historical perspective the schools clearly did embody the political/cultural critique raised by the student movement of the 1960s.[38]

After 1964, the rising surge of student activism found a powerful unifying cause, as President Johnson dramatically escalated U.S. military involvement in Vietnam. To many young people, this war was so unjustifiable, so blatantly imperialist and contrary to American ideals of democracy, that it solidified their disillusionment into outright opposition. SDS membership grew from 2,500 in December 1964 to 10,000 by October 1965 to 100,000 by 1968. One student leader spoke for thousands when he recalled that "We'd been brought up to believe in our hearts that America fought on the side of justice. The Second World War was very much ingrained in us. . . . So, along with the absolute horror of the war in Vietnam, there was also a feeling of personal betrayal. I remember crying by myself late at night in my room listening to the reports of the war." At the first major anti-war demonstration, sponsored by SDS in Washington, D.C., in April 1965, SDS president Paul Potter told a crowd of 20,000 that "The incredible war in Vietnam has provided the razor, the terrifying sharp cutting edge that has finally severed the last vestige of illusion that morality and democracy are the guiding principles of American foreign policy." New Left radicals opposed the war not only out of pacifist principles, but because they saw the war effort as the immensely destructive logical result of a technocratic society. For Paul Goodman, the striking feature about the Vietnam War was "the input-output accounting, the systems development, and the purely incidental significance of the human beings involved." Potter's 1965 speech urged people to resist this impersonal, indeed inhuman, autocratic management of human lives.[39]

For the next seven years, it was the war, more than any other social or political factor, that radicalized the young generation and impelled them to seek out alternative institutions, including alternative forms of education. Dissident scholars began to claim that "the war is very largely a product of the academic community's cultural default," and criticism of established educational practices mounted. At the University of Michigan, faculty and students gathered for the first "teach-in" on the war in 1965—a radical forum that broke down conventional educational roles and enabled students to express their feelings and ideas. This model was another important step toward the free school movement.[40]

The war generated increasing alienation, frustration, and rage as demonstrators discovered that the bulk of the American population supported military action against communism and responded to protests with police force. Valuing "law and order" above the abstract moral arguments of seemingly unpatriotic protesters, public officials put a violent end to many demonstrations, and in 1970 students were killed at Jackson State and Kent State Universities. Many young people were even more deeply radicalized. Jonathan Kozol later reflected that this period was "a time when people who grew up to love their nation felt a sense of shock and shame." These feelings were frequently expressed within the free school movement. The editors of a 1969 anthology of radical writings on education said the critics believed American society was "sick" due to "its competitive ethos, its cultural vulgarity, its neglect or suppression of minority groups, its inherent racism and imperialism. . . . Their critique of the schools derives from this questioning of society." One educator, reflecting on the experiences that led him from teaching in public schools to running an alternative high school, claimed that "America is an empty seduction that offers no roots, no love, no spirit, only insatiability." The events of the 1960s, particularly the civil rights movement and war in Vietnam, "helped crystallize my growing disillusionment with the political system. . . . As we analyzed the war's causes more thoroughly, we had a more difficult time remaining in America's mainstream. . . . I began to feel part of a nebulous movement—people who were determined to shatter the mythology that had made the war possible."[41]

It was this effort to "shatter the mythology" of mainstream culture (i.e., the interlocking values and beliefs that made up the technocracy) that defined the free school movement as an explicitly countercultural thrust. The war in Vietnam quite clearly contributed to the anger and feelings of marginalization that fed the rise of free schools. In addition, there are indications in the free school literature (supported by anecdotes told during later interviews) that some participants in free schools were conscientious objectors who were teaching there as a form of alternative service to the military draft. How many of these young men would have chosen to be poorly paid teachers in alternative schools in peacetime may never be known, but we can justifiably state that the war boosted the free school movement in various ways. Indeed, the war became such a focus for countercultural protest and resistance that when American troops finally pulled out in the early 1970s, the force of 1960s-era dissent rapidly diminished. One historian has claimed that "radicalism became more difficult to sustain" after the end of the Vietnam War, and without this angry radicalism the free school movement quickly declined.[42]

TRANSFORMATION OF CONSCIOUSNESS

Many accounts of the "Movement" (the surge of political, academic, and cultural dissent during the 1960s) point to the contrast between the more sober, serious, and intellectually rooted political critique of the early years—exemplified by the Port Huron Statement—and the ecstatic, hedonistic, anarchistic impulses that flowed profusely after 1967 as seen in the "hippie" subculture and psychedelic drug craze. Photographs of early demonstrations, even many of the events during the Free Speech Movement, show students to be conservatively dressed (the young men with narrow ties and heavy glasses could easily be mistaken for technicians at NASA's Mission Control), but within a few years the youth movement was characterized by its flamboyant, even outrageous flaunting of accepted styles of dress and decorum. Historian Kenneth Cmiel was struck by the rapid shift from the civil rights movement's "Christian message of hope and redemption"—its quest for "a social order permeated by love"—to the counterculture's outlandish forms of protest. He commented that "in the name of personal freedom [the counterculture] attacked the restraints and compromises of civil society." Allen J. Matusow has written that once the Dionysian thirst for freedom and unthrottled self-expression was released by student dissent in the mid-1960s, its darker side emerged as well, and he speaks of "the New Left's decline into madness."[43]

To be sure, the combination of raw frustration (the Vietnam War raged on and mainstream America repudiated the New Left's vision) and the delegitimating of cultural mores opened paths for violence (such as the Weathermen and their "days of rage" in Chicago), licentiousness, intoxication, and self-indulgent withdrawal, and there is no question that various delinquents, dropouts, and "predators" gravitated to the Movement. Indeed, as I discuss later, one of the serious flaws of the free school movement was its *excessive* emphasis on freedom at the expense of other educational, cultural, and even psychological values. Nevertheless, in order to fully appreciate the meaning of the counterculture and the educational ideology it produced, one cannot be content with the label of "madness" any more than with the charge of "contempt for rationality." Acknowledging the excesses of the counterculture, its Dionysian "madness" reflected a wholehearted effort to experiment with radical cultural renewal—an extension, not a reversal, of the social and political critique the New Left had spawned. Bruce Schulman has pointed out that most historical scholarship "draws a rigid distinction" between the sober political phase of protest and the apparently self-indulgent rebellion of the counterculture, but he argues, as I do, that these two aspects of dissent in the 1960s were closely related. Together, they represented a search for authenticity, and this involved a holistic critique of modern culture—an existential dimension ("personal liberation," in Schulman's words) as well as a more overtly ideological dimension ("political revolution").[44]

As Theodore Roszak explained so well, the counterculture sought nothing less than a *transformation of consciousness*, and any cultural rupture so fundamental must inevitably be disorienting, messy, and, in the established culture's terms, irrational by definition. Roszak explicitly argued that the counterculture was a rebellion against technocracy—"a world which more and more thinks of society as the subordinate adjunct of a gigantic technological mechanism requiring constant and instantaneous coordination from the center." Technocracy was more than a political program or economic arrangement—it was (indeed, still is) a worldview, a culturally induced way of perceiving and defining reality, and thus deeply ingrained in consciousness. Roszak called this worldview "the myth of objective consciousness"—a scientific/technological way of knowing that purges the world of human qualities, leading to a "progressive alienation of more and more . . . personal contents" of our own identity. "To a mournfully great extent," Roszak charged, "the progress of expertise, especially as it seeks to mechanize culture, is a waging of open warfare upon joy. It is a bewilderingly perverse effort to demonstrate that nothing, *absolutely nothing* is particularly special, unique, or marvelous, but can be lowered to the status of mechanized routine. . . . It is as if the organism could not be trusted with a single one of its natural functions, but this brain of ours must be brought forward to control and supervise and make sure everything is running along as efficiently as a well-programmed machine." This brief passage reflects the heart of the countercultural critique, and explains why dissident students went beyond protesting racial injustice, petty university rules, or the Vietnam War and saw existing social institutions as being thoroughly corrupt. Free school ideology precisely reflected this critique that technocratic society educated young people to control their "natural functions" in order to efficiently serve as parts in the social machine. I think it makes sense to characterize the free school movement, in Roszak's terms, as an effort to defend "joy" against what was perceived as an onslaught of mechanization, standardization, and routine.[45]

The rebellion against technocracy took political forms, but it was soon clear that the entrenched political system would not adequately respond. The rebellion had deep intellectual roots, but American culture proved, as it generally does, to disdain intellectual critique. Ultimately, the rebellion had to strike at the very *worldview* of technocracy, the *structure of consciousness* that the mass of the population had absorbed from their culture. Hallucinogenic drugs, frenzied music, liberated sexuality, and Asian religious practices were all experienced as ways of discovering a reality that was larger, more fluid, more alive, and more joyful than the technocratic world. While both mainstream liberals (who have faith that the system can be reformed) and radical activists (who attempt to build enough political pressure to cause the system to collapse) have argued that these forms of personal liberation are self-indulging distractions from serious political work, the counterculture welcomed them as a vital element of their rebellion. Todd Gitlin has argued that social change through consciousness followed in the tradition of Emerson and Thoreau; according to Doug Rossinow, seekers of cultural transformation believed that "an alternative that answered the deep and unmet needs of the population would eventually cause the wholesale abandonment of the existing social system." Explaining the motivation of many in the free school movement, Allen Graubard had made very much the same point. "The dream of the counter-institutional 'greening of America' perspective is that the dominant institutions will collapse as more and more people go off and build their own good places, self-sufficient and uncompromised by the taint of corruption in the dominant institutions." Many in the counterculture believed, quite realistically, that significant political change was not on the horizon, and that a massive change in consciousness could only come from an inner revolution of values and lifestyle that demonstrated its superiority to the old system. Out of this hope emerged the phrase that characterized the women's movement: "the personal *is* political."[46]

George Leonard, the insightful *Look* magazine journalist who coined the phrase "human potential movement" in 1965 and then actively promoted this movement, testified to the direct link between the movements for radical social change (civil rights, free speech, and anti-war) and the consciousness revolution. He himself had been raised in the segregated South, and as he began to wonder about the morality of racial discrimination, he developed a critical perspective on American culture as a whole. "If conventional wisdom can be wrong on something as important as race," he asked, "then might not conventional wisdom be wrong about other matters as well? It became a habit of thought to look for alternative explanations for everything that was presented to me, especially if it was presented as gospel truth by the leading authorities on the subject." This willingness to question authority, to deconstruct culturally shaped knowledge, was the key that unlocked radical dissent and the counterculture of the 1960s. While most of the national media was still focused on the "silent generation," Leonard, himself developing this critical "habit of thought," recognized what was stirring on campuses and told the nation in the December 20, 1960 issue of *Look* that "Youth everywhere is exploding into action." He covered the civil rights movement and was deeply moved both by its leaders and by the heroism of rank-and-file participants. In July 1964, he published a powerful anti-segregation essay in *Look*, "A Southerner Appeals to the North," and in 1965 he marched in Selma. The important point here is that for Leonard, these social and moral concerns were intimately connected to the existential and psychological. If the racial transformation of the South was possible, he reflected years later, "then what was not possible? The civil rights movement had shown me something. Now people of all races, all of us, needed to start liberating ourselves from the unacknowledged, unseen oppression that keeps us from achieving our potential."[47]

Leonard had discovered this oppression at work in schools. Alongside his involvement (both as journalist and participant) in the civil rights movement, he was an astute critic of American education. As early as the mid-1950s, his award-winning, widely reprinted pieces in *Look* told what classroom life was really like for teachers and children. In his memoir he recalled his assessment of modern education: "When you really looked at it, the whole idea of children sitting motionless at desks listening to the same material being presented at the same rate was appalling," he wrote. "I began to see first grade as a violent shock to the healthy human organism. . . . [The child] is, in fact, a master learner, happy to explore, eager to try new things. Then comes school, and he gets some stunning news: He must try to learn what the teacher says when the teacher says it, whether he's ready for it or not." During the early 1960s, Leonard's perspective on education and civil rights merged together into a passionate concern for "human potential." He reached the very conclusion that Roszak had identified as the basis for the countercultural critique: modern technocratic culture suppresses our vitality, our erotic energies, our joy, and thus reduces our full organic potential. Not only must schooling be radically transformed, as Leonard went on to propose in *Education and Ecstasy* (1968), but all people whose lives had been diminished by the constraints of modernity needed to take part in a liberation of consciousness, aided by meditative practices, humanistic therapies, communal rituals, biofeedback, and other approaches. Clearly, in Leonard's view this psychological revolution was not a substitute for political action but an extension of it—a fundamental necessity for any deeply meaningful social change. Just the *belief* that human nature might hold potential for creativity, joy, and mystical experience that had been suppressed by a narrowly focused culture was liberating in itself, and an invitation to radical critique.[48]

The personalities and events that comprised the consciousness revolution—Timothy Leary, Ken Kesey, Alan Watts, Gary Snyder, Allen Ginsberg, the Grateful Dead, the Woodstock festival, to name a few—made for a colorful history that is (unfortunately!) outside the scope of this study. Two points are relevant to the free school movement, however. First, the liberating (if not sacramental) qualities of "sex, drugs, and rock & roll" were welcomed at many of these schools (at least, those serving teenage students). The literature shows a relaxed, accepting attitude toward these recreational pursuits, in contrast to their repression in conventional educational institutions. Significantly, one of the central points A. S. Neill made in *Summerhill*—several years before the "hippie" counterculture emerged—was that repression of sexuality was one of the most damaging, life-denying practices of modern education. He did not advocate licentiousness but observed that teens at his school had a healthy and self-controlled interest in sexuality rather than compulsive behavior caused by repression. As George Dennison put it, in defending Neill's controversial views, young people "want a great deal more than sexual freedom. They want *wholeness*. They do not want to lie and evade and suffer guilt, but to affirm themselves in the largest possible harmony of self and society, passion and intellect, duty and pleasure."[49]

The consciousness revolution was, indeed, about a search for wholeness and harmony, qualities that were not valued by a technocratic society or the image of human nature that prevailed in its scientistic theories of psychology and pedagogy. Like child-centered educators of the 1920s,

Neill was influenced by the psychodynamic theory of Sigmund Freud, which acknowledged the powerful and vital forces of the nonrational unconscious. In addition, Neill was a personal friend of Wilhelm Reich, who interpreted Freud's work to signify that repression of erotic energies led to personal misery as well as a closed, controlling, fascist society. It is worth noting that Norman O. Brown, whose books *Life Against Death* (1959) and *Love's Body* (1966) were recognized both by Roszak and by Matusow as important influences on the Dionysian side of the counterculture, also derived his critique from Freudian theory.

This fact is related to the second point I wish to make here. The consciousness revolution fueled an insurgent movement within the field of psychology that included both "humanistic" and "transpersonal" approaches to theory, research, and psychotherapy, and these approaches would have a significant impact on education, by supporting much of the free school ideology but extending it to a less culturally radical audience well into the 1970s and 1980s. (This, indeed, was my own intellectual introduction to countercultural ideologies.) The most direct link is found in the work of Carl Rogers, who translated his "client-centered" psychotherapy into a student-centered educational method in his popular book *Freedom to Learn* (1969). Although more academic in tone than the fiery writings of Neill, Goodman, and Holt, this book was radical and was often on the list of recommended readings for free schoolers. George Leonard's *Education and Ecstasy* was also apparently familiar to many in the free school movement, although his popular critiques of schooling from ten years earlier seem to have been forgotten. Neither Rogers nor Leonard became actively involved in the free school movement, apparently focusing their own involvement in workshops, seminars, and retreats for *adult* learners seeking liberation.

While Rogers was pioneering his work well before the 1960s, it is quite clear that the counterculture stirred much greater interest in the "human potential" movement than could possibly have been imagined in the previous decade. Timothy Leary and Richard Alpert (later known as Ram Dass) began exploring LSD as psychology professors at Harvard, and what could have remained an academic interest in states of consciousness was transformed into a radical cultural critique by the unique historical context of the time. Even as a purely scholarly pursuit, transpersonal psychology would probably not have attracted as much interest as it has without the young generation's quest to transcend their culture's worldview. (For example, Charles Tart's notion of "consensus trance" [explaining how reality is defined by cultural conditioning] would make no sense to an observer who is himself or herself thoroughly entranced.) I am trying to emphasize again that free school ideology does not stand alone, as an ephemeral outburst of spite against conventional forms of education, but fits into an intellectual pattern of critique and searching that affected many areas of thought during and after the 1960s. Free school ideology was influenced by the consciousness revolution just as it was influenced by the civil rights movement, campus dissent, and the Vietnam War.

The free school movement was an explicit and radical effort to go beyond liberal reforms of public education. There was already a great deal of ferment in American education in the late 1950s and early 1960s, and major foundations as well as the federal government began commissioning and funding massive programs to overhaul the curriculum and teaching practices. But for those who had rejected corporate liberalism, these innovations were insufficient. Surveying the radical education literature in 1969, Beatrice and Ronald Gross declared that "The school crisis has finally broken through to basics. The debates of the fifties about academic rigor and 'life adjustment,' the sputnik-sparked worries that we were falling behind the Russians in producing scientists, Dr. Conant's concerns about marketable skills and Dr. Flesch's formulas to make Johnny read—all suddenly seem irrelevant. In the big cities the Black communities are demanding full control of their schools, and in the suburbs the students are demanding control of theirs." Indeed, they continued, liberal reforms did not address the fact that "larger social forces were calling into question the relevance of the entire enterprise of formal education."[50] As I turn next to the substance of free school ideology, I will show that it was essentially an effort to remedy this loss of relevance.

CHAPTER 2

Free School Ideology

Free school ideology, articulated in radical educational writings between 1960 and the early 1970s, reflected a shared experience of existential dissatisfaction. The free school movement was not simply a body of educational techniques but a radical response to troubling feelings of disillusionment and alienation. It makes little sense to interpret the dissident educational writings of the period outside of this context, since their obvious passion and often extreme rhetoric distinguish them from the more measured texts on educational philosophy and practice to which many readers, particularly scholars and education professionals, are accustomed. The radical critics were not concerned with improving schools or bolstering student achievement; rather, their writings reflected a deeply felt sense that the established system of schooling as such was an oppressive institution that thwarted young people's social, emotional, moral, and even intellectual development. Free school ideology conveyed an urgent desire to rethink the most basic assumptions about teaching, learning, education, and schools. The leading critics who gave voice to educational dissent—authors such as A. S. Neill, John Holt, George Dennison, Paul Goodman, Jonathan Kozol, and Edgar Z. Friedenberg—did not aim to provide careful scholarly analysis of specific educational issues but a frank moral critique of schooling in modern society. Never in the history of American education had such a concerted radical attack been launched against schools, and the purpose of this chapter is to explain why it took place in the 1960s.

THE STUDENT REVOLT AGAINST ALIENATION

The generational rebellion of the 1960s represented a *counterculture*, not strictly a political or intellectual movement, because it pursued a total transformation of American society. The youth movement encompassed far more than campus demonstrations and anti-war marches—it also involved hundreds of underground newspapers (including many published by high school students) that gave voice to radical ideas and experimental self-expression; thousands of young people joined communes, often leaving modern urban life for rustic, simple lives on the land; folk and rock music provided a popular, unifying voice of protest; the young developed distinctive fashions in clothing and appearance (radical males, especially, were often identified by their long hair); and many experimented with marijuana, LSD, and other drugs to alter or enhance consciousness.

What were these people looking for? Theodore Roszak argued in his perceptive study that youths above all sought to escape the depersonalization of mass technological society; they felt that modern institutions objectified and manipulated people and instead they sought open, emotionally authentic, face-to-face relationships; they rejected technocratic systems and celebrated mystery, sensuality, emotion, and immediate experience. Reviewing the underground high school press, journalist Diane Divoky found this to be a common theme. Students were saying that "in this depersonalized, technological society, what is most needed is feeling. . . . The adult is told: 'You don't understand.' Often this means 'you don't feel anything about this. It's just an intellectual exercise for you.'" The counterculture, including the educational rebellion to which it gave rise, was at its heart a search for wholeness, for existentially genuine experience. Paul Goodman stated that dissenting youth were rebelling against a system that meant "death to the spirit," while Erich Fromm claimed that student protest represented "a deep hunger for life." Todd Gitlin recounts the feeling that young people were attempting to rescue "the natural, the primitive, the unrefined, the holy unspoiled child, the pagan body" from their repression by the "plastic" culture of mainstream America. A manual for free schoolers was devoted to "finding ways to free our children from the controls that warp their growth. . . . Instead of a reality based on measurement, the new ways are feeling what you really are and trusting that."[1]

Young people were alienated because they felt disempowered. Two critics wrote, "The students see the shape of the future as one in which their needs will be disregarded, and in which the emergence of free men, as they define the term, will be an impossibility, because of the need for social control and because of hypertrophic organization." Peter Marin, a well known figure in the free school movement through his eloquent writings and involvement in the alternative Pacific High School in California, stated young people's predicament in a potent essay published in 1969 by the (liberal) Center for the Study of Democratic Institutions. He claimed that "Students are encouraged to relinquish their own wills, their freedom of volition; they are taught that value and culture reside outside oneself and must be acquired from the institution. . . . It is almost as if we hoped to discourage them from thought itself by making ideas so lifeless, so hopeless, that their despair would be enough to make them manipulable and obedient." Marin placed the radical educational critique squarely in the larger political and social critique by concluding that "one realizes that what is done in the schools to persons is deeply connected to what we did to the blacks or are doing now in Vietnam."[2]

The rebellion of the 1960s spread to thousands of young people because they perceived that human beings could not find meaningful fulfillment in a society that had become technocratic, a society that *used* human energies for impersonal economic purposes or worse, for destructive ends. They experienced a gap between their desires for community, transcendence, and ecstatic experience on one side, and a culture that demanded competition, adherence to well-defined roles, and satisfaction through consumption of commodities on the other. The counterculture spawned a distinctive educational ideology because young people, idealistic educators, and even some parents recognized that schooling was a major agent for harnessing youths' vital energies and narrowing their ideals in the service of a smoothly managed corporate society. One student, reflecting on her reasons for dropping out of school and becoming involved in an alternative school, recalled being deeply disappointed at the way learning was reduced to "predigested material" and "isolated meaningless units of information." She reported that "I was also learning to hate school because learning was inseparable from a system of control which I found oppressive and humiliating. . . . We saw the educational system as an extension of a society which wanted to train its young people to accept the Vietnamese war and to leave ecology, the arms race, and other significant issues forgotten. . . . The sedative effects of the school's structure was [*sic*] destroying my only resources—energy and enthusiasm." One group of students at a college near Chicago believed that the young generation must find new "social and psychological attitudes which are necessary to the development and maintenance of personal autonomy in a technologically routinized, bureaucratically organized society." In a book that emerged from their study they reported that "It was clear to us that an alternative to our present future of diminished freedoms must be based upon an alternative to our present view of man as a creature to be externally coerced, shaped, or otherwise conformed to pre-existing and ultimately arbitrary norms and standards."[3]

Many students similarly felt that their schooling was irrelevant, or worse, repressive. The underground press, free school literature, and even occasional articles in the mainstream press all revealed that in the mid- to late 1960s, large numbers of students felt that what they were taught in school was entirely disconnected from important events in the world and in their lives. At a time that the culture was in turmoil, most schools attempted to carry on business as usual—preparing students for their slots in the corporate economy—and many young people found this dishonest and disillusioning. In its second issue in August 1966, the pioneering radical education journal *This Magazine is About Schools* commented that "most people have decided that the schools had nothing to do with the quality of life and everything to do with training for jobs. . . . High school students, taking their cue from university students, protest, grumble, and are restless about having to get most of their real education outside school walls." Divoky noted that "the student voice in the underground papers is a totally different one from that which speaks in English class compositions. . . . The disparity in the voices is a telling comment on the schools." A group of Milwaukee students who had dropped out to form a free school were quoted in a *New York Times* article in 1970 as saying that "Kids are pumped through the system like products, never learning to think at all" and "Here was this nice sterile little cubicle, and you'd turn your mind off when you went inside. When you got out you'd turn it back on." An article about a free school in Bloomington, Indiana, quoted a 16-year-old girl who had been an honor student: "I really was bored. The school institution crushes an individual."[4]

These representative samplings illustrate widespread and deeply felt experiences among young people in the 1960s. A critic of higher education reported that "when college freshmen arrive they are bewildered, fearful and alienated rather than enthusiastic or hopeful. Parents tell me their kids are so turned off by the schools that they go only to avoid the loneliness and emptiness of the home." The movement for alternative education was stimulated, to a great degree, by this alienation. Alongside their radical responses to social and political issues of the time, students demanded substantive change in the institutions that touched them most directly—their universities and schools. As early as 1962, the Port Huron Statement had called for students to "wrest control of the educational process from the administrative bureaucracy," and by 1965 the idea of "free universities" was being discussed at an SDS convention. This idea sought to apply the vision of human scale, participatory democracy to educational institutions. Jane Lichtman observed that "in place of anonymity, coldness, regulations, rigid time schedules and remote rulings, free u's welcome people with warmth, encouragement, and cooperation."[5]

Similarly, many free schools were started in immediate response to adolescent students' growing alienation. To cite one example, an alternative school in Maine (which is still in existence over thirty years later) was founded in the late 1960s because students felt local public schools were increasingly irrelevant. "Their concerns were deeper than the issues their school work and teachers addressed," one of the school's longtime staff members reflected. "Outside of school they discussed war, the draft, injustice, racism, freedom, love, birth control and environmental destruction. Above all, they felt a lack of freedom to be themselves, a lack of space to follow their individual interests, and a lack of adults to listen to their passions and fears." Free schools sought to remedy this disconnection between learning and real-life issues, concerns, and needs. One participant specifically defined the free school as "a place which responds directly to the individual needs of the community which composes it—everything flows from that." She defined the free school as a learning environment in which "the child's place, values, inclinations, curiosities, passions, interests are taken seriously. I see it as a place where an organic connection can be made between form and content, where the past, present, and future can be explored fully, honestly and critically, where neither method nor content is censored or confined according to arbitrary philosophy or authority, where learning is not distinct from living and is, consequently, joyous though not always comfortable."[6]

This passage contains several key words and phrases that define free school ideology and distinguish such schools as counterinstitutions. Education in free schools was intended to be "organic"—learning would be rooted in meaningful experience rather than made abstract and remote. Learning was intended to be "joyous" and passionate rather than strictly cognitive and informational. Honesty, directness, and spontaneity were to be honored, not bound by "arbitrary" academic or bureaucratic controls. In these ways, free school ideology responded directly to a widespread experience of cultural disillusionment and disempowerment by redefining education as an open-ended, responsive process that made room for a wide range of human experiences, feelings, desires, and needs.

VOICES OF EDUCATIONAL DISSENT

Against this background of alienation and the search for authenticity by thousands of young people, a small group of writers—a few of them social scientists, others classroom teachers—produced a body of literature that came to define the free school ideology. They inspired many of the young people and disaffected educators who fled from public schooling to free schools; the writers articulated their experiences and showed that alternative forms of education were possible. From the perspective of intellectual and social history, these writings help explain the ideas, beliefs, and hopes that motivated thousands of people to turn against the previously respected institution of public education. None of these writers, with the possible exception of Paul Goodman, are generally considered to be important intellectual figures. However, they were acutely sensitive to the temper of the 1960s and fashioned a critique of schooling that anticipated the more systematic, academically sophisticated "critical pedagogy" of the 1980s and 1990s. Although their books are not widely read today, their critique remains relevant. These writers accurately described the alienating environment of contemporary schools, a dehumanizing environment that still produces disillusionment and, in recent years, outbursts of murderous violence.

Around mid-century a handful of social scientists, such as William H. Whyte in *The Organization Man* (1957), C. Wright Mills in *White Collar* (1951) and *The Power Elite* (1956), and Vance Packard in *The Hidden Persuaders* (1957) and *The Waste Makers* (1960), observed that postwar American culture had become over-organized, conformist, and dominated by inauthentic values of mass marketing, public relations, and the relentless pursuit of consumer goods. Two critics in particular explored the effects of this mass consumer culture on the social and psychological development of young people—sociologist Edgar Z. Friedenberg and anthropologist Jules Henry. In *The Vanishing Adolescent* (1959), Friedenberg argued that modern society had become existentially sterile and through its system of schooling it prevented young people from defining their own individuality and authenticity. He claimed that the task of adolescence is to learn "the complex, subtle, and precious difference" between one's individuality and conventional social definitions of identity. We individuate, said Friedenberg, by gaining self-acceptance and self-understanding through developing competence, but "as more and more enclaves of autonomous activity are opened up commercially, the role of individual competence declines, to be replaced by discrimination in choice among mass-produced articles." In this context, education does not enable young people to establish *meaning* in their lives but is merely "the source of the certification prerequisite to getting a decent job in a society grown much too impersonal to depend on face-to-face assessment of competence." In his preface to the 1964 edition of the book, Friedenberg made reference to an "absurd, dangerous, and rather contemptible economic system" that bred manipulation, anxiety, and alienation. Here, indeed, was a frontal assault on the cultural foundations of American schooling, among the most penetrating critiques of education since social reconstructionism in the 1930s.[7]

In *Coming of Age in America* (1965) Friedenberg described teens as a colonized population, economically dependent and exploited. He railed against the techniques high schools used to control students' behavior, and observed that mass society in general was unable to accommodate authentic individuality. "An extremely important social function of the school," he wrote, "is to protect society from 'subjectivity.'. . . The school is not there to help John find himself; its purpose is to help youngsters 'make something *out* of themselves,' some useful thing." Friedenberg reiterated his earlier contention that the primary developmental task for the adolescent is self-definition, but that contemporary society "is too contemptuous of human dignity" to allow for this. He argued that education must be disengaged from the purpose of economic or career security and scorned an economic system that imposed "an infantile and unproductive status on adolescents and indoctrinat[ed] them with a need for trashy goods and shallow, meretricious relationships that they know to be degrading."[8]

In a 1962 essay published in his collection *The Dignity of Youth & Other Atavisms* (1965), Friedenberg expressed the core of his critique of technocratic society, a belief that would later be the foundation of the youth counterculture: "Liberation and spontaneity are more valuable than anything else I could name; and more of them for one individual means more for all, rather than less." In other essays he argued, again, that American society feared spontaneity, particularly in adolescents, and sought to constrain it through the confining roles and petty rules of schooling. Referring to John Dewey, Friedenberg proposed that "education, if it is to have any depth, must start with and be derived from the life-experience of the student, which is in some measure unique for every boy or girl" but that public schooling serves "to establish a common response to certain key stimuli"; as John Holt would also argue, the student is primarily trained to produce the right answer. "Of course, his inner voice gradually gets a lot softer and more plaintive." Friedenberg's writings constituted a coherent and penetrating critique of modern schooling's effects on young people. He identified the widening separation between the values and purposes of an impersonal social order, and the innate need of young people to find meaning and authentic identity. This separation was a major cause of the disillusionment and alienation young people experienced in the 1960s, and Friedenberg was among the first social critics to address the problem. With this iconoclastic analysis of American education, he became established as an elder within the free school movement and later contributed writings to its publications and spoke at several of its gatherings.[9]

Jules Henry's *Culture Against Man* (1963) was another early work in the literature of radical educational critique. Henry attacked American culture's "lopsided preoccupation with amassing wealth and raising its standard of living"; he pointed out that controls on impulse and greed built into more traditional cultures have been abandoned, and the modern economic system is driven to create new needs and wants to consume its output. Individuals must renounce their true selves, must become "fuzzy-minded and impulsive" in order to continue pursuing the elusive goals of consumerism; Henry singled out the advertising industry for enticing people "to respond to pseudo-values as if they were responding to real ones." Henry, though, more explicitly considered the effect these trends were having on education. After studying classrooms for several years, Henry concluded that children "are taught to adopt alienation as a way of life"; they are taught to compete—to "wring success" from other students' failure. They do not learn to love knowledge but to fear failure. Henry argued that schooling conditioned young people to measure themselves by others' expectations rather than their own.[10]

Henry was no romantic anarchist. As an anthropologist, he recognized that education in any culture must serve the ambiguous function of conserving the cultural heritage while allowing creativity and discovery. But his critique of American culture, which also included lengthy discussions of mental illness and retirement homes, suggested that there was little of value in this culture to conserve. Schooling was alienating, not because it used incorrect or outdated methods, but because American culture itself was hostile to authentic individuality. Although Henry was not, as far as I can determine, active in the free school movement (he died in 1969), his critique provides a basis for distinguishing the free school movement from progressive reform movements within public education (a distinction that will be explored further in subsequent chapters). Free schools arose because radicals believed that the culture *as a whole* acted to deaden authenticity, therefore its system of education *could not* be saved by improving instructional methods or revising the curriculum. So long as schooling was set up to serve the interests of a competitive, consumerist, mass-mentality society, it could never fully educate young people for lives of meaning and personal integrity, no matter how well-intentioned were its reformers.

One social critic of the early 1960s had even more influence on free school thinking than Friedenberg or Henry. According to educational historian Henry Perkinson, *the* founder of the radical education movement of the 1960s was Paul Goodman, and Theodore Roszak called Goodman "the foremost theoretician of participative democracy" influencing the New Left. Taylor Stoehr spoke for the dissident generation when he wrote that "Goodman changed the lives of many of us simply by naming [the] outrages" of technocratic society, and called him "by far the most important" of "modern American decentralists or anarchists." In several widely read books, Goodman applied his radical democratic views to the topics of schooling, education, and the enculturation of youths, and provided a coherent philosophical framework for free school ideology; he stands out as one of the major theorists of free school ideology.[11]

In the book that established his reputation, *Growing Up Absurd* (1960), Goodman argued that young people are made to conform to a society that does not represent fully human values but is essentially a mechanical system that has lost "genuine culture," human scale community, a sense of quality, and meaningful, useful work. His analysis paralleled that of Friedenberg and Henry, claiming that "our economic society is not geared for the cultivation of its young or the attainment of important goals that they can work toward." Throughout his work, Goodman integrated political, moral, and psychological (or existential) concerns, and this is why his critique was attractive to the New Left and to free schoolers. He called for decentralization of political and economic institutions, and the creation of intimate, participative communities, because he believed that in order to thrive the human psyche requires authentic, meaningful contact with other persons. Whether he wrote about work, the arts, or education, his main goal was to expose the rigid structures that over-formalize human relations and make them inauthentic and irrelevant to people's organic needs and desires. He was a harsh critic of technocracy, writing at one point, for example, "It is notorious that the physical plant and social environment have grown out of human scale. To achieve simple goods it is often necessary to set in motion immense masses. . . . The child sees that competence does not exist in ordinary people, but in the system of interlocking specialties." Schooling was set up to prepare people for these specialties, to temper their creative energies so that they could fulfill narrowly defined roles in the economic system. Why was this wrong? Like Friedenberg, Goodman believed that spontaneity is a vital element of a full and meaningful life. "If society becomes too tightly integrated and pre-empts all the available space, materials, and methods," he explained, "then it is failing to provide for just the margin of formlessness, real risk, novelty, spontaneity, that makes growth possible."[12]

In a later book, *Compulsory Miseducation* (1964), Goodman continued this critique, asserting that the structure of modern society excludes people from meaningful participation or opportunities for personal initiative because corporations and government "dictate the possibilities of enterprise." He claimed that school and the mass media train youth "that life is inevitably routine, depersonalized, venally graded; that it is best to toe the mark and shut up; that there is no place for spontaneity, open sexuality, free spirit." Inundated by this monolithic worldview of materialism and competition, "it is hard for an American child to grow toward independence, to find his identity, to retain his curiosity and initiative. . . . The pervasive philosophy to which children are habituated as they grow up is the orthodoxy of a social machine not interested in persons, except to man and aggrandize itself. . . . The social machine does not require or desire its youth to find identity or vocation; it is interested only in aptitude. It does not want new initiative, but conformity." Here

Goodman explicitly described the evil that free school ideology sought to address: the "social machine" (in other words, technocracy) did not recognize the unique individuality of each person, and did not allow people to value their own inclinations and aspirations.[13]

In order to place Goodman's views in historical perspective, one should recall that during the first sixty years of the twentieth century, many, if not most, leading social theorists and educators explicitly believed that this "orthodoxy of a social machine" was a *positive* approach to managing a complex industrial society. The "technological rationality" that Marcuse, Fromm, Roszak, Goodman, and other critics began to assail in the late 1950s and 1960s was seen as a sign of *progress*—the replacement of faulty beliefs and corrupt politics with scientific rigor and disinterested expertise. In some ways, the technocratic worldview made sense; it did seem reasonable to believe that a diverse society of many millions of people, highly urban and industrialized, rapidly evolving as new technologies continually emerged, could easily disperse into chaos if not carefully managed. In this worldview, efficiency and uniformity came to be valued over spontaneity and individuality so that large-scale productive and administrative functions could be adequately performed. "Identity" and "vocation" are subjective, hence unmanageable, while "aptitude" can be quantified, allowing for each person to find a career, a place in the system, that is objectively more likely to be appropriate.

Goodman and the New Left sought to demonstrate that these considerations clashed with values of democracy and authenticity, and that such values are ultimately more important. In a smoothly managed social order, who did the managing, and what power did they gain from their position that the mass of the population did not enjoy? Furthermore—and here is the heart of the politics of authenticity—what sense of ultimate meaning, purpose, or relevance can people experience when they are merely performing in roles that have been carefully scripted for them by unknown experts? Doesn't being human, asked the radical existentialists, involve more than rational, utilitarian concerns and the pursuit of material wealth? Underlying Goodman's specific criticisms of modern society was a set of ideas about human nature. He believed that "Living functions, biological, psychosociological, or social, have very little to do with abstract, preconceived 'power' that manages and coerces from outside the specific functions themselves. Indeed, it is a commonplace that abstract power—in the form of 'will power,' 'training,' 'discipline,' 'bureaucracy,' 'reform schooling,' 'scientific management,' etc.—uniformly *thwarts* normal functioning and debases the persons involved." Essentially, Goodman believed that the human organism's spontaneous, holistic response to lived situations (that is, authenticity) was more healthy and beneficial than behavior controlled by powerful external agencies, whatever efficiency this control may seem to produce. "Anarchism is grounded in a rather definite proposition: that valuable behavior occurs only by the free and direct response of individuals or voluntary groups to the conditions presented by the historical environment. . . . Anarchists want to increase intrinsic functioning and diminish extrinsic power."[14]

If this is a correct understanding of human nature, then any society that suffocates authentic experience under a regime of control and efficiency is thwarting healthy development and ought to be changed. Goodman, like Lewis Mumford, was aware that the tendency toward systemic control of human activity predated modern technocracy. He commented that "Corporate and bureaucratic societies, whether ruled by priests, mandarins, generals, or business managers, have always tended to diminish the importance of personal needs and human feeling, in the interest of abstractions and systematic necessities." Nevertheless, he believed that the suppression of organic functioning was especially pronounced in the modern age. "I suggest that for a couple hundred years, and suddenly at an accelerating rate, modern societies have colonized and disoriented themselves, imposing on themselves a technology, urbanization, and centralized social organization that they cannot morally and psychologically cope with."[15]

Although Goodman was a self-described "anarchist," he traced his democratic theory back to Jefferson and nineteenth-century American populism rather than to the more desperate European anarchist tradition. His critique of American society apparently reflected a simple desire that America live up to its own ideals. As the youth movement erupted in the mid-1960s, Goodman welcomed it, saying that it expressed, "with remarkable precision, point by point, the opposition to the overcentralized, interlocking, and empty society." (He did become critical of student protest later, however, for what he perceived as anti-intellectual tendencies.)[16]

Goodman believed that cultural renewal could be accomplished, in part, through "progressive" education, which he defined, quite broadly, as "the attempt to naturalize, to humanize, each new social and technical development that is making traditional education irrelevant." He added that "if society would once adopt this reconstruction, we could at last catch up with ourselves and grow naturally into the future." He seemed to be implying by such statements that "progressive" education was not so much a specific technique but any educational approach that enabled young people to engage the world organically, meaningfully. By trusting their inherent capacity to make meaning and fashion a coherent identity, "progressive" education would enable them to build a participatory society that supported rather than hindered human needs. Goodman commended John Dewey's theory of democratic education, but felt that the libertarian pedagogy expressed by A. S. Neill in *Summerhill* went beyond Dewey by addressing the compulsory nature of modern schooling. For Goodman, then, free school ideology was the natural extension of progressive education, adapted to an increasingly bureaucratic society in which the managerial structure of public education sabotaged its own democratic intentions.[17]

For Goodman, progressive education consisted of several key principles: "To learn theory by experiment and doing. To learn belonging by participation and self-rule. Permissiveness in all animal behavior and interpersonal expression. Emphasis on individual differences. . . . Community of youth and adults, minimizing 'authority.' . . . Trying for functional interrelation of activities" and several others. Consistent with his overall philosophy, Goodman argued for the drastic reduction of school bureaucracy and individual school size, and suggested that the ideal environment for urban youths would be storefront learning centers from which students could go into the real world and participate directly in society's affairs. Above all, he criticized the abstract, formal structure of schooling that worked against authentic learning experience: "The whole extrinsic rigmarole of credits, prescribed syllabus, competitive grading, and promotion up the ladder is pedagogically destructive and should simply be scrapped. There is little evidence that a student learns anything of value if he has learned it merely to pass."[18]

Underlying Goodman's educational theory was his anarchist faith in organic, unmanaged human nature. "We can, I believe, educate the young entirely in terms of their free choice, with no processing whatever," he claimed. "It seems stupid to decide *a priori* what the young ought to know and then try to motivate them, instead of letting the initiative come from them and putting information and relevant equipment at their service. . . . Free choice is not random but responsive to real situations; both youth and adults live in a nature of things, a polity, an ongoing society, and it is these, in fact, that attract interest and channel need." *Free choice is not random.* Here, again, is Goodman's emphasis on the holistic meaning of the lived situation. Freedom is not simply a negation of authority, a desire to escape responsibility, but a necessary condition for purposeful and authentic action. Without this freedom, people cannot engage their social world intelligently (as Dewey himself emphasized most highly) but become automatons, performing their assigned roles mechanically and obediently, often in violation of their own true needs and interests. On the basis of this understanding, Goodman's educational theory provided a coherent foundation for the free school movement. Indeed, his entire social critique lent a powerful voice to the discontent and alienation that fueled the rise of free schools, and Goodman participated in free school gatherings until his death in 1972.[19]

Nevertheless, it was another voice, that of a radical British educator named Alexander Sutherland Neill, that rang across the 1960s and, for many, defined the educational rebellion. A. S. Neill opened a boarding school called Summerhill in the 1920s, and although he published several books about his unorthodox educational approach, he failed to attract much interest. In 1960, an American publisher named Harold Hart, who had visited the school, published a compilation of Neill's writings under the title *Summerhill: A Radical Approach to Child Rearing*. At first, this book, too, seemed destined for obscurity, but its message spoke directly to the growing disenchantment with conventional schooling among young people, some progressive parents, and politically galvanized educators. Even before the protest movements of the 1960s had stirred the culture, readers began discovering that Neill gave voice to their misgivings about schooling. Once the cultural critique gained momentum, *Summerhill* became the bible of educational protest and sales climbed: in 1968 alone 100,000 copies were sold, in 1969, 200,000, and in 1970, reported Hart, the book was required reading in 600 university courses.

The few scholars who have studied free school ideology, such as Joel Spring and Robin Barrow, have seen Neill as a key figure in the educational protest movement. His book led to many of the early free school efforts: the Summerhill Society and its *Bulletin* spread the ideas of libertarian pedagogy in the United States during the early 1960s; Herb Snitzer founded one of the first of the 1960s free schools, Lewis-Wadhams, in upstate New York, after visiting Summerhill in 1962; George Dennison named Summerhill as an inspiration for his pioneering free school in New York City; and subsequent books, including *Summerhill: For & Against* (Hart, 1970) and *Summerhill USA* (Bull, 1970), extended the consideration of Neill's ideas. Indeed, various people involved in the educational struggles of the 1960s and early 1970s considered Neill's book to be the single greatest influence on the radical education movement, and one of them explained why: "Like the many young people I had talked to about Summerhill, I realized that I saw in Neill's principles a potential for a benignly radical evolution in western civilization—a deep and basic change in our consciousness."[20]

A. S. Neill's philosophy was actually quite simple; from the perspective of intellectual history one might even call its argument simplistic. In a didactic and self-righteous tone, Neill hammered away at a few major points. First, "My view is that a child is innately wise and realistic. If left to himself without adult suggestion of any kind, he will develop as far as he is capable of developing." There was no subtlety here—this position totally denied the role of adult direction or guidance that virtually all accepted educational theories, even Deweyan progressivism, have accepted as a normal aspect of the social context of learning. Neill was convinced that "true interest is the life force of the whole personality, and such interest is completely spontaneous . . . though one can compel attention, one cannot compel interest." Neill valued this self-generated interest above all other pedagogical considerations, in large part, I believe, to correct what he perceived to be the complete suppression of individual interest by society. Like other critics of the time, he connected educational discipline with the demands of a technocratic economic system. "The world is full of jobs that hold no intrinsic interest or pleasure," Neill charged. "We seem to be adapting our schools to this dullness in life. By compelling our students' attention to subjects which hold no interest for them, we, in effect, condition them for jobs they will not enjoy."[21]

Enjoyment, then, was the second of Neill's simple goals. More specifically, he believed that *happiness* is the primary aim of life, and he demonstrated in his book that students at Summerhill, free from adult coercion and the fear that goes with it, were uncommonly happy. As I explained in Chapter One, Neill was highly influenced by his reading of Freud and his friendship with Wilhelm Reich, and in *Summerhill* he passionately appealed for young people's right to pleasure, including sexual pleasure. He argued that the acceptance of organic impulses was a celebration of life, and their repression a denial of life. He attacked religious teachings that promote guilt and self-hatred, and appealed to his readers "to foster a civilization that will not have sin thrust on it at birth." He stated that unhappiness is the cause of all social problems, including prejudice, violence, and even war. "One day humanity may trace all its miseries, its hates, and its diseases to its particular form of civilization that is essentially anti-life. . . . Because emotions are dynamic, their lack of opportunity for expression must and does result in cheapness and ugliness and hatefulness. . . . Children are deadened by all the forces of reaction and hate. . . . They are trained to say *nay* to life . . . and taught to say *yea* to all that is negative in life."[22]

Like Henry, Friedenberg, and Goodman, although even more polemically, Neill claimed that modern society sacrifices happiness for mechanical, intellectual achievements, and toward the end of the book he analyzed the human situation in terms of stark polarities: "Pro-life equals fun, games, love, interesting work, hobbies, laughter, music, dance, consideration for others, and faith in men. Anti-life equals duty, obedience, profit, and power. Throughout history anti-life has won, and will continue to win as long as youth is trained to fit into present-day adult conceptions." Neill seems to have adopted Freud's theory of the struggle between Eros and Thanatos—the exuberant life force and the dark forces of destructiveness—and uncritically fashioned this theory into a simple model of education. To allow young people to follow their interests, impulses, and passions was to be "pro-life," but to suggest that individuals have any "duty" toward a larger community was to deny life. While a more sophisticated theorist can easily debunk this simplistic dichotomy, Neill's formula struck a responsive chord at a time when the technocratic social order and consumer culture of the twentieth century were taken to represent any community beyond the individual.[23]

Neill's third major point, which followed from the first two, was an emphasis on "self-government." Summerhill was governed by all-school meetings in which all children, even the youngest, had an equal vote. Other than upholding a basic respect for individuals' property and personal rights (Neill insisted that by "freedom" he did not mean "license"), Summerhill did not regulate young people's behavior. Neill wrote at length about his *therapeutic* approach toward children's antisocial actions; rather than punish them he would provide counseling, often of a Freudian nature, which sought to allay anxiety presumably caused by sexual fantasies or tensions. He described instances where he *rewarded* children for damaging property, sending a message that they had no reason to attack authority because there was none. Indeed, he emphasized that Summerhill was a healing environment, and that young people who transferred from oppressive homes and schools, psychologically damaged and angry, simply needed time in a free environment to learn self-regulation.

Educationally, as well, Neill insisted upon self-government. No child was required to attend any class, and Neill was not concerned about grade levels, curricula, or even "basic" academic skills such as reading. His experience at Summerhill demonstrated that young people, freed from anxiety, would learn when and what they chose, and their learning would be meaningful to them. Perhaps Neill's most radical departure from the conventional purposes of schooling was his attitude toward competition and success; he wanted his students to be happy rather than successful in the world's terms, if this meant losing their sense of selfhood. He proudly related stories of Summerhill graduates who were content as craftspeople or mechanics, doing work they loved rather than pursuing status and wealth that did not bring happiness.

Writing several years later, in the foreword to a book about the Summerhill-inspired Lewis-Wadhams School, Neill restated the essence of his educational outlook. Free schools, he said, give children "from the sick environment a chance to live life fully and bravely and charitably"; we need to "let kids be themselves, and in a few generations the world will become healthy and happy." He stated that "The function of Lewis-Wadhams, and of Summerhill and the new schools, is to fight the mass molding that makes the world an evil place. We pioneers think of education as living, not the exam system set by the Establishment. . . . Picasso could not get a job teaching art in a British or American school because he had not passed any exams." Here, Neill was making a point that was emphasized repeatedly in the free school literature: education should be directly, organically connected to the young person's own life, and not consist of abstractions (curricula, standards, credentials, exams) imposed on the child's life by external authorities. Healthy personal development and a healthy, peaceful society demand that individuals be allowed to enjoy their own authentic experiences.[24]

For all its simplicity, Neill's anti-authoritarian philosophy of education resonated for many readers of the time. Erich Fromm, the leading social critic to come out of the psychoanalytic movement, recognized and applauded Neill's assault on an economic system that alienated authentic human needs and subverted genuine freedom. In the foreword to *Summerhill*, Fromm gave his own position that modern society produces men "whose tastes are standardized, men who can be easily influenced, men whose needs can be anticipated," and then pronounced that "Neill does not try to educate children to fit well into the existing order, but endeavors to rear children who will become happy human beings, men and women whose values are not to *have* much, not to *use* much, but to *be* much." In a later essay, Fromm gave a concise description of technocracy and claimed that Neill's views were an antidote. "Our system tends to make people part of the machine, or subparts of the parts—all unified by the selfsame program transmitted to everyone through the same education, the same radio, the same television, the same magazine." Fromm maintained that "Summerhill presents the possibility of a life-oriented rather than a death-oriented culture. Neill's fundamental goal is to bring up children who are alive, who are inwardly active individuals rather than passive spectators and consumers." At Summerhill, Fromm continued, the child became "in tune with Nature, in tune with the rhythm that pulses through all existence."[25]

In this way, Neill's ideas spoke directly to the emerging counterculture. By identifying technocratic society as "evil" and pronouncing the repressed energies of the psyche and the body as wholly good, Neill gave dissident educators, young people, and even parents full permission to reject their culture and its schooling. *Summerhill* freed its readers from allegiance to established social and economic structures and passionately invited them to create new ones. Michael Rossman, the Berkeley activist, wrote that the young generation responded enthusiastically to *Summerhill* because they had been "born into a culture dominated by pathological authoritarian control" and were now seeking to escape it.

In the same volume, Eda J. LeShan commented that "Neill ought to be triumphant about these young people on the barricades. . . . They are the first generation who was raised with more kindness than fear, more understanding than punishment" and this accounted for their sensitivity to injustice and their desire for authentic relationships.[26]

Joel Spring, an educational historian sympathetic to radical and libertarian critiques, commented that Neill's intention was fundamentally political; along with Reich he ultimately aimed to rid the world of fascism by challenging the suppression of vital energies. Curiously, Neill himself disavowed political intentions. In *Summerhill* he stated that he would not attempt to change society because he would only meet with resistance, perhaps violence. Later he wrote that "to treat adults is not the way" to change the world, and bluntly said that a free school represents no political creed. Neill's daughter, Zoe Readhead, confirmed that "Neill was a very un-political animal. He never really said much about his political leanings." Although Spring, Fromm, Rossman, LeShan, and others saw definite political implications in Neill's ideas, many readers did not, and *Summerhill* became the bible of the extreme romantics in the free school movement, those who idealized individual freedom and self-expression and sought retreat from the evils of society rather than political engagement. Consequently, critics of *Summerhill,* both sympathetic readers like Bruno Bettelheim and Fred Hechinger, and disapproving ones like Robin Barrow, rightly warned that Neill's polemics were oversimplified, bordering on anti-intellectual, and needed to be considered in a larger context.[27]

Barrow, for example, questioned Neill's "string of disconnected and dubious pronouncements," unsupported by any systematic evidence. Neill assumed, he pointed out, that human happiness depends upon children's desires being immediately and consistently gratified, ignoring the possibility that long-term happiness depends on a measure of self-discipline and sacrifice. Neill overemphasized the role of interest and neglected the important fact that children inhabit a vast, complex world that their elders know and to which they can and should introduce young people. Barrow charged that Neill, in common with radical educators in general, substituted his own emotional judgments for careful empirical description; consequently, he considered the individual to be unrealistically good and society to be the source of all evil, and did not consider the possibility that "individuals might be responsible for evil and misery because they are selfish and nasty."[28]

From a logical point of view, Barrow's critique is accurate, and a more careful educational theorist, someone of the caliber of John Dewey, for example, would avoid such unbalanced and unsupported arguments. But the fact remains that Neill's writing inspired thousands of people in the 1960s, while Dewey's did not. Disaffected students and educators were looking for an escape from a culture they experienced as deadening and repressive, and in Summerhill they found a route of escape and a beacon of hope. They would find through their own experiences where an extreme anti-authoritarian ideology could lead.

As Neill approached the end of his long life, he remarked that his work would be carried on by another radical educator/author, John Holt. After the publication of *How Children Fail* in 1964, Holt soon became established as a major voice of educational critique. He had taught in progressive private schools in Colorado and Massachusetts since 1953, but even in these select environments, he discovered that the established routines of schooling were in basic opposition to children's natural ways of learning. "Most children in school fail," he declared. "Except for a handful, who may or may not be good students, they fail to develop more than a tiny part of the tremendous capacity for learning, understanding and creating with which they were born and of which they made full use during the first two or three years of their lives." For the next twenty years, Holt returned again and again to this theme, seeking ways to help teachers and parents sustain young people's "tremendous capacity for learning." He wrote numerous articles in popular and professional publications as well as a series of additional books that became increasingly radical as he became more discouraged about the prospect of genuinely changing schools; he moved from helping classroom teachers, to supporting alternative schools, to promoting the then-outrageous notion, first suggested by Ivan Illich around 1969–70, of complete "deschooling." In 1977 Holt established the newsletter *Growing Without Schooling*, which became an important catalyst for the rise of the home education movement.[29]

Holt was a major contributor to the free school movement. He traveled around the country, giving talks and visiting hundreds of schools by 1969. He corresponded with hundreds of parents, students, educators, authors, editors, political leaders, and activists. In a 1970 letter he commented that he had been to over 100 meetings in the preceding month and a half alone, and had a nearly eight-inch stack of mail to answer. He gathered information on educational experiments and in the early years of the movement he was a primary contact for people looking for schools or wanting to start one.[30] He also inspired the movement through his writings. He bluntly argued in *How Children Fail* that "children are subject peoples. School for them is a kind of jail. Do they not, to some extent, escape and frustrate the relentless, insatiable pressure of their elders by withdrawing the most intelligent and creative parts of their minds from the scene?" Holt punctuated his point with an ironic statement: "To a very great degree, school is a place where children learn to be stupid."[31]

In *The Underachieving School*, a collection of magazine articles that was published in 1969, Holt expanded on his critique, arguing that "There is much fine talk in schools about Teaching Democratic Values. What the children really learn is Practical Slavery. How to suck up [to] the boss. How to keep out of trouble, and get other people in. . . . Set into mean-spirited competition against other children, he learns that every man is the natural enemy of every other man." As an alternative to this controlled, competitive educational process, Holt asserted that education must revolve around the learner's own experiences, interests, and inclinations: "I believe that we learn best when we, not others, are deciding what we are going to try to learn, and when, and how, and for what reasons or purposes." Holt's critique evolved into a radical student-centered position that echoed Neill's insistence on each individual learner's own interests.[32]

Holt's educational theory contained a strong political dimension, which, although not always apparent, was more explicit than Neill's. At various points in his writings, particularly during the height of the antiwar and counterculture movements between 1968 and 1972, Holt demonstrated that his concern about education reflected a broader critique of modern society. Like other free school authors, Holt was essentially concerned with the displacement of democracy by the rise of technocracy. "Part of the trouble of our times," he wrote, "is that so many people feel that their lives and the institutions around them have somehow slipped out of their control, or even the possibility of their control." At first mainly concerned with ineffective teaching techniques, he came to believe that schooling as such played an integral part in the management of a hierarchical society. The educational system, he concluded, was in "the business of turning people into commodities, and deciding who goes where in our society and who gets what." In a 1973 letter to Ivan Illich, he stated his view even more specifically, claiming that all large social institutions are "machines whose parts are human beings. Like all other machines, they depend for their swift, smooth and sure functioning on the reliability, precision and interchangeability of these parts. . . . As you have pointed out, it is the function of education in the modern state to turn people into serviceable parts for their institutional machinery." This is a very clear definition of the notion of "technocracy" as it was understood by social critics at the time.[33]

In common with other authors associated with the free school movement, Holt essentially argued that conventional forms of schooling did not serve young people's authentic growth, but were intended to mold children into compliant servants of the corporate state, alienated from their genuine interests and passions. Even more explicitly than other education critics, he expressed fear that actual fascism was on the rise in the United States, and in such a cultural climate, he did not believe that institutional forms of education could possibly nourish children's full development into happy, autonomous persons. Consequently, in the early 1970s he became disillusioned with all efforts to reform schooling, and began to advocate learning outside of conventional institutional forms. The evolution of Holt's educational and social critique sheds a great deal of light on the historical context of free school ideology, and I will describe his ideas in greater depth in the following chapter.

One other author, George Dennison, deserves recognition as a major proponent of free school ideology. Although his masterpiece, *The Lives of Children*, did not appear until 1969, well after the movement was under way, the quality of his writing gave the free school position its most coherent expression. Holt called this volume "by far the most perceptive, moving, and important book on education that I have ever read, or indeed ever expect to."[34] Dennison was a fiction writer, youth worker, and gestalt therapist who helped open The First Street School in the lower east side of New York City in the fall of 1964. He kept a journal of his daily experiences as a teacher, and although he left the school after only one year (it closed the following year), he immortalized it in the stirring book that grew from his journal.

Dennison was genuinely concerned, as both teacher and writer, with the lives of the twenty-three children in the school, most of them poor and many from Puerto Rican or African American families. He sought to understand their world and their struggles, and to make their education responsive to the actual needs of their lives. He described an educational approach that was concerned with the *wholeness* of human experience, and his writing reflected his search for balance, harmony, and openness to a wide range of feelings, ideas, and actions. Like Neill, he demanded freedom for young people—but then he was careful to define freedom in relation to the communal and social context without which freedom has no meaning. Issues of authority and freedom, he said, cannot be decided abstractly or remotely, but involve concrete situations in actual human relationships. When "arbitrary rules of order are dispensed with," he wrote, children's hunger for knowledge and understanding meets the teacher's genuine interest in their lives, and in this relationship of collaboration and trust, a decent and human education takes place. Without an artificial order, an "internal" order emerges through caring relationships. "Education must be *lived*. It cannot be *administered*. And we have become, as a nation, a wretched hog wallow of administrative functions. . . . We abolished tests and grades and Lesson Plans. We abolished Superiors, too—all that petty and disgusting pecking order of the school bureaucracy which contributes nothing to the wisdom of teachers and still less to the growth of the child." *The Lives of Children* is filled with stories of Dennison's (and the other teachers') caring, authentic, creative responses to their students' struggles to grow and learn. It portrays education as a human engagement, an ever-evolving effort to find meaning in shared experience rather than an obsession with the content of the curriculum or academic results determined by a fixed timetable.[35]

Dennison's work is particularly coherent for three reasons. First, his phenomenological descriptions of children are unsurpassed. He sensitively described their personal struggles to find meaning, self-esteem, and emotional security against obstacles of race, class, language, and a culture that in many ways was hostile to them. The reader comes to know his students intimately and understand their struggles from their own point of view. Dennison's argument for libertarian education is rooted in these children's lives, not in some sociological critique or romantic utopian vision. The First Street School comes alive in a way that Neill's Summerhill does not (although Dennison, like Fromm and others, acknowledged the vital qualities of Neill's personality and school despite his bombastic prose). A second source of the book's clarity is that Dennison did not simply proclaim a personal vision of social transformation, but explicitly grounded his ideas in a historical intellectual tradition—specifically, Dewey's philosophy of experience. Dennison took from Dewey the notion that a "scientific" approach to experience (or, more specifically, to education) "is instrumental, wholly alive in the life of the present, yet it is open to the future and is no enemy of change. Free thought is its essence, yet it is disciplined by its devotion to emergent meaning. It places the highest value upon ideas, cannot function without them, defines them scrupulously, yet never enshrines them into final truths. . . . It might be well to contrast Dewey's thought, and the style of his thought, his habit of mind, with the prevailing style of our educationists."[36]

It is also instructive to contrast Dewey's—and Dennison's—"habit of mind" with the prevailing free school style. Other than Paul Goodman (who personally influenced Dennison), few free schoolers recognized the usefulness of Dewey's radical yet carefully balanced philosophy. Following Neill's example, most tended to proclaim the absolute value of freedom without recognizing, as did Dewey, the social and intellectual meanings of individual experience. Dewey sought to correct what he perceived as excessive individualism in progressive education in his 1938 book *Experience and Education*, and Dennison cited this argument to distinguish his own approach from common free school assumptions. Using Dewey's balanced thinking as a touchstone for reflecting on his own educational practice, Dennison was neither obsessively anti-authoritarian (he wrote at length about the "natural authority" of caring adults in children's lives) nor anti-intellectual. With this perspective Dennison also bridged the split between the "political" and "existential" (or romantic) elements of free school ideology, a point I address later in this chapter. This is the third reason I see his work as especially coherent.

ELEMENTS OF FREE SCHOOL IDEOLOGY

Several core themes recurred consistently in the writings of Goodman, Neill, Holt, Dennison, and other writers connected to the free school movement. Although these authors brought idiosyncratic, if not unique, perspectives to the social and educational critique I am calling free school ideology and disagreed on various points, I believe that the common themes identify a distinctive educational theory that reflected the struggles and ideals of the 1960s counterculture.[37]

Len Solo, who as coordinator of the Teacher Drop-out Center (TDOC) was familiar with hundreds of free schools, discussed the common beliefs of people in the "new schools" movement in a 1972 doctoral dissertation. He identified one primary belief as the conviction that "humans are naturally curious and, if given support and love in a rich environment, they will continuously learn and grow." This core idea logically led to a cluster of others: "Schools must be small so people can have close, face-to-face contact because schools are, first and foremost, places for personal relationships; schools should be democracies—places where the participants are directly and equally involved in the decision-making processes that affect their lives, places that provide for many alternatives, ones that involve real choices that are meaningful to students; schools should have heterogeneous populations because heterogeneity provides a basis for growth . . . ; schools should not be compulsory, for a student must be free to choose and grow in his own directions if he is to be an independent, integrated being; schools should provide a wide variety of learning situations, hopefully meeting the needs of each student; schools should be places where there are adults who deeply care for children . . . ; schools should be communities, places where there is a true sense of belonging, togetherness, caring and sharing." Each of these beliefs reflected a desire to provide individuals support and love (or caring) rather than seeing students as raw social or economic material to be molded into some preferred form. This was the heart of free school ideology.[38]

The archives of TDOC, as well as the New Schools Exchange papers at Yale University, contain flyers and brochures from many of the free schools, and a thorough review of these documents largely confirms Solo's list of common beliefs. To cite just one example, an excerpt from the flyer of a free school in Colorado weaves together several of these themes:

> What goes on in the Community School is determined by the needs and interests the children show through their relationships among themselves and with their teachers. For this to work, everyone must be known well by everyone else. That is why the school is small. For this reason, too, the school is experimental: trying new things as they are suggested by the changing requirements of changing children. . . . The school does not insulate the children with child experts. Inclination is more useful than training, and so the school welcomes young and old volunteers who are inclined to work with children.[39]

Dozens of school brochures made similar statements. In free schools, individuals' needs and interests held priority over any predetermined curriculum. There were no authoritative texts, subject areas, or lesson plans for students to digest—rather, they were free to enjoy their own experience as whole human beings within an intimate and caring community. Such schools did not want teachers' involvement limited by professional roles or methods of instruction but encouraged teachers to become interested and involved in young people's lives, and responsive to their needs and experiences. Free schools attempted to build genuine communities in which people could learn naturally, organically, and freely—honoring their own internal rhythms and styles of learning and their own inherent curiosity and desire for growth.

The belief system of free school ideology is quite plain to see. Interpreting it is another matter. To the small number of people who have been involved in alternative schools since the 1960s, free school ideology is simply common sense—a democratic educational theory for a society that presumably aspires to be democratic: free schools for free people. To some critics, however, this way of approaching education is merely "romantic"—unrealistically radical and hopelessly naïve about the educational requirements of modern society. However, I wish to understand the free school literature from a broader and more historical perspective. The radical educational critique of the 1960s represented a specific response to American culture at the time. Sociologist Ann Swidler, in her analysis of free school beliefs, identified the ideological agenda that lay behind the rise of the free school movement. In common with other countercultural organizations of the late 1960s, free schools were dedicated to abolishing "competitive individualism, attacking traditional forms of inequality, rehumanizing 'dehumanized' services, and reintegrating the divided, specialized individual." This agenda exactly reflects the pattern of 1960s-era dissent: it is an existentialist politics, a search for authenticity, in reaction against a culture perceived as overly competitive, materialistic, and technocratic. When free school people said they were striving for "community" or "relationships," they were not simply offering a pedagogical technique they thought would help students learn more effectively, but were trying to provide a social space in which human beings—adults as well as children—could explore and enjoy the fullness and richness of their experience.[40]

The elements of free school ideology make sense in terms of this cultural context. As Allen Graubard pointed out in 1974, the free school movement did not stand alone but represented "the same spirit of radical critique that has appeared in many sectors of American society over the past decade. . . . If one holds attitudes radically critical of the dominant values and institutions, how can one seriously expect public schools or any other official institution to represent or support attitudes that are significantly subversive of the status quo?" Free schools represented a redefinition of "education" itself—an exploration of what education might become in a culture that was authentic rather than hierarchically managed. The radical educational ideology was subversive because it was not just calling for friendlier environments for children, but for a thorough overhaul of society's attitude toward young people and their learning. Still, despite using the charged term "subversive," Graubard hinted at a notion that I discussed earlier: 1960s-era radicalism was not antithetical to American ideals but sought to reclaim them in a fuller and more authentic fashion. Graubard saw free schools as "keeping with a great American tradition of self-help." Similarly, Theodore Sizer, who was not connected to the free school movement (he was then recently dean of the Harvard Graduate School of Education), commented in 1973 that the radical education critics were simply expressing a key American value—the belief in essential human dignity.[41]

Indeed, free school ideology was a peculiarly American combination of "self-help" (a search for self-expression, self-actualization, and personal authenticity) and ideals of justice and democracy that must apply to all persons, black as well as white, young as well as old. Although there were tensions within the movement between those who emphasized one or the other of these ideals, each side realized that it was inextricably allied with the other. In American mythology, "freedom" carries ambiguous meanings, connoting both personal sovereignty and universal human rights.[42] The radicals of the 1960s believed that the growing bureaucracy of corporate liberalism was rapidly eroding freedom on both fronts, and they desperately tried to restore it. It is only in this light that one can appreciate the phenomenology of free school ideology, the meaning it held for the thousands of people who opened or attended free schools.

This ideology rested on a particular conception of human nature—the belief that human beings are *naturally* inclined to grow and learn in healthy ways if not thwarted by oppressive or shortsighted social practices. A pamphlet for a free school in Georgia declared that "a student's natural curiosity, freed from the burdens of competition and threats, and guided by an affirming environment, will lead him to a quest for knowledge of himself and his world. . . . Young people have a natural curiosity and need little further inducement to learn." Similarly, a school in New Jersey, started by an educator who had taught for four years at Summerhill, stated that "We have experienced that students in the proper natural environment want to relate to the world around them and that they have more motivation for developing their skills in such a setting."[43]

This insistence on the natural process of learning was fundamental to the radical education critique, regardless of specific applications in practice. While technocratic society sought to *manage* human impulses in order to ensure greater social efficiency and productivity, free school ideology *celebrated* these impulses. Trusting in an inherent urge toward growth and development, radical educators sought wholeness rather than efficiency, and saw value in all the natural tendencies of growing persons. Paul Goodman lamented that an over-regulated society wasted human abilities "because a playful, hunting, sexy, dreamy, combative, passionate, artistic, manipulative, destructive, jealous, magnanimous, selfish and disinterested animal is continually thwarted by schooling." Clearly, Goodman was not making the Rousseauian argument that human nature is altogether "good"; even in this brief passage he embraced several qualities that are generally perceived as undesirable. Rather, Goodman—who was a leading advocate of the holistic gestalt psychotherapy approach—valued wholeness above artificial cultivation of the good, for he perceived that when a mechanical, repressive society attempts to shape human nature, it inevitably saps vitality, creativity, and joy. It followed, then, that "the main purpose of pedagogy should be to counteract and delay socialization as long as possible."[44]

George Dennison, who studied gestalt therapy with Goodman, based his educational theory on this point. Education, he wrote, "does not rest upon our ability to control, or our will to instruct, but upon our human nature and the nature of experience." Human nature is "the source of talents far stronger than our gift for bureaucratic planning. . . . I have been urging that we trust them, that we show some little faith in the life principles which have in fact structured all the well-structured elements of our existence, such principles as our inherent sociability, our inherent rationality, our inherent freedom of thought, our inherent curiosity, and our inherent (while vigor lasts) appetite for more. What this means is that we must rescue the individuals from their present obscurity in the bureaucratic heap." As both Goodman and Dennison made clear, a basic trust in the human organism suggested a very different kind of learning environment from the typical school classroom. Swidler exactly identified the pedagogical shift that this view of human nature entailed, observing that "Teaching in these free schools was not defined as imparting information that teachers possessed and students lacked. Rather, teachers sought to liberate or nurture students' own best selves. Indeed, this redefinition of the goal of education provided the essential justification for abandoning authority."[45]

As Solo put it, learning in free schools involved authentic, "face-to-face" relationships between persons, and this was the antithesis of authority derived from a hierarchical institution. A school in suburban Washington, D.C., stated that "the role of adults is to support and facilitate each child's individual growth. . . . By honestly expressing and sharing our own individuality and interests with the children, we encourage them to openly express their own needs, talents and emotions." A free school in New Mexico declared that its goal was "to develop within the child a total 'aliveness.' He is accepted as himself and brought into relationships with other people within an exciting, growth-producing, warm environment." Trusting in human impulses, accepting each individual "as himself," was rooted in the conviction that wholeness involves more than the disciplining of intellectual and rational capacities. Herb Snitzer spoke for many in the free school movement when he wrote that "Man's intellectual attitudes come out of his feeling state. Freud, Jung, Reich, Erickson and others have shown this to be so. The age of rationalism has come full circle, completing its own revolution. We as a nation and as a world body have brought, through rational thinking and practices, more despair and destruction to mankind than all of recorded history. I do not advocate the total scrapping of rational thought, but I do suggest that we have given it its day and have found it wanting. . . . Education *must* aim for more than intellectual development if we are to survive."[46]

This assertion was, indeed, a core article of faith among free school participants. Radical educators frequently argued that learning must involve more than the academic goals that define schooling in modern society. One author who observed several alternative schools found that "each student is valued as a unique individual; the school's goal is that the child grows as a whole person, undivided, much more complex and complete than a head stuffed with learning." Jonathan Kozol had expressed this position eloquently in his 1967 classic *Death at an Early Age*. Seeking a more full and human relationship with his students in an inner-city public school, he found that "There was a chance suddenly to find out who a student might actually be as soon as he did not have to be designated as so much teachable or unteachable material sitting in such and such a row and such a such a chair. . . . The difference between the real child and the child in the chair at school was immense in all cases. It was the difference, specifically, between somebody artificial and somebody real." Analyzing a public school "curriculum guide for character traits," Kozol said, "You look in vain through this list for anything that has to do with an original child or with an independent style. You also look in vain for any evaluation or assessment or conception of the human personality as a full or organic or continuously living and evolving firmament rather than as a filing cabinet of acceptable traits."[47]

Although Kozol would become the leading advocate for the social and political mission of free schools and a harsh critic of the Summerhillian emphasis on emotion and personal self-expression, we see in these passages that even his politics shared in the spirit of the politics of authenticity. For Kozol, no less than for Snitzer or Holt or Goodman, the institution of schooling produced "artificial" persons, while free schools could enable people to be "real." And this meant wholeness. For those in free schools, learning was not solely a process of intellectual molding but was intimately connected to emotional and psychological realities that were lost or distorted by the practices of technocratic schooling. "Understanding students' personal lives was central to the teachers' conception of their proper role" in free schools, according to Swidler. The human community that free schoolers sought to provide represented a search for fellowship, warmth, acceptance, and love. "Practically no one of any age here has altogether given up his rights to love and be loved as a child," wrote Snitzer and Ransohoff about Lewis-Wadhams School.[48]

Given this emphasis, education could simply not be understood as a merely academic activity, but had to be expanded to serve as an expression of "total aliveness." This understanding explains a great deal about the anti-authoritarian and seemingly anti-intellectual quality of the free schools. Outside the confining boundaries of academic disciplines, textbooks, fifty-minute periods, and achievement tests, young people could learn authentically in an atmosphere of freedom. This way of teaching and learning, emphasizing the living experience of each person, was often called "natural" or (as we see even in Kozol's writing) "organic." In a 1967 pamphlet, one of the early free schools, The Children's Community in Ann Arbor, stated that "organic learning takes place when the child's life, his needs, desires, and experiences, are taken into account along with the subject matter to be learned." A California school also explicitly advertised itself as being organic, by which it meant that it was "a culmination of all the things that all the people here bring with them.

The school is a living thing which grows and changes and expands—a whole, greater than the sum of its parts."[49]

This point deserves further emphasis. Free schoolers saw themselves as being *responsive* to changing life conditions, in contrast to educational institutions that remain rigid and hence irrelevant to students' actual concerns or society's present issues. As I said earlier, free schools proliferated, in large part, because thousands of young people rejected the irrelevance of the tidily packaged curricula being delivered through conventional schooling. Free schools sought to be absolutely, urgently relevant. "We live in a world of constant and rapid change," announced one school, "and the Rancho Mariposa School [California] is a part of this world. We have no desire to become established by finding the 'best way' to operate a school and holding on to it for years. Rather, we will be responding to new needs, new possibilities, new individuals, new perspectives, and constantly reassessing our methods and goals in search of a better way to further the growth of children."[50] The persistent, at times obsessive, desire for *freedom* by these radical educators makes sense in this context. In order to be authentic ("natural" or "organic"), responsive, and relevant, it was believed that the educational experience had to be unfettered by preestablished expectations or arbitrary authority. Young human beings *could* be trusted to learn in a free and supportive atmosphere, and therefore they *must* be allowed to learn in ways, times, and places of their own choosing. As Goodman and Friedenberg and Neill had argued, spontaneity produces health and useful growth, while rigidity and control frustrate normal development.

John Holt emphasized this point throughout his writings, and succinctly stated it in a 1971 letter, when he explained that he and Ivan Illich "speak of a de-institutionalized society in which people will be able to move much more directly to meet their own needs, instead of always having to go through the medium of a Black Box called an institution, be it corporation, government, or profession." For Holt and other radical educators, institutions tended to prevent organic functioning because they maintained their structure by rigidifying courses of action. The particular needs of any individual could not be addressed unless they happened to coincide with the preestablished responses of the institution. Countercultural ideology envisioned a society that would respond to human needs directly, flexibly, without the hindrances of impersonal bureaucracy. Free schools embodied this vision, and Peter Marin spoke for nearly all free schoolers when he wrote, "We eliminated from the school all preconceptions about what was proper, best, or useful; we gave up rules and penalties; we refused at all levels to resort to coercive force and students were free to come and go at will, to do anything. What we were after was a 'guilt-free' environment, one in which the students might become or discover what they were without having to worry about preconceived ideas of what they had to be."[51]

With the preconceptions about schooling discarded, the meanings of teaching and learning became more open-ended. Jack Spicer, who taught at Marin's school, later reflected on the sense he had that "we're not doing a school here; we're doing learning." In free school ideology, this came to be an important distinction. Goodman, in *Compulsory Mis-education*, argued that the "disastrous overestimation of schools and scholarship" which had arisen since the *Sputnik* episode in the 1950s was "an educational calamity" that prevented young people—even the most academically talented—from learning in ways natural to them. Schooling, Holt had pointed out in *How Children Fail*, did not encourage young people to think, but to produce answers expected of them, and by 1970 he began to question whether authentic thinking and learning could take place in *any* school situation. John Bremer, director of the Parkway Program in Philadelphia, a celebrated "school without walls" that placed high school students in seminars and internships in diverse locations around the city, explained that "Learning is not something that goes on only in special places called classrooms, or in special buildings called schools; rather, it is a quality of life appropriate to any and every phase of human existence, or more strictly, it is human life, itself."[52] Although Parkway was supported by the public school system, it was a radical (and short-lived) model that free schoolers appreciated. They fully agreed that learning equals "human life, itself," and since they believed that what goes on in most schools was detached from people's lives, it did not qualify as real learning.

George Dennison elaborated on this point in *The Lives of Children*, saying that "where the public school conceives of itself merely as a place of instruction, and puts severe restraints on the relationships between persons, we conceived of ourselves as an environment for growth, and accepted the relationships between children and ourselves as being the very heart of the school. . . . What a vast perversion of the natural relations of children and adults has been worked by our bureaucratized system of public education! . . . No teacher is just a teacher, no student just a student. The life meaning which joins them is the *sine qua non* for the process of education, yet precisely this is destroyed in the public schools because everything is standardized and the persons are made to vanish into their roles. . . . The world *as it exists* is what the young are hungry for; and we give them road maps, mere diagrams of the world at a distance." Dennison and other free school advocates believed that schooling as an institution was inimical to "real" learning, to the "natural" development of human capacities. In a technocratic society, educators and parents had forgotten (or had no way to know) what the human organism truly needs for healthy growth. The demands and procedures of the system had replaced the lived experience of learning.[53]

Free school educators particularly singled out and rejected one of the endemic practices of conventional schooling—evaluation of students' learning through grading. On this issue, Solo quoted responses free schoolers had given to his survey about their beliefs and practices. They emphasized the discrepancy between grading as an institutional procedure and learning as an organic function within a caring democratic community. One radical educator asked, "How do you evaluate life? Do you have to?" Another reported that "There are no evaluations of students. People are just with themselves and each other." Another insisted that "Acceptance and understanding come first." One survey respondent argued that grades had no relation to "job success, satisfaction in life, good citizenship . . . creativity in any realm, to the ability to find fresh solutions to problems." Solo himself concluded that "People who live and work together in small groups know what each other can do and cannot do so there is usually no need to judge anyone. . . . Also, the schools say that evaluations are labels and labels often become self-fulfilling prophecies. They would prefer to relate with people who are constantly changing and growing rather than to labels. . . . How, some schools ask, can the really important things that happen inside a person or between people be evaluated—the personal growth, the voyaging into new territory, the excitement of the discovery of self or another?" Conventional schooling was seen as irrelevant because it did *not* deal with things that were really important to people's lives. *Learning*, according to free school ideology, enables people to pursue lives of meaning and fulfillment, while *schooling* confines them to static roles (labels) that are inauthentic and alienating rather than fulfilling.[54]

This analysis of schooling closely paralleled the New Left's search for participatory democracy. Although one finds few specific references to the Port Huron Statement in the free school literature, these writings contained numerous ideas that were congruent with the manifesto of the student movement. For example, anti-war activist Eric Davin was an organizer, in 1971, of the Centerpeace Clearinghouse in Cambridge, Massachusetts; through its newsletter and at least one conference, he promoted the radical educational ideas of the time (he was associated with Jonathan Kozol, Allen Graubard, and Nat Hentoff, author of *Our Children Are Dying* [1966]). In one of his newsletters, he wrote a ringing statement of free school belief that clearly reflected key themes of the politics of authenticity: "If it is a definition of a human being that he/she determines his/her own life and participates in a community of one's fellows, then largely we are no longer human beings. . . . The natural products of our schools are passive, 'silent' majorities of adults and frustrated, freaked-out, self-destructive youth, who find no channel in the schools or society for their individuality and so turn their energies inward. . . . We want: The creation of environments supportive of human meaning, purpose and community. We want: The creation of channels of power through which the individual can become a citizen in the truest meaning of the word—a determiner of his/her life and his/her society. We want: The creation of a social democracy within which the individual is encouraged and enabled to become all it is possible for him/her to become." This was a particularly eloquent expression of a longing for democratic community that was frequently described in the free school literature.[55]

Free schools sought, above all else, to be "environments supportive of human meaning, purpose and community." And most of them tried to accomplish this by actually practicing participatory democracy. In a 1970 article in the free school newsletter *Outside the Net*, Jerry Friedberg of the Lorillard Children's School in New York City wrote that "We operated without any rules. There were no formal duties, penalties, hierarchies, or ways of enforcing anything even if somebody wanted to. Decision-making was communal, by consensus. We never once took a vote or felt moved in that direction. We operated, rather, on the basis of personal encounter, dealing with our feelings as they emerged, working through our differences, and confronting our angers, fears, frustrations and joys. . . . The style which developed permitted no easy refuge in theories, abstract commitments, or rules, but demanded personal and fairly constant contact." Significantly, the participants in this program eventually concluded that the level of commitment, compatibility, and community that they sought could not be practiced within a school setting, which they came to see as a "specialized environment" removed from people's whole lives; it felt "artificial and phony" with its own driving goals, so they had begun to build an intentional community in which adults and children could share their lives "organically."[56]

However, other radical alternative schools did manage to practice participatory democracy, and some have maintained this practice for thirty years. Stuart Rosenfeld commented that the successful free schools were those that developed effective democratic decision-making practices. It does appear, in fact, that schools such as Sudbury Valley in Massachusetts, The School Around Us (SAU) in Maine, and the Albany (New York) Free School may well have endured to the present because each involved its entire community so intimately in the life of the school. Reflecting on their success, Claudia Berman of SAU reported that "participation in a democratic governing system, where each person has a voice, empowers everyone. . . . Participating in democracy and practicing good citizenship is a strong part of the SAU curriculum for students of all ages." Chris Mercogliano of the Albany Free School recently related that "teachers and parents hammered out, in a series of heated sessions, the policy that only those actually present in the building could determine the school's day-to-day operating policy. . . . Anyone who wanted to resolve a conflict or to change school policy could call a general meeting at any time." He comments that this "council meeting system quickly became the heart and soul of the young school. It, more than anything else, would provide the wherewithal for the school to operate as a community in which everyone had an equal stake in the school and in which mutual responsibility and interdependence were daily realities."[57]

The key issue, for free schoolers as for the counterculture at large, was the role of *authority* within social groups. They believed that large, monolithic institutions wielded an impersonal authority that stifled genuine self-expression and interpersonal communication. A technocratic society imposed order on human interactions by giving professionals, including, in particular, educators, authority to manage behavior and enforce conformity to established roles. The radical critics identified this authority as a primary barrier to authenticity and democracy and attacked it directly. Kozol, for example, declared that "only the authority of visible character demands respect. No other kind deserves it. No child in his heart, unless drugged by passivity, will pay obeisance to authority unless authority has earned it, and authority based upon political maneuvering and upon the ingestion and assimilation of platitudes is an authority which no person, white or Negro, adult or child, should respect." Critics such as Ann Swidler as well as participants who experienced chaotic, tempestuous, short-lived free schools have claimed that a purely participatory democracy, one that categorically rejects all formal authority and attempts to operate entirely by consensus, is inherently unstable. There is some truth in this observation, but the fact is that a number of free and alternative schools have successfully practiced participatory democracy over an extended period of time. As one observer put it, "This to me was one of the most impressive features of these schools. It is startling to find that a truly democratic form of self-rule not only can work with adults, but with kids as well. The kids themselves handle most of their own problems among themselves. It is a fact that at the best free schools the kids are first and foremost in control of their own lives—visibly and actually in control."[58]

Free schools, then, embodied the political agenda of the New Left, with the understanding that this agenda involved an uncertain mixture of existentialist and more conventional political elements. Clearly there was a tension between these elements. Many participants in the movement, primarily from upper-middle-class backgrounds, could be perceived as "romantics" looking for personal liberation from alienating structures of consciousness. An unsigned editorial in *New Schools Exchange Newsletter* claimed that "the heart of the vision behind 'free schools' was never really political in the narrow sense; it was more clearly therapeutic." Drawn especially to Neill's seemingly apolitical pedagogy, these participants made "a minimal political demand on the larger society," according to Graubard. Some activists, however, found this to be a problem. "Subjectivism and psychologism are inadequate as responses to world hunger, global war, and the rise of the large corporate superstructures which are sterilizing the human spirit," argued a writer named Jim Shields. Around 1970, according to one account, staff members of the Summerhill Society dissolved the board of directors and established "workers' control." In a statement they announced that "We plan to push the free school movement away from its apolitical and elitist traditions towards an understanding of the intensely political nature of education, i.e., the role it has in nurturing racism and sexism and the manner in which it stratifies people some for war, some for college, some to factories, and some to drugs."[59]

The single most striking critique of the "romantic" educational dissidents was Jonathan Kozol's fiery 1972 book *Free Schools*, in which he derided the upper-middle-class white counterculture for its "artificial context of contrived euphoria" and argued that free schools should be "in the midst of true and human confrontation with the real world of exploitation and oppression"; for him, the free school was a "community of conscience" that must join with marginalized people in their struggle for dignity and basic human rights. In this book and other writings, Kozol displayed an intense sensitivity to the suffering of impoverished children, "children who are congenitally malnourished, infants who are victims of lead-paint poison in slum-apartments," and he argued stridently that "in face of pain, in face of hunger, in face of misery on every side," it was not right for anyone "to tend to his own needs, and to advance his own enlightenment, reward, self-interest." Kozol, who had become closely associated with Paulo Freire during the latter's recent stay in the Boston area and was inspired by Freire's "pedagogy of the oppressed," asserted that educators cannot be neutral about injustice; either they stand for a more just social vision or stand back and allow society to manipulate their consciousness. In a letter to Len Solo, Kozol baldly asserted that Summerhill was "one of the most racist schools in England" and that John Holt's "noncritical adulation of Neill's work is consistent with his own lifelong involvement with the education of the ruling class." In a memorable passage in *Free Schools*, he compared the child-centered free school to "a sandbox for the children of the SS Guards at Auschwitz."[60]

I want to step back a moment to consider this rhetoric. From the standpoint of intellectual history, the free school movement embodied an ideological tension similar to that which characterized progressive education earlier in the century. In both cases, "romantic" or "child-centered" educational approaches were responding to existential or psychological dimensions of experience, while more explicitly political or "social reconstructionist" approaches maintained that all persons concerned with social change, even those from privileged backgrounds not directly touched by poverty or racism, must take action to reduce social and economic inequity. Kozol's 1972 critique of free schools echoed George Counts's 1932 diatribe against "romantic" progressive educators, when he literally dared them to "build a new social order." Without attempting to analyze this tension exhaustively, I want to suggest that sociologically and psychologically, it does make sense that upper-middle-class people would respond to suffering or oppression as *they* experience it, which is qualitatively different from the suffering of poverty. But this difference does not mean that the two branches of progressive education or free school ideology need be hostile to each other. Rather, I argue that they are complementary.

Perhaps the divergence is best explained by Abraham Maslow's theory of the hierarchy of needs, which identifies existential enrichment ("self-actualization," in Maslow's terms) as a "higher order" developmental goal. It is not likely to become a pressing concern until more basic subsistence and "belonging" needs are adequately met, but it clearly emerges as a major life task when these needs are satisfied. This theory suggests that different layers of moral concern are not necessarily in conflict but represent elements of an organic continuum, just as the New Left's politics of authenticity had asserted. As George Leonard had suggested in his observations on the various movements of the 1960s, social justice and existential wholeness are *both* necessary for enjoying a fulfilling life; freedom from obvious and violent oppression opens possibilities for freedom from implicit cultural limitations on experience. Justice is clearly primary, but that does not render the quest for wholeness irrelevant or antithetical. The challenge for the socially privileged individual seeking existential fulfillment—and for the upper-middle-class alternative education and human potential movements in general—is to maintain a sense of empathy and moral concern for the struggles of those who are seeking justice, dignity, and simple economic opportunity. Too often, advocates of humanistic psychology and cultural "transformation" have not adequately taken up this challenge, most likely due to an unacknowledged class bias. Kozol was pointing out that free schoolers, similarly, failed to address these struggles.[61]

The radicalism of the 1960s was fueled by deeply felt existential needs among privileged students exacerbated (and complicated) by the call to conscience proclaimed by the civil rights movement. The question was what sort of action this call demanded. Was it enough to withdraw from technocratic society and begin the task of building a new culture rooted in a new consciousness—a task that the privileged could afford to attempt? Or was it necessary to break out of one's class-defined comfort zone and personally engage actual violence, hunger, and racial and economic oppression? Kozol, himself a Harvard graduate from a comfortable background, made the latter choice, and the highly moralistic tone of some of his writing in the early 1970s (no one has the right to tend to his own needs? Auschwitz?) seemed to suggest that it was not an easy one; he seemed genuinely angry toward those who had chosen the presumably easier course of action. (Remarkably, apparently only months before his letter to Solo denouncing Holt, Kozol published a statement proclaiming his "admiration for John Holt and my belief in his integrity. . . . [Holt is a] very decent man who has been my friend, co-teacher, and sometimes like a father to me, throughout the past six years." If Holt was "like a father," then it makes sense that Kozol would need to reject him as he sought to distance himself from his class identity. This is not to deny the real philosophical differences between Kozol's emphasis on social activism and Holt's on personal values, but it helps account for the stridency of Kozol's criticism.)[62]

Most free school participants, practicing the New Left's politics of authenticity, would have claimed that they *were* building communities of conscience in resistance to technocratic social institutions. If the free school movement is to be considered "therapeutic," it was not merely practicing *psycho*therapy but a radical critique that some later activists have called "culture therapy." Solo wrote that the radical educators "created what Myles Horton calls 'islands of decency' in a not-so-decent world." Salli Rasberry and Robert Greenway went further, claiming that "It is a revolutionary act to be involved in a free school. Saying 'no' to the heart of a culture—their schools—and establishing an alternative system for learning is an explicit rejection of a set of beliefs, and the web of premises, myths, rituals—the underlying faith—that goes with a set of beliefs." In a review of *Free Schools*, Greenway insisted that "the vast majority of alternative attempts are struggling mightily with . . . this present and the possible future culture, with moral ways of earning a living, with the critical dilemmas facing this whole earth." Steve Bhaerman and Joel Denker (who had risked his life participating in Freedom Summer) wrote that "free schools are more than just a tactic to achieve social change. They may equip us with the strength and staying power we need to re-enter the system and confront it."[63]

Like historians who would later interpret the "counterculture" as being separate from the serious, activist Left, Kozol's critique downplayed the countercultural view that a transformation of consciousness was integral to the magnitude of social change that was needed. Rasberry and Greenway were correct in saying that free school ideology sought nothing less than to undermine "the underlying faith" of modern American culture; this ideology was radical even when it was not explicitly "political." Even Eric Davin, the activist quoted earlier who argued forcefully for social and political change (he was closely associated with Kozol, in fact), wrote that he, like Michael Rossman and so many others, was inspired to promote radical educational ideas by reading *Summerhill.* And Jim Shields, in the same article in which he denounced "subjectivism," allowed that liberation could not be achieved solely through standard political means but required human "fellowship" that nourished the affective dimension of our lives. We need, he said, to integrate a political revolution to address social problems with a personal/cultural revolution to liberate consciousness. Free school ideology contained both of these elements, even if one or the other was often implicit.[64]

Among the major writers in the literature, George Dennison offered perhaps the most balanced and insightful perspective on the political nature of free schools. "Life in our country is chaotic and corrosive," he wrote, "and the time of childhood for many millions is difficult and harsh. It will not be an easy matter to bring our berserk technocracy under control, but we *can* control the environment of the schools. . . . If, as parents, we were to take as our concern not the instruction of our children, but the lives of our children, we would find that our schools could be used in a powerfully regenerative way."[65] This brief passage encompasses several important points. First, of course, Dennison has explicitly identified "technocracy" as the basic problem—not public schools, not the federal government, not capitalism, but the *worldview* underlying all modern institutions, the "underlying faith" of modernity. Later in the book he referred to technocracy as being "heartless," meaning that it deprives persons' lives of authenticity and wholeness; again we see that for the critics of the 1960s, technocracy was not simply a political problem but a moral and existential one.

Second, this passage succinctly explains why educators and parents abandoned public education for free schools. To change a worldview (to "bring our berserk technocracy under control") is a difficult task that cannot be accomplished on a large scale alone; it requires personal participation in new social forms. Free schoolers sought small, intimate, and democratic communities that they could collectively control. They made a choice to empower themselves by leaving the hierarchically ruled institutions of modern society and creating more democratic counterinstitutions.

Third, in Dennison's juxtaposition of "instruction" and "lives of our children," the reader again sees the distinction between schooling and learning. The very title of Dennison's book—*The Lives of Children*—captured this primary element of the free school ideology, and he addressed this topic at length. Education as instruction lodges cultural power in impersonal institutions, while a caring concern for the unique personal identities and struggles of individual children redefines education as a person-to-person encounter. Even when a school does not explicitly address issues of racism, class privilege, and the like, it makes a strong political statement by challenging the legitimacy of cultural authority residing only in the institutions of mass society. In his claim that "schools could be used in a powerfully regenerative way," Dennison was suggesting that a free school, by its very nature, constituted an effective agent of social and political renewal.

Dennison explained these ideas further in a March 1972 letter he sent to *New Schools Exchange Newsletter* and other publications. (Kozol's book *Free Schools* had just been published and caused quite a stir in the movement.) He argued that free schools were not political only if "politics" meant struggling against the government; he envisioned, instead, a nonviolent anarchist revolution, meaning that people should simply begin the work of building an alternative society. "The distinguishing thing about the community free school is that it fills an ongoing and fundamental social need: The rearing and educating of the children. Thus there is much in the relations of parents, teachers, neighbors, and children which is *already* the very pattern of rational, post-revolutionary politics in the anarchist mode. *This politics is precious and must not be diminished.* It does not need to be 'politicized.' It is already political in the deepest sense. It is not only a pattern of what's to come, but is an actual increment of the social revolution. . . . To bring into being the sexual-intellectual-moral wholeness of the individual, and to act upon this wholeness as the only rational source of social decision, is revolutionary."[66]

Here is the very heart of the free school rebellion, indeed of the entire counterculture: *"to act upon this wholeness as the only rational source of social decision, is revolutionary."* I have not encountered any other single sentence that so fully captures the phenomenological meaning of free school ideology. The purpose of radical dissent was to rediscover wholeness—the full, integrated personality that spills beyond the bounds of institutional roles; to express this wholeness in community with other persons was to introduce meaningful social change, even if it did not follow conventional political channels. Dennison's letter was also significant because, although he conducted his own school for poor Puerto Rican and African American children in New York City, he responded to Kozol's critique of "basket-weaving free schools" for upper-middle-class whites by saying that even they were on the right path because "the children will gain." While it was certainly true that impoverished and marginalized people suffered greater social and economic injustice than comfortable whites, the "heartless technocracy" diminished the life experience of all, and it must be fought on all fronts. In a similar vein, John Holt wrote that "I don't agree with anyone who says that if a free school is not for poor kids, preferably black, it is a waste of time, if not a crime. In a society where most kids are middle class, no one need apologize who wants to put time and energy into making a decent school for middle class kids." Despite his disagreement with Kozol on this point, Dennison highly recommended *Free Schools* in his letter. In an earlier essay he had asserted that "when Kozol talks of political action, he's coming to politics through people and problems" rather than an abstract agenda. I believe that Dennison's position strongly suggests that whatever tension or class differences existed between the more overtly or angrily "political" free schoolers and the more utopian romantics, there was a common ideology that involved both of these elements—a politics of authenticity which insisted that social change must address existential wholeness as well as social reform.[67]

This discussion also supports my argument that a social movement initially concerned with race relations, free speech, and opposition to war easily became translated into an *educational* ideology because its critique of existing social institutions was holistic. Dennison was correct that "the rearing and education of the children" is a "fundamental social need," and those who sought to alter the very foundations of the existing culture (its underlying mythology or worldview) could not leave educational practice untouched. Radical college and high school students themselves clearly saw that they were being educated specifically to fit into the corporate-military state (the technocracy) which they found so immoral and alienating, and they demanded an alternative. The crucial difference between free school ideology and progressive public school reform was the former's holistic and radical critique of modern culture; in the ideas of Neill, Goodman, Holt, Dennison, Kozol, Marin, and the other voices of educational dissent, one does not find a concern for "pedagogy" or "instruction" or student "achievement" but a strong recognition of the cultural role of education. Stuart Rosenfeld, directly contradicting the belief that free schools were primarily "therapeutic" in an apolitical sense, specifically concluded that the free school movement was essentially political rather than pedagogical: it was not about school reform but education for a new kind of society.[68] Clearly, however, it was "political" in the expanded sense of the term as the New Left defined it.

Moreover, by including "the rearing and educating of the children" as an essential part of an agenda for social change, radical educators implicitly (although rarely explicitly!) embraced what had historically been the domain of women. Suggesting that the most personal, intimate, and familial elements of people's lives contain social and political significance, free school ideology unintentionally endorsed a feminist understanding of society: history is not made only by "great men" in positions of power, but by the personal decisions of men and women in their daily lives. It is true that nearly all the publicly visible writers and activists in the free school movement were men—a situation that would appear unbalanced in virtually any professional organization or political action group today. Yet it is also remarkable that so many men were involved in the free school movement, even as teachers of young children. By demonstrating that the education of children is important, useful, creative work, the radical education movement helped to blur traditional gender lines.

In light of these considerations, it is evident that free school ideology was not simply an educational position as "education" is commonly understood, but a holistic social critique that saw education as an important arena of cultural dissent and change. Consequently, it was a natural extension of the countercultural vision of the 1960s.

CHAPTER 3

The Legacy of John Holt

> Anyone who works for a just, peaceful, humane and decent world for all people, a world without needless suffering, exploitation, degradation, or cruelty, is my ally.
>
> —John Holt[1]

John Holt was one of the key figures in the free school movement. His writings suggested to thousands of readers that American education was seriously flawed, and his efforts gave many groups the inspiration or contacts they needed to launch or sustain alternative schools. Moreover, Holt was a sensitive, inquisitive observer and social critic whose journey from fifth-grade teacher to free school activist to homeschooling advocate reveals a great deal about the whirlwind course of events during the 1960s and early 1970s. Holt was an accurate barometer, as well as shaper, of the rapidly evolving radical educational ideology of the time. In addition, Holt provided a coherent analysis of schools, teaching, and learning that is at least as relevant to the problems of the present time as the work of many other, more widely recognized theorists. Holt's work deserves a closer look because it has been almost completely ignored by mainstream educational scholarship. If it is useful to reappraise, after twenty years of neglect, the cultural critique raised by the free school movement, then it is useful as well to consider Holt's important contribution to that critique.[2]

BIOGRAPHICAL SKETCH

Born in 1923, John Holt was educated at Exeter Academy and an Ivy League university which, throughout his public career, he refused to name. He later reflected that this elite education had deprived him of the opportunity to learn practical skills. (Significantly, many educators involved in free schools had received a similarly privileged education, and like Holt, they found that it did not address the important practical, as well as moral, issues of their time.) Holt was a generation older than the student dissidents of the 1960s, and his response to the events of that decade was moderated by experience and maturity. In temperament and lifestyle he has been described by associates as being "conservative." Nevertheless, he had developed an unusually acute social conscience during the years of cold war culture, and "he was sometimes more profoundly radical than somebody who had the trappings of the sixties' culture."[3] He had served as a submarine officer during World War II, but was horrified by the introduction of the atomic bomb. In a letter written shortly after Hiroshima and Nagasaki, the 22-year-old Holt demonstrated the humanitarian concern that would later characterize his educational thought. "We have been threatened a long time that the day would come when man would have to change his ways or be eliminated from this planet. The day is here and he has not started to change yet."[4]

Holt attempted to facilitate this change by joining the World Federalists (an organization promoting the notably un-American notion of world government) in 1946, and working as an organizer and lecturer for this group until 1952. He then turned to education, becoming a teacher at a private progressive school in Colorado between 1953 and 1957, and at similar schools in the Boston area between 1957 and 1967. Significantly, he claimed that "Schools were always a means to an end for me. I had to work in schools in order to answer my questions on learning and children's intelligence. But I never identified myself as a *schoolteacher*." Although Holt had not received training in education (or, perhaps, because of this fact), he proved to be an uncommonly gifted observer of children's diverse styles of learning and development. Working with a colleague, Bill Hull, Holt began documenting his observations and came to the conclusion that routine school procedures primarily worked against, rather than with, children's natural ways of learning. He realized early on that his perspective challenged conventional wisdom. In 1963 he wrote that "The questions that concern me, in the words of a member of the Harvard School of Education, [are] 'not respectable.' Neither are my views on intelligence, or the enormous intellectual potential of all children, or almost anything that I know of." According to Susannah Sheffer, Holt was fired from one of the progressive schools where he taught for suggesting innovations that were simply too radical. In 1964, Holt published his emerging critique in *How Children Fail,* and very soon found himself "catapulted into public life." According to one friend, "Mounds of mail flooded in. Papers were in piles all over his apartment floor. . . . People hungered to talk to him, ask him questions, tell him how they felt about themselves and their kids. He traveled thousands of miles in those days . . . and he made hundreds of good friends."[5]

Because he was "one of the first to see through educational jargon and theory and to write about what life in school was really like for children and teachers," Holt received letters from parents discouraged or even distraught about their children's experiences in school throughout his career.[6] In addition, he tapped into an emerging undercurrent of discontent with American education. Although his critique did not acknowledge the sociological analysis of Paul Goodman or C. Wright Mills, or the political critique of the Port Huron Statement, Holt's book appeared during a pregnant moment in the rise of cultural dissent in the 1960s. The year 1964 witnessed Freedom Summer and the Free Speech Movement, and the cause of civil rights had moved to the forefront of the national agenda. With a rising awareness of the possibilities of "freedom," the time was ripe to revisit educational questions that had been raised by progressive educators earlier in the century but suppressed by cold war ideology in the 1950s. Holt did not refer to the progressive education tradition; his observations were based entirely on his personal experiences in teaching. Nevertheless, Holt's objections to conventional education echoed those of Francis Parker and John Dewey seventy years earlier. Like them, he was interested in learning as an organic process, and came to see that schooling failed to recognize or nourish this process.

At first Holt did not speak to radical dissidents, but to liberal parents and idealistic teachers. In 1965 he published articles in mainstream publications such as *Life,* the *Saturday Evening Post*, *Redbook*, the *New York Review of Books*, the *New York Times* magazine, and *PTA Magazine*. Over the next few years he spoke to hundreds of groups and gatherings, published more articles and books, and found himself involved in a grassroots movement that sought to rebuild American education on entirely new premises. Because of his extensive traveling and correspondence, as well as his bold critique of conventional educational practices, Holt became the key link in the emerging network of free schools. During the height of political and cultural struggle in the United States, between about 1968 and 1972, Holt became more explicit about the political dimension of his educational critique. According to Sheffer, "The more that America and society in general seemed to be going in wrong directions in so many ways, the more it began to seem absurd to him to worry only about classrooms." A pacifist since the end of World War II, Holt was deeply troubled by the war in Vietnam, which he called "obscene," and like thousands of young people, he was radicalized by the American government's foray into imperialism. For several years he refused to pay taxes, and he actively supported draft resisters. (Bill Ayers recalls that Holt even helped him when he was a fugitive with the Weather Underground.) Yet his focus remained on education. He wrote at one point that he felt "the work I do in education is more valuable, even in terms of ending war, than any witness I might make in going to jail." By the early 1970s this work involved questioning the institution of schooling as such, and until his death in 1985 Holt was primarily concerned with supporting families who attempted to educate their children outside of school altogether. Indeed, the moral vision and tireless effort that had placed Holt at the center of the free school movement now made him a national spokesman and catalyst for the rise of the homeschooling movement. He continued to travel, speaking to groups of parents and educators. He continued to reach a wide audience, appearing as well on television talk shows. His newsletter *Growing Without Schooling*, and his organization Holt Associates, provided encouragement and resources to thousands of "unschooling" families and have continued to do so in the years since his death.[7]

Holt was not a scholar or theorist, but a moralist and reformer. His views arose primarily in response to his own experiences rather than to intellectual influences. Although he was an avid reader and wrote numerous book reviews, he rarely credited other authors with shaping his ideas. He did, in fact, acknowledge that J. H. van den Berg's *The Changing Nature of Man*, a critique of scientism, had "stimulated and advanced my thinking," which I take as evidence that he *would* have given credit to others had they similarly influenced him. Holt occasionally quoted authorities when they supported his thinking, but he rarely cited them as sources for it. Remarkably, he told one reviewer in 1969 that he had not even read John Dewey. It is safe to say, then, that Holt's view of education did not spring from a philosophical analysis of pedagogical ideas but directly from his experience and deeply felt response to the moral and cultural challenges of his time. In the published collection of his letters Holt frequently revealed profound distress over the failure of modern society to uphold what he felt were decent and humane values; on more than one occasion, according to the biographical narrative in this book, Holt openly broke into sobs when he reflected on modern culture's inhumanity and wasteful destruction of the beauty of the natural world. In various passages of his writing he qualified his predictions or hopes for the future by saying "if civilization survives" or "if we have a future." He keenly felt the possibility that humanity in the twentieth century was on the verge of terrible catastrophe, and his educational critique must be appreciated in this context. Holt exemplified what David Purpel has called the educator's responsibility to be a "prophetic voice" in a suffering world.[8]

A MORAL RESPONSE TO A TECHNOCRATIC CULTURE

John Holt was an inquisitive and open-minded observer of American society. He did not adopt a theoretical position and attempt to develop or defend it, but spoke out for human dignity and freedom wherever he saw these threatened by social and political forces. He was not an ideologue and endorsed no "-ism"—indeed, very much like Dewey he explicitly warned against the quest for ideological purity and "over-abstractness," as he put it. "Life, people, change, even Richard Nixon, are more complicated than the labels we stick on them." Further, he wrote, "the worst thing that can happen to any great pioneer of human thought is for his ideas to fall into the hands of disciples and worshippers, who take the living, restless, ever-changing thought of their master and try to carve it into imperishable granite. . . . The words may remain, but the spirit is soon lost."[9] These comments convey the very essence of Holt's moral vision. Similar to Paul Goodman, Norman O. Brown, and other intellectual parents of the counterculture, Holt advocated an *organic* worldview—an appreciation for the living, dynamic, evolving, interacting, and responsive nature of reality. He valued spontaneity, complexity, process, and connectedness, and saw that "over-abstractness" was the epistemological core of a technocratic culture. Holt's moral vision celebrated life. It is no accident that his educational philosophy celebrated, not the abstract curriculum or the routines of schooling, but the living child.

Holt's own intellectual development was "living, restless, ever-changing." Peter Marin wrote that "what always impresses me about John Holt is how he himself learns. He is less interested in his own positions than in coming to terms with the best of what is being said and thought about schooling—and his real passion is for passing those ideas along to others, in putting them to work."[10] Still, Holt did hold several fundamental principles such as the dignity and value of human existence and faith in the human capacity to learn. He was passionately concerned with freedom and believed that it was being seriously eroded by the impersonality of large organizations and the forms of surveillance and control practiced in social institutions, particularly schools. Of course, Holt's ideas did have ideological implications, but it is a mistake to classify Holt's thought according to any fixed philosophical position (such as "libertarian" or "individualist") for this will not capture the moral sensibility of Holt's response to the cultural crisis of the 1960s. Free school ideology raised complex questions about the relationship between education and democracy, and it is too simplistic to count defenders of public schools progressive democrats and label "deschoolers" like Holt conservatives or classical liberals—a point I explore further in Chapter Five.

Throughout Holt's career one can see a driving concern for the need of each person to find a meaningful, fulfilling sense of identity in a mass society that makes this difficult. That is, Holt was primarily concerned with what I have been calling "authenticity." Unlike the student intellectuals in the New Left, Holt did not seem to be influenced by existentialism or the literature of social critique that began to develop in the late 1950s—at least, he never acknowledged such influence. Nevertheless, he seemed attuned to the postwar technological and economic transformation that had led Friedenberg and Goodman, among others, to observe that young people were losing opportunities to establish their place in the world through meaningful work. In a 1961 letter (a year after the publication of *Growing Up Absurd*), he pointed out that automation was producing unemployment, and claimed it was unjust that a wealthy society could not offer decent work to people. "I am more often than not gloomy about the state of our country," he wrote. "There is something dinosaurish about a society that cannot adapt, or that can only adapt slowly and ponderously, to new conditions."[11]

This letter reveals not only the focus of Holt's critique, but also the fact that his mood was so contrary to the optimism of the Kennedy era. Holt was already disillusioned with American institutions and was supportive of grassroots efforts to change them. He wrote that the "American disease, a belief in unlimited progress, unlimited growth, unlimited greed . . . has largely corrupted whatever good there may have been in this society"; indeed, he argued that the modern economy "has lost all touch with reality, with human nature and human needs" and criticized the national obsession with economic growth because it "dehumanizes and trivializes people" and contributes to environmental degradation. He was, in fact, concerned with conservation and sustainability well before the environmental movement was popular. Beyond this, he was passionately opposed to racism and segregation and outraged by what he saw as a gross imbalance between the wealthy and the poor. He supported union efforts and legislation to improve working conditions, and social change movements such as women's liberation. He worked actively in the 1972 presidential campaign of George McGovern and he wrote that "the rebellion of the young is one of the most hopeful and constructive phenomena of our times." In a remarkable essay in the *New York Times Magazine* in 1970 that stirred up an angry response from readers, Holt described how campus protests at Berkeley were subjected to repeated police violence, even though they were raising concerns that were, to him, perfectly legitimate. "To our students and young, who cannot tolerate our society as it is, we only offer more and more of what they can't stand. Bigger, noisier, dirtier cities, more war, more exploitation, more corruption, more cruelty, more ugliness, more depersonalization, and at the end of it, the virtual certainty that if the world is not destroyed by war it will be made uninhabitable by the waste products of an ever larger gross national product." Above all, because he valued life so passionately, he was a pacifist. "Since 1946, when I left the submarine service of the U.S. Navy, I have been involved or concerned, in one way or another, with the movement to bring nuclear weapons under control and to establish world peace—certainly the most urgent issue of our time." To label Holt as an ideological conservative simply because he is associated with the homeschooling movement is clearly a misreading of his life's work![12]

Like Paul Goodman and the New Left, Holt sought a thorough renewal of culture that would be as concerned with personal wholeness and authenticity as with social justice. Like them, Holt understood that technocracy was the cultural/epistemological source of the most serious social and cultural problems. "All of these [modern] societies are basically alike," he declared. "They all want the same things, they all worship the same gods: science, bigness, efficiency, growth, progress. . . . I think that any society which is based on the notion of progress, growth, change, development, newer, bigger, higher, faster, better is almost inevitably going to move toward Fascism because, in a nutshell, it arouses so many more hopes than it satisfies." Holt went on to describe a book he was considering writing (although he never completed it) on "Progress: The Road to Fascism." He said that he would be writing "about a society of much smaller scale institutions, smaller scale tools with very drastic limits on the uses of energy and growth. Now, I'm not at all optimistic about the possibility of developing such a society, but the only kinds of social change that seem fundamentally important to me seem to be in those directions."[13]

In response to the growth of a bureaucratically managed mass society, Holt did not so much seek to reform social institutions as to circumvent and thus deflate them. Very much in the tradition of Thoreau, he argued that "one can do a great deal to change a bad social system or arrangement by refusing to take part in it." He saw himself as a "decentralist" who "leaned in the direction of anarchism," but he did not follow a prescribed ideological position. He insisted that conventional political agendas were "mostly irrelevant" to the cultural crisis of his time.[14] Holt was one of the earliest of the decentralist critics of technocracy whose ideas have come to be associated with movements such as "social ecology" and "constructive postmodernism." In addition to Goodman and Roszak, these critics include such diverse thinkers as E. F. Schumacher, Murray Bookchin, John Cobb, Herman Daly, Jeremy Rifkin, Charlene Spretnak, Wendell Berry, and others. Of course there are numerous differences in the ideas of these writers, but they all agree in opposing centralized political and economic power that rests on scientific-technological management of natural and human resources. As a pioneer in this genre, Holt may appear to be unconnected to the literature that has appeared during the past twenty years, yet in retrospect it is evident that his response to technocracy was very closely aligned to the ideas of such thinkers, for they too have envisioned "a society of much smaller scale institutions, smaller scale tools with very drastic limits on the uses of energy and growth."

Of course, Holt was primarily concerned about human growth and learning, a focus that distinguished his writings from most of these other social critics, but more than many learning theorists, he examined the cultural context of human development. Holt was an important educational thinker, in part, because he explored the relationship between social institutions and personal development. "Perhaps my deepest interest could be described as 'How can we adults work to create a more decent, humane, conserving, peaceful, just, etc. community, nation, world, and how can we make it possible for children to join us in this work . . . ?' Except insofar as we find answers to *those* questions, there is very little we can do under the name of 'education' to help young people grow up into whole, intelligent, sensitive, resourceful, competent, etc. human beings."[15] Throughout his work, as in this passage, Holt emphasized the *connection* between the social and the individual, between the political and the existential. Human beings could not grow whole in a fragmented or violent culture, but at the same time a decent culture would only emerge when people personally experienced meaning and fulfillment.

What distinguished Holt's position from a more social democratic (what we would today call "progressive") critique was his insistence that reform of social institutions alone was not sufficient for cultural renewal. The source of violence, hatred, and exploitation, he argued, is not in institutions as such but in the psychological reality people experience as they live in society. As Michael Lerner (a Berkeley activist in the 1960s) has argued more recently, the conventional Left's focus on legislative and institutional reform has neglected the existential dimension of *meaning*, leaving people desperate for experiences of belonging, community, and moral commitment, which the political Right has gladly provided. Lerner maintains that "the quest for meaning is the central hunger in advanced industrial societies," and by "meaning" he specifically means a satisfying connection between the individual and the larger world, a sense of worthwhile purpose. The need for meaning, for connection to something larger than oneself, "plays the central role in shaping human reality," and much of the "violence, destructiveness, and other irrational behavior" of modern life "is produced by the frustration of a deep yearning for connection with others, a pessimism about one's ability to ever get one's needs met, and a deep shame about one's own imagined failures."[16]

Holt's social vision represented, in Lerner's terms, a "politics of meaning," one that directly addressed this existential dimension. Holt insisted that social problems and violent conflict were closely associated with personal feelings of inadequacy, alienation, and resentment. In one particularly explicit passage he claimed that "efforts for peace are doomed to fail unless we understand that the root causes of war are not economic conflicts or language barriers or cultural differences but men—the kind of men who must have and will find scapegoats, legitimate targets for the disappointment, envy, fear, rage, and hatred that accumulates in their daily lives. . . . The fundamental educational problem of our time is to find ways to help children grow into adults who have no wish to do harm." He similarly argued that "whatever makes men feel less free, even if it does not take away any particular right or liberty, lessens and threatens the freedom of all of us." Many people mistrusted freedom, he said, and opposed both anti-war protesters and free schools, not simply for rational ideological reasons, but because they themselves did not feel free and resented others exhibiting such autonomous and spontaneous behavior. He suggested that racism and inequality would diminish only when young people learned to grow into caring adults who did not hate themselves or their work.[17]

This emphasis on the personal, emotional dimension of social reality was a consistent emphasis in Holt's writing, to the end of his life. "People are best able, and perhaps only able, to cross the many barriers of race, class, custom, and belief that divide them when they are able to share experiences *that make them feel good*. Only from these do they get a stronger sense of their own, and therefore other people's, uniqueness, dignity, and worth." In this passage and throughout his work, Holt was speaking about existential authenticity—the individual person's assurance that his or her life is meaningful and fulfilling. When people "feel good"—by which Holt did not mean hedonistic pleasure but the experience of one's life as integrated, whole, and guided by worthy values and aspirations—then they can participate freely and constructively in social and public life. "One of the most urgent social tasks of our time is to rebuild, both in our festering cities and our deserted countrysides, communities where people feel, 'I belong; this is my place; I have something to say about what happens; I can help and count on others to help me; I can do something to make this a better place to live.'" Holt recognized, as did the students who adopted the Port Huron Statement, that *participatory* democracy demands more than opportunities to vote or write letters to a newspaper. As Dewey had argued, genuine democracy can only take place within a genuine community, a group of persons who feel themselves joined by common purposes and meanings, and who therefore feel that they belong. Social institutions, particularly education, must strive to nourish experiences of belonging, authenticity, and worth for a just and peaceful world to be possible, because when the inherent human need for meaning and connection is frustrated, people are likely to vent their disappointment or hatred through violence or the sublimated violence of political and ideological oppression.[18]

The search for authenticity in the countercultural ideology of the 1960s, expressed so clearly in Holt's writings, was a search for meaning and connection that Holt and other dissidents felt was lacking in a technocratic culture, in which people were increasingly defined according to their functional roles in an impersonal economic system. Nevertheless, Holt's perspective was not merely psychological or individualistic. Unlike A. S. Neill, he explicitly recognized that "much of our task is political." Holt did not prescribe education, even deschooled education, as a solution to poverty. He specifically stated that society needs to "make a fairer distribution of the world's resources, make a serious attack on poverty," and ridiculed the standard liberal assumption that education in itself could help impoverished people: "We promise poor kids that if they will do what we want, there are goodies waiting for them out there. They know that these promises are false." Answering a correspondent who had specifically asked how he defined his political views, especially in light of Kozol's critique of the romantic free school wing, Holt wrote in 1978, "I am not on some 'individualist' side as opposed to 'community development' side. Such differences as I might have with Jonathan Kozol do not revolve around the issue of whether community development or political actions are important, but about what *kinds* of community development or political action are likely to produce useful and lasting results." Holt meant that political action which fails to address the psychological domain of meaning and hopes and moral values is unlikely to succeed—but he did not mean that we could *only* attend to the existential.[19]

Holt recognized that very real political forces were at work, and he found them frightening. He believed that the cultural worship of progress and growth was inevitably leading to fascism, and during the height of social conflict between 1967 and 1972, he quite frequently expressed his fear that a "headlong movement towards Fascism" was taking place in American society. "Either we become a genuinely integrated society," he wrote, ". . . or we will become a genuinely, wholeheartedly, unashamedly racist society, like that of Nazi Germany or present South Africa—with perhaps our own Final Solution waiting at the end." Writing to A. S. Neill in September 1968 about the George Wallace presidential campaign, Holt said that "a sickness is growing terribly rapidly here that may wipe out the world." In *What Do I Do Mon-*

day? Holt explicitly suggested that the alienation bred by authoritarian education could well "prepare the ground for some native American brand of Fascism, which now seems uncomfortably close," and in a letter to Paul Goodman in 1970, he wrote, "I keep looking for and hoping to find evidence that [Americans] are not as callous and greedy and cruel and envious as I fear they are, and I keep getting disappointed. . . . What scares me is the amount of Fascism in people's spirit. It is the government that so many of our fellow citizens would get if they could that scares me—and I fear we are moving in that direction." He wrote to Ivan Illich in 1972, "I think if U.S. society collapses, it will collapse into some kind of fascism, some sort of violence-worshipping totalitarian government. . . . I'm terribly afraid of fascism for my country."[20]

What is the reader to make of these dire warnings? Fear of fascism was common in the counterculture. During this time many young radicals called the United States "Amerika," the Germanic spelling apparently implying some sort of Teutonic/Nazi infiltration of American culture. It must, indeed, have been terrifying to face the military draft, the forceful suppression of anti-war protests, and the "conservative restoration" in American politics after 1968, and highly discouraging to realize that Richard Nixon's "silent majority" soundly rejected the dream of cultural renewal. For Holt, who was alienated from the social/political mainstream throughout the decade, the realization that substantive social change would not take place was a tremendous disappointment, as he indicated in a letter to George McGovern after the 1972 election.[21] How could ideals such as peace, justice, personal freedom, and authenticity, so vibrantly and courageously articulated by civil rights and student activists, be so decisively repudiated? Some formidable cultural force, more than simply a resistance to change, must have been opposed to these ideals. Holt called this opposition fascism, and like Wilhelm Reich he viewed it as a deadly political ideology resting on a mass psychological condition bred by frustration of the need for meaning.

In retrospect, America's democratic heritage was not in imminent danger of collapsing into a Nazi-style culture of repression and violence, and Holt's "prophetic voice" might have overstated the situation. However, in the years since, critics of technocracy have commented that the continuing centralization of economic power and mass media influence, combined with covert government activity and the popular appeal of fundamentalist religious values, are indeed leading toward a "soft fascism" that relies on the hegemony of consumerist values, rather than overt state power, to ensure the maintenance of an efficient social machine managed by a privileged elite. Holt foresaw the coming of the New World Order, and he did not like what he saw.

EVOLUTION OF HOLT'S EDUCATIONAL THOUGHT

John Holt's thinking evolved in response to his perception and interpretation of rapidly changing events in the 1960s and 1970s. In order to understand his work as a whole, it is not sufficient to identify him as an advocate of homeschooling, without considering how he arrived at this position. Allen Graubard, among others, has observed that in Holt's early writings on education, he was concerned with educating "good, skilled, inquiring, and critical people" and did not raise "large-scale political questions." Holt's early books spoke to teachers, in both public and independent schools, who simply wanted to help children learn. In articles published in 1968 he argued against *compulsory* school attendance because he observed that schools could not educate well so long as children experienced them as jails, but he claimed that the idea of teaching children at home was "essentially elitist" and argued that a good school offered benefits not available at home. As late as 1970, Holt still expressed the hope that public schools could change for the better, and that free schools could increase pressure on public education to do so.[22]

However, around this time Holt began to voice in his published writings the social and political critique he had already been expressing privately, and he began to realize that school reform was not an effective avenue for social change. In an essay in *New Schools Exchange Newsletter* in 1971, Holt made his thinking clear. "I do not believe that any movement for educational reform that addresses itself exclusively or even primarily to the problems or needs of children can progress very far," he wrote. "In short, in a society that is absurd, unworkable, wasteful, destructive, secretive, coercive, monopolistic, and generally anti-human, we could never have good education, no matter what kind of schools the powers that be permit, because it is not the educators or the schools but the whole society and the quality of life in it that really educate. . . . More and more it seems to me, and this is a reversal of what I felt not long ago, that it makes very little sense to talk about education *for* social change, as if education was or could be a kind of getting ready. The best and perhaps only education for social change is action to bring about that change. . . . There cannot be little worlds fit for children in a world not fit for anyone else." Holt already had his doubts about American society by the early 1960s, but it appears that the rise of student dissent and the escalation of the Vietnam War demonstrated just how absurd and unworkable the system had become. By the late 1960s, the growing critique of American institutions increasingly invited radical dissent. Historian Joseph Kirschner, who interpreted the free school movement as part of a religious "great awakening" in American culture, specifically commented that Holt could not stay "a-political" once this movement began gathering momentum. A sensitive moral critic of American culture, Holt could not remain unmoved by the awakening of radical dissent. Sheffer, also, has suggested that the turmoil of the 1960s caused Holt to examine fundamental assumptions about education. In *Freedom and Beyond* (1972), Holt turned decisively to questions of social justice, racism, poverty, and class conflict, and argued that schooling was contributing to these problems rather than helping to solve them.[23]

Still, Holt's evolution into more political concerns did not take the route that social reconstructionist progressives had taken in the 1930s. Despite the enthusiasm of the counterculture, he realized that few educators were actually attempting the reforms he had suggested, and as he looked more critically at the role of schooling in modern society, he came to believe that schools simply could never "build a new social order," as George Counts had suggested during the Depression. The "reversal of what I felt not long ago" was a rethinking of the cultural significance of schools that would soon lead Holt to become the preeminent proponent of deschooling. In 1971 he wrote that public schooling had failed to realize Jefferson's vision of education for citizenship because in its very foundations it "saw society as a machine, with human beings for parts." In other words, he was beginning to suspect that the institution of schooling was *essentially,* by its very nature, technocratic. He thus concluded that it was futile to use schools as an agent for genuine social change. In *Freedom and Beyond* he wondered whether "we are trying to salve our consciences by asking our children to do what we can't and don't want to do," and the following year, 1973, he even questioned the usefulness of free schools: "I think free schools make a great mistake if they think of themselves as incubators for later world changes." In a 1976 letter to George Dennison, he expressed irritation at Jonathan Kozol's emphasis on activist education, scoffing that "to suppose that someone who is really concerned about poverty and injustice in this country can best oppose it by talking against them in public schools seems to me so nonsensical that I can hardly think about it."[24]

Unlike most others in the free school movement, Holt reached the conclusion that Ivan Illich proclaimed in his 1970 jeremiad, *Deschooling Society*: school *as such* is an impediment to a rich, liberating, meaningful education. By 1977, Holt wrote, he had come to "hate" schools. "I don't believe in schools. It's not just that I don't believe they are reformable. I don't believe they are needed. I don't believe they were a good invention in the first place." Holt's move in this direction was troubling to many of his allies in the free school movement. Several reviewers of *Freedom and Beyond* lamented that the book was based on speculation and brainstorming rather than Holt's intimate knowledge of real children. Nat Hentoff claimed that "Holt has not yet done nearly enough hard thinking to be able to show how . . . individual and community needs would be met through deschooling" and that by taking "his leap into the Illich faith," he had "uncharacteristically become hortatorily vague." Although admiring Holt's intellectual integrity, Peter Marin found his new emphasis "too naïve, artificially innocent."[25]

However, given my understanding of Holt's view of society, it makes sense that he arrived at this iconoclastic position. Because he emphasized the personal, psychological experience of individuals-in-society, he did not accept that social institutions by themselves could bring about meaningful social change. As early as 1968 he acknowledged the large-scale social and political forces that shape institutions (he recognized that schools are "strongly conditioned by life in a capitalist society"), but he explained that, "in general, I don't believe in the top to bottom approach to things. I am enough of an anarchist to feel that things are improved in general when they are improved in their particulars." As he saw it, when ideas or values are represented by an institution, they become abstract—that is, removed from people's daily lives and existential needs. The search for authenticity, for meaning, for connection, is intensely personal because it arises from the lived experience of each person. Sheffer has commented that "this belief that change must happen within people's own lives is perhaps more characteristic of Holt's thinking than anything else." For Holt, attempting to change society through schools was an evasion of personal responsibility because authentic meaning could not be cultivated, much less delivered, en masse. He insisted that "important and lasting social change always comes slowly, and only when people change their lives, not just their political beliefs or parties or forms of government. . . . People don't change their ideas, much less their lives, because someone comes along with a clever argument to show that they're wrong."[26]

In the evolution of Holt's thinking one can trace the condensed history of the politics of authenticity. Starting with a moral sensibility that found conventional society and politics wanting, Holt, like the New Left, became increasingly radical as his awareness of social injustice and cultural limitation became more sharply focused. For a brief time in the late 1960s, it seemed possible that a new generation could build a new culture, grounded in values of peace, community, and human fulfillment, but as these hopes proved problematic and unrealistic, activism began to turn inward. If the politics of authenticity could not whittle away the power of the so-called Establishment, at least it could create retreats, oases, "islands of decency." Most of these were collaborative, such as communes, free schools, and food co-ops. But when activists began to see that old cultural habits died hard and collective action was fraught with internal conflict and disorder as well as friction with the dominant social order, many turned to still more private pursuits, such as "human potential" work and homeschooling. These pursuits were not entirely private—participants in both movements saw themselves as carrying on the work of cultural renewal and made connections with like-minded pioneers—yet they clearly reflected a growing belief that authenticity could ultimately be achieved more readily through personal rather than social action. As an anarchist, Holt had leaned in this direction, but with the failure of the counterculture he appears to have become more firmly convinced of this understanding.

Thus, the politics of authenticity was transformed from an energetic mass social movement that fused existential and political concerns (as practiced at Berkeley in 1964) into a matter of personal choice of lifestyle. One result of this transformation (to highlight only one element of a very complex process) has been the notable impotence of the Left in American politics during the past twenty years and the domination of a conservative agenda that thrives on its advocacy of personal freedom and choice combined with moralistic restraint. It is ironic that the "fascism" Holt abhorred may creep into American culture in a "soft" form under the guise of consumer choice, and it is significant that the homeschooling movement has grown dramatically, involving a million families by 1998, largely because religious fundamentalists have promoted it as a way of subverting secular social democracy.

However, I do not believe that either apolitical individualism or anti-secular fundamentalism is the most logical extension of Holt's ideas. As I have pointed out already, it makes more sense to associate Holt with decentralist movements that are deeply concerned with issues of ecology, community, and social responsibility. Unfortunately, American culture is heavily influenced by very different moral orientations, such as a "possessive individualism" (a term used by education scholar Gregory Smith) that defines democracy as the freedom to pursue personal success with minimal regard for communal obligations, and a Calvinist religious heritage that emphasizes personal piety and ultimate salvation over human conceptions of justice. Seen through the lens of the dominant culture, Holt's vision of social change through personal effort does seem compatible with a consumerist individualism, and his radical model of "unschooling" can be used as a means of escaping entanglement with secular society. It is only within the context of the *countercultural* understanding of decentralization and personal authenticity that Holt's ideas, and free school ideology generally, make sense as a radical democratic critique of modernity, a critique that progressives today would do well to reconsider if they are to reclaim the sphere of meaning and values from the Right. I will explore these issues further in Chapter Five. They are important here, not so much to critique Holt's intellectual journey as to appreciate the difficult terrain he sought to traverse.

Holt came to see that traditional politics, relying on reformed institutions to shape social behavior, perpetuate the power relations that maintain the dominance of the technocratic state—so long as the individual is seen as a product of institutions, the quest for meaning and wholeness cannot be fulfilled. Holt also experienced the difficulties of building more authentic counterinstitutions and the constraints these faced in a monolithic culture. What options were left to him? In retrospect one might say that Holt could have pursued the route taken by the European Green parties, or what Mark Satin called "new age" or "third force" politics, or Michael Lerner's politics of meaning—efforts to maintain a balance between the existential and the political, the personal and the social.[27] One might say that Holt gave up on collective action too totally. Yet Holt chose the route of deschooling because he came to believe firmly that the quality of people's lives would only improve when they took personal action, unfettered by extraneous demands and conflict, on behalf of their highest ideals. Those who shared Holt's pacifism, ecological sensitivity, and faith in children's organic development were and still are a minority in this culture, and Holt realistically perceived that until cultural values evolved, political action on behalf of these ideals would fail. So far, in fact, none of the "green" or "third force" political movements have achieved many concrete results in American society, while thousands of homeschooling families (including many who are culturally and politically progressive) are practicing what anarchists Thoreau, Goodman, and Dennison preached: they are living in accordance with their ideals rather than waiting for the approval of society at large.

In summary, then, I am arguing that Holt did not arrive at his advocacy of homeschooling because he was a "conservative libertarian," as critic Susan Douglas Franzosa has argued, but because he struggled to find an approach to education that would address the hunger for meaning and authenticity in a technocratic society. His concern for personal freedom was not rooted in laissez-faire individualism but in an Emersonian sense of the inherent dignity—the nonsocialized organic core—of the person. Although he may have been "conservative" in habit and style, Holt explicitly rejected right wing politics that failed to address issues of alienation and injustice. He commented that the term "conservative" was often used in a "nutty way . . . to describe many people who are in love with cruelty, destruction, and death" and criticized the "crazy Adam Smith way of looking at things"—that is, the belief that free enterprise could solve all social problems; in *Freedom and Beyond* he wrote at length about the need for political action to relieve inequality and poverty, at one point even calling for a guaranteed income for all people. Patrick Farenga observed that "libertarians have a tough time with Holt—he never said that public funds shouldn't go to the common good. He was just trying to broaden the definition beyond providing mandatory educational services." Susannah Sheffer added that "people often mistake Holt's individualism"—specifically in reference to his theory of learning—for an attitude of "'every man for himself; I don't care about the social good,' which I think was very untrue. Holt was an anarchist in the sense of individual action, but he really was concerned with the society as a whole. . . . Holt was not saying 'just let each family be happy and that's enough'; he was very concerned with the entire social structure. . . . He was very, very interested in community. Where people miss that is because it wasn't necessarily institutional."[28]

Holt was forced into defending a private sphere of education by his conclusion that mass schooling serves social functions antithetical to values of human development that he shared with the New Left and youth counterculture. Like Illich, although unlike others in the free school movement, Holt reached the conclusion that *all* schools in a mass society tend to take learning out of its living context and turn it into an abstraction, a commodity. Ultimately, his conception of human learning and the educational process could not tolerate interference by the political and economic forces of modern culture. In order to understand this better, it is useful to focus more specifically on his conception of learning and education.

HOLT'S THEORY OF LEARNING

Holt observed children in numerous settings, and according to many accounts he had an uncommon ability to engage spontaneously and genuinely in their play and conversation. Based upon his experience, apparently without drawing upon any specific educational or psychological theory, he came to believe that the young human being possesses an enormous capacity to make sense of the world—that is, to construct meaning—when free to inquire, explore, experiment, and actively participate in real-life affairs. The heart of his educational thought was his passionate defense of this capacity: he insisted that adults allow children this freedom to initiate contact with the world in order to come to terms with it. He argued that knowledge is only authentic, relevant, and meaningful to persons when it is acquired in response to one's own interests and questions. In *How Children Fail* he stated simply, "Schools should be a place where children learn what they most want to know, instead of what we think they ought to know."[29]

This trust in the human ability to learn and make meaning was shared by all the advocates of free school ideology. Critics such as Robin Barrow have identified this trust as a "romantic" (i.e., naively optimistic) view of human nature, because it does not account for the darker impulses and inherent weaknesses of the personality. Theorists who emphasize the "social construction of reality" would call this faith in the individual learner solipsistic because it appears to ignore the ways that meaning is created through language and other cultural forms. I will consider these criticisms at some length later on, for they do suggest limitations of free school ideology.

For now, however, it is important to explicate just what Holt meant by his interpretation. I do not consider his understanding to be merely romantic (in a pejorative sense) or solipsistic, but a phenomenological effort to interpret how real children acquire knowledge and make meaning. The key to Holt's perspective, I suggest, lies in Paul Goodman's statement that "free choice is not random." Like Goodman and the other radical education critics, Holt did not view freedom solely as the opportunity for spontaneous release of blind impulses, but as a necessary condition for the individual to actively seek and construct meaning through deliberate engagement with the world. He insisted that the growing child is deeply and inherently motivated to build a structured understanding of reality, but could only do so—could only learn effectively—in an environment that nourishes and supports the purposeful construction of meaning. By limiting the child's opportunities to explore and inquire, authoritarian social forms, such as modern schooling, severely limit the ability to learn. "The main reason for giving young people self-direction, autonomy, and choice in their learning," Holt explained,

> is not so that they will grow up to be revolutionary fighters against Fortress Amerika [sic], or preserve some mythical childhood innocence and purity, or know how to live in harmony with nature and the universe, but quite simply because that is how people learn best. . . . We learn best when *we* are deciding what we want to learn, when we learn for our own reasons and not someone else's, when we have the maximum control over the pace and the manner in which we learn.

This passage, from one of his more obscure articles, makes it clear that Holt did not advocate freedom for ideological purposes (his reference to "Fortress Amerika" was meant to be ironic), or to put forward some "romantic" defense of human nature; he was not saying that the human organism is perfectly reliable, or perfectly capable of learning in a social vacuum. He was saying only that human beings possess an innate capacity to learn which can be diminished or severely damaged by insensitive limitations. And the structure of modern schooling places numerous limitations on this capacity. "Almost every child, on the first day he sets foot in a school building, is smarter, more curious, less afraid of what he doesn't know, better at finding and figuring things out, more confident, resourceful, persistent, and independent, than he will ever again be in his schooling, or, unless he is very unusual and lucky, for the rest of his life."[30]

We might ask whether, in Holt's view, the community or society ought to have any influence on what the child is to learn. Isn't his advocacy of the child learning whatever he or she wants the very definition of romantic individualism? Recall once again that in the anarchist's organic vision of society, "free choice is not random" because the individual acts in response to a larger whole that gives one's life meaning. Holt was, in fact, deeply concerned with the *connection* between individual and society. True, he emphasized the innate ability to learn and sought to defend it from social practices that he felt would damage it. But it is incorrect to leap to the conclusion that Holt therefore simply celebrated the individual in some mythical state of nature. Holt clearly described, particularly in *Freedom and Beyond*, his understanding that learning—authentic learning—is a social endeavor, a process of connection between person and society. He stated that "man is a social, a cultural, animal. Children sense around them this culture, this network of agreements, customs, habits and rules binding the adults together. They want to understand it and be a part of it." In another book he plainly proclaimed, "Learning is a growing out into the world or worlds around us" and explained his position in detail. Even in *Teach Your Own* (1981), his manifesto for unschooling, he placed himself outside the "romantic liberal view of children" and insisted that children need and want socialization—"They are born social, it is their nature." Holt attacked school-mediated learning because, like other radical educators of the time, he clearly distinguished between schooling and living. When young people have a *vital* interest in knowing more about some aspect of themselves or the world, when knowledge will make a difference in the quality of their experience, they learn actively, eagerly; but when they see that their needs and concerns are not as important as the "curriculum" that enshrines the approved answers to adults' questions, they become passive and lose interest in learning.[31]

Holt deconstructed this notion of "curriculum" far more radically than most educational theorists. "I am totally opposed to all kinds of curriculum building," he wrote as early as 1968, "and indeed all decisions on our part about what children shall be made to learn. . . . We each of us explore the world in our own way, find certain things important and other things less important, need to know certain things at certain times and other things at other times. . . . Let's sum it up. What goes on in school is boring, stupid and pointless. Virtually all children find it so; virtually no children do any learning in school; the best that most children do is to fake it." I would accuse Holt of rhetorical overkill in saying that "virtually no children do any learning in school," but it is clear that his purpose was to emphasize the difference between *authentic* learning and acquisition of "fake" knowledge, factual material that is not meaningful or relevant to people's lives. Students may do well on tests and learn much of the material in the curriculum, but Holt insisted that something valuable was being sacrificed in the process. He asserted that "the things we do in the name of education . . . probably are to a devastating degree destructive of spirit, character, identity. The harm I think we do goes much deeper than the kinds of bad intellectual strategies that I talked about in *How Children Fail*. . . . What we do in the school (never mind what nice things we preach) says in effect to young children, 'Your experience, your concern, your hopes, your fears, your desires, your interests, they count for nothing. What counts is what *we* are interested in, what *we* care about, and what *we* have decided you are to learn.' This, as I think about it, seems to be a kind of spiritual lobotomy."[32]

Again, Holt's rhetoric seems extreme. Numerous educational reformers, Dewey for example, have sought to make teaching more responsive to children's needs and interests, yet still have maintained that there is a legitimate place for adult guidance of students' learning. In this excerpt, Holt appears, as Richard Hootman suggested he did generally in his writing, to be setting up a false dichotomy for the purpose of portraying his own position in the best possible light: to support curriculum of any kind is to condone "spiritual lobotomy," therefore one must oppose adult-guided learning as such. Even if Holt pushed this point too far, we can at least acknowledge that he was attempting to look at children's lived experience of learning free of conventional assumptions about teaching and school routines, and trying to demonstrate that the "curriculum" was *not* essential to genuine education. Quite simply, Holt became convinced that genuine learning was something other than the rituals that take place in school. "I want to do away with the idea of compulsory learning, and the idea that learning is and should be separate from the rest of life. Above all, I want to break down the barriers that separate children from adults and their work and concerns."[33]

This had been a consistent theme in Holt's writing throughout his career, but he wrote this particular passage in his *Growing Without Schooling* newsletter in 1980, and now he went further, following it with a critique of free schools: "Most alternative schools meet my objections to only one of these three basically wrong ideas, the idea of compulsory learning. . . . They leave untouched the great isolation between learning and serious work, or other parts of life, and between children and adults. It's ok to have some special places for kids, since they have certain needs that in some respects are different from the needs of adults. . . . But they should not have to spend all their time in these special kid places." For Holt, during the last phase of his career, learning that took place in school, in a "special kid place" removed from the vital realities of the social world, could not be counted as authentic learning. He insisted that adults could teach young people in a meaningful way only when they were being true to themselves, and stated that "children should be with adults who are doing what they love, not people who are paid to help children find things to be interested in."[34] Throughout his work Holt advocated for an authentic connection between the growing child and the larger world: to be "authentic" meant that the child's organic urge to explore, gain knowledge, and construct meaning must be nourished rather than exploited, and this meant providing access to real activities, real concerns, real passions, and real problems in the adults' world. If I were to encapsulate John Holt's educational philosophy in one oversimplified phrase, it might be: *schooling is not authentic.* His educational vision accurately reflected the 1960s counterculture's existential critique of technocratic culture.

More specifically, Holt's critique focused on how the structure and methods of schooling embodied this culture. Even in his earlier (and less overtly political) writings, he pointed out that competition for grades, a core element of modern schooling, replaced the possibility of authentic community with authoritarian control. In a 1966 article in the *New York Times Magazine*, he criticized the pressure that society and parents placed on young people to compete and succeed. "Outside forces hurry them along with no pause for breath or thought, for purposes not their own, to an unknown end. Society does not seem to them a community that they are preparing to join and shape . . . ; it is more like a remote and impersonal machine that will one day bend them to its will." Here, of course, is the basic concern of free school ideology and the countercultural critique at large—the moral difference between an organic, participatory community and the impersonal social machine of modern technocracy. It is noteworthy that Holt expressed this concern so early in the evolution of the counterculture; clearly he understood the larger social issues at stake in the emerging struggle over education. Throughout his writings Holt insisted that genuine education could not take place in an environment that stifles free participation. "We cannot be in the business of education and at the same time in the business of testing, grading, labeling, sorting, deciding who goes where and who gets what." He argued that this competition and sorting inhibit learning because they produce fear in children, reducing young people's willingness and ability to reach out to the world. The controlling, high-pressure methods of schooling, and the ever-present possibility of failure, damage or destroy the self-confidence and initiative that authentic learning requires. But schooling is not interested in authentic learning, Holt charged: "it is in the business of turning people into commodities, and deciding who goes where and who gets what."[35]

In defending community against technocracy, Holt directly attacked the cult of expertise and credentials. The academic system, he charged, had "taken the great common property of human knowledge and experience, which ought to belong to all of us, and made it into private property." He argued that the system of grading, sorting, and credentialing had created a social hierarchy that was inimical to a truly democratic community. Schooling involves "an intense struggle between classes and social groups for . . . scarce educational resources," a struggle, Holt explicitly recognized, that is biased against nonwhite and poorer people.[36] To expand upon a point that was made earlier, just as Holt differentiated learning from schooling, he distinguished between knowledge and academic credentials. For Holt, learning and knowledge were authentic and organic—they connect the individual to the life of the surrounding community. Schooling and credentials, on the other hand, serve the smooth, impersonal functioning of the technocracy, and assign individuals to their roles in the social machine.

The contrast between Holt's educational philosophy and the educational views prevalent in American culture was highlighted in a dramatic encounter when Holt testified before the subcommittee on education of the U.S. House of Representatives on December 17, 1969.[37] The committee was trying to make sense of the explosion of educational dissent and had heard Paul Goodman the day before. The committee chairman, Representative Roman Pucinski, opened by stating that progressive education had not worked. Holt replied that "compulsory teacher-directed learning" was overwhelmingly the norm in American schools, and it was this, not progressive education, that had not worked. He explained that children learn naturally when adults do not force them, but committee members were skeptical; one said he had a boy who was "kind of a discipline problem" and who would "probably never be a businessman, lawyer, politician" if he were not made to work harder in school. Holt replied, "I hesitate to talk about your boy, not knowing him." This was an archetypal clash of perspectives! The congressman, a member of society's ruling elite, viewed education as a path to similar success for his son, and assumed that success on this path required a measure of coercion. Holt, concerned as always with the experiences and strivings of actual persons, simply refused to discuss the young man's educational goals in the abstract.

Representative John Brademas asked Holt what standards public officials should use to judge the success of public money spent on education. Holt replied by questioning the need for objective standards. He pointed out that children learn at various rates and often make sudden leaps, so their progress cannot be measured with precision. Policymakers should not demand strict accountability, but provide nourishing learning environments in the hope that young people will benefit. "We do certain things because we think they are the right things to do, because we have a faith or conviction that this is the right course to follow. . . . It seems to me that fundamentally, at the root of things, education is a kind of act of faith." The subtext of this exchange is the clash between culture and counterculture in the 1960s. The policymaker viewed education as an investment, and sought tangible, measurable assurances that resources would not be wasted. The organic, human dimension of learning was less important to him than efficient management of the system. In subsequent years policymakers would increasingly demand proof of suitable "outcomes" in return for their investment. Holt, however, would have none of this. For him, education was not an arm of a mechanistic social/economic system, but a moral and existential commitment to children's lives—an "act of faith." Technocratic culture sees such faith as "romantic," because it cannot specify results. Holt told the committee that his view of human nature was "hopeful rather than romantic . . . though I don't shy away from the term 'romantic.'"

Holt went on to propose that public school systems should offer diverse choices to families (a notion that Mario Fantini popularized a few years later), including schools that they would run themselves (an idea that gained acceptance in the 1990s under the concept of "charter" schools). He did not advocate for free schools or suggest deschooling, yet the transcript leaves the reader with the distinct impression that the lawmakers saw Holt as a wildly impractical radical. Despite the enthusiastic reception his writings and talks had been receiving for several years, it is easy to understand why Holt would conclude, in the months after this encounter, that American society as a whole was really not interested in his ideas about children's ways of learning.

HOLT AS AN EDUCATIONAL THINKER: AN EVALUATION

Clearly, John Holt was at the very center of the countercultural educational critique of the 1960s and early 1970s. His views stirred radical dissidents, including those who abandoned public education for free schools and home education, but were largely unappreciated by most of those in mainstream society. Was he, then, a "romantic" education theorist? Holt's ideas hover around the edges of this dissenting tradition, and depending on the nuances one reads into the term, one might be justified in applying it to his work. Holt himself denied that his perspective was "romantic," by which he seemed to imply a naïve faith in the perfectibility of human nature, but he did not repudiate the notion entirely. Richard Hootman argued that the romantic position was an expression of "that aspect of human nature which one way or another asserts the claims of the individual against the claims of society and its institutions." Following Neil Postman and Charles Weingartner, he believed that Holt's early work represented a romantic phase, while his later writing, because it acknowledged the social context of education, was no longer romantic.[38]

I wish to examine this elusive notion more closely, for it is more complicated than Hootman suggested. In a broad sense, the term "romantic" connotes a preference for the wild and organic, for giving freer rein to emotion, intuition, and self-expression, and placing less emphasis on the managed, rationalized, and predictable routines of social organization. It would seem that free school ideology, and Holt's thinking throughout his public career, may reasonably be called "romantic" according to this meaning. The important question is whether this "preference" for the organic is flexible enough to admit the need for structure and social control in appropriate situations. Archetypal romanticism is not flexible. When Rousseau tells us in *Emile* that "the first impulses of nature are always right; there is no original sin in the human heart," he is proposing an absolute organicism that must view all social organization as an undesirable limitation on human freedom.[39] A. S. Neill seems to have accepted this premise to a great extent, and Robin Barrow's critique of this strand of radical educational ideology correctly identifies it as a problematic position: the "first impulses of nature" do seem to contain various unsavory potentials for prejudice, greed, rage, self-aggrandizement, and the like, which a healthy democratic community (or any sort of community, for that matter) must contain in order to function.

In a harsh critique of Holt's thought, Susan Douglas Franzosa placed him firmly in the Rousseauian camp. "Holt has consistently, if not always explicitly, portrayed the child as a kind of noble savage representing authentic human nature, associated social life as unnatural and corrupting, and *laissez faire* individualism as the terrible but true state of nature. . . . In fact, Holt's contention is that the full growth of the individual is incompatible with any form of institutional control built on community consensus."[40] I believe that Franzosa, attempting to defend a Deweyan social democratic view of schooling (which I will explore further in Chapter Five), failed to consider Holt in historical context and overlaid a caricature of archetypal romanticism on his ideas. In my reading of Holt, I do not see him endorsing Rousseauian organicism. Rather, I think that, like most of the other serious writers around the free school movement, Holt was seeking to restore a *balance* between the organic and the organized, a balance that they perceived had been badly distorted in modern society in favor of bureaucracy, top-down management, standardization, commodification, and other forms of social control. They perceived that technocracy was not an expression of democratic "community consensus" but an autocratic system increasingly governed by elites. Holt warned that a society he saw moving toward fascism was in danger of losing freedom, spontaneity, and individuality altogether. This is a "romantic" position, not in an absolute sense, but only in contrast to conventional discourse which accepts the increasing centralization, standardization, and mechanization of society as normal and necessary. Progressive social democrats do not advocate the mechanization of society, but from the perspective of the politics of authenticity or the politics of meaning, many progressives do not seem to realize the extent to which technocratic values distort and undermine even well-intended efforts toward social reform when these take place within centralized institutions.

A related strand of "romantic" thinking is the radical individualism derived from the excessive rhetorical outpouring of the Enlightenment faith in reason during the late eighteenth and early nineteenth centuries. This strand is not so much organic as rationalist, but it holds a Rousseauian, uncompromising view that the human mind is untarnished in its pure, independent state before being contaminated by the irrational, coercive forces of society. This view leads to an extreme anarchism or libertarianism, as in the thinking of Max Stirner in the nineteenth century and Ayn Rand in the twentieth century, whose goal was to detach the individual from collective engagement as much as possible. I have made it clear that John Holt, who emphasized the relationship between person and society, was not strictly a libertarian, and not romantic in this sense.

A third meaning of the romantic tradition is the Transcendentalist version, which is found in thinkers such as Coleridge, Goethe, Emerson, and, in the twentieth century, Rudolf Steiner, who were all *opponents* of Enlightenment rationalism. They attacked modern institutions for being overly materialistic and asserted that the sublime truths of the spiritual realm could only be experienced inwardly by individuals, without the clumsy mediation of social institutions. Holt's critique of materialism, and his views on the process of learning which emphasized the young person's freedom to construct meaning according to one's own experience, bear some resemblance to this tradition. It makes sense, as I have already pointed out, to compare his notions of freedom and human dignity to Emerson's and Thoreau's thought—but only to a point, because Holt never posited a Platonic "spiritual" realm that presumably contains eternal truths. Instead, he saw meaning as being contingent on a fluid and open-ended relationship between person and environment. Despite never having read Dewey, Holt was more of a pragmatist than a Transcendentalist romantic. He did not place as much importance on the social construction of reality as did Dewey's epistemology, but he did, as we have seen, recognize that the individual lives within a social and cultural context and strives to adapt to it. In his writings, at least, this relationship took precedence over any notion of transcendent reality.

In its least specific sense, the term "romantic" is often used to refer to a temperament rather than a particular ideological position—a posture of idealism that resists compromise with an existing social reality that one finds unpalatable. *Any* radical idea that would seem to have no reasonable possibility of acceptance by the established culture may be termed "romantic." Any extremist, of the communalist left, the libertarian right, or some other utopian persuasion, may be called a romantic if one persists in believing that his or her views are superior to conventional thinking. Those who consider themselves "realists" use the term "romantic" to dismiss radical ideas, especially when the radicalism in question rests on a Rousseauian celebration of untainted human nature. But in an unhealthy culture, being a realist may not be such an intellectually courageous stance. The counterculture, the New Left, free school ideology, and Holt's educational thought were all "romantic," to some degree, in this general sense of the word, because they could not be satisfied with moderate reforms in existing institutions. They sought—desperately at times—to remake society according to their ideals of authenticity, wholeness, community, and participatory democracy, ideals they were not willing to compromise. Alienation and romanticism are closely associated, because when one has given up hope of finding meaning in an existing culture, there is little to lose in imagining or joining a marginal counterculture.

Given this connotation of the term, I would reverse Hootman's analysis: Holt was "romantic" (in this general sense) throughout his career, and his mature view that educational change was not sufficient to bring about cultural renewal was, if anything, further removed from mainstream discourse than his early work. Establishment educators since the time of Horace Mann have repeatedly pinned their hopes for social reform on public schooling, and this faith in the "culturally redemptive power of schooling," which one scholar has called an "educational messiah complex," is an integral part of the American democratic faith.[41] Focusing on school reform has been a convenient way to avoid dealing with far more difficult issues of race, class, inequality, and economic exploitation. Consequently, to demand changes in classrooms is to speak a language that may resonate with policymakers, even if these changes are, as in Holt's case, quite radical. (As I will explain in the following chapter, Charles Silberman's *Crisis in the Classroom* condemned educational practices almost as severely as did the free school literature, but by retaining the culturally sanctioned faith in the ideal of public education, it helped stir up significant foundation and government support for the open classroom movement of the early 1970s.) By becoming more explicit in his critique of American society, arguing that school reform could *not* address its problems, and then taking the uncharted and marginal path of deschooling, Holt moved farther from mainstream educational discourse. He became more radical, more uncompromising. From the point of view of the liberal Establishment, he was less realistic and hence, more romantic. Holt did not "assert the claims of the individual *against* the claims of society and its institutions," but he most certainly defended the integrity of the individual *within* society. He was not a romantic in the sense of extreme or naïve individualism, but he was firmly opposed to the opposite extreme—the sacrifice of individual freedom and wholeness to a consuming technocracy.

It is for this reason that I consider Holt to be an especially relevant educational thinker for our time. Today, with the exception of small pockets of dissent—advocates of critical pedagogy and holistic education, remnants of progressive education, and alternatives surviving from the 1960s and 1970s—the dominant thrust of contemporary educational scholarship, professional discourse, and public policy is in support of a utilitarian, technocratic conception of schooling. Educational literature since the 1980s is saturated with the language of "standards," "outcomes," "accountability," "school-to-work," and other concepts largely tied to narrowly defined economic interests. Students, and schools, are increasingly expected to compete in order to be recognized for "excellence." They are increasingly subjected to objective testing and evaluation. School systems are managed by businesses or retired military officers who promise efficiency and hierarchical control. John Holt's moral vision penetrated to the roots of this discourse and offered a fundamental alternative. While many progressives may not agree that deschooling is the only (or even an appropriate) response, they cannot afford to ignore Holt's observations on the organic process of learning and his reflections on the social and pedagogical implications of that process.

It is obvious that life at the turn of twenty-first century has become enormously complex, with information and communication technology dramatically increasing the pace and sheer volume of cognitive stimulation, global economic trends increasing interdependence and local uncertainty, ethnic conflicts increasing the transfer of populations, and other complicating factors. More than ever, the technocratic mentality seeks to manage social life in order to control this complexity—it seeks to replace spontaneity with abstraction—and nowhere is this more evident than in educational policy. Global economic competition fuels the desire for "world-class" academic achievement; the proliferation of subcultures and languages in schools triggers a renewed effort to standardize the curriculum around objective "basics." Most policymakers seem to accept the inevitability of social management as the only logical response to complexity, but as the world grows ever more complex, where will this social control end? Holt feared that it would end in fascism, and he offered instead a radically decentralist understanding of the role of education in a democratic society. Holt's legacy is more than "homeschooling," if that term refers only to a small minority of families who keep their children out of schools. Holt envisioned a more organic and fluid society, in which education would nourish rather than diminish young people's autonomy and sharpen rather than co-opt and commodify their critical intelligence. Unlike many scholars and policymakers shaping modern education, Holt squarely addressed the possibility that technocracy, which he saw as being inimical to meaningful learning, makes all institutionalized forms of education problematic.

Admittedly, the effort to decentralize these institutions is problematic as well, for if not pursued carefully it can dangerously weaken ideals of social democracy that Dewey and other progressive theorists have considered vitally necessary for a free and just culture. Critics of homeschooling (and those few, like Franzosa, who have bothered to critique Holt) are understandably nervous about losing these ideals to the persisting influence of possessive individualism and religious fundamentalism. The tension between free school ideology and social democratic theories of education is an important issue and I address it at length later in this study. In the meantime, I want to return again to the core argument I am making in this book: 1960s-era dissent, particularly as expressed in the radical critique of modern schooling, remains relevant to the social and cultural challenges of our time because it signaled a desperate alarm about the viability of personal authenticity in a technocratic society. This alarm has not been heeded, and technocracy's power continues to expand.

CHAPTER 4

The Rapid Rise and Fall of the Free School Movement

In the turbulent cultural climate of the late 1960s, the radical educational critique inspired thousands of young people, parents, and educators to make bold, unconventional efforts to create new kinds of schools. Free school ideology was not an academic discussion but a call to action that helped produce an unprecedented popular movement for serious educational reform. The formation of hundreds of free schools in the late 1960s represented a truly dramatic phenomenon in American education. Before this time few independent schools (other than those serving specific religious purposes) were founded explicitly to practice a radically alternative philosophy of education. Since that time, the "one best system" of public schools has been challenged repeatedly by reformers and dissidents, leading to a proliferation of alternatives, including magnet and charter schools, an explosion of both religious and secular private schools, and a rapidly growing homeschooling movement. The free school movement represented a major turning point.

The emergence of the counterculture in the late 1960s provided a unique opportunity to explore educational approaches that American culture had largely designated as "romantic" or too radical to deserve the support of the corporate capitalist society. After Goodman, Neill, Holt, Kozol, Dennison, and other critics had thoroughly deconstructed conventional assumptions about learning, teaching, curriculum, discipline, and the proper cultural role of education, dissident educators found themselves free to experiment with new forms, new methods, new conceptions of education. Free schools were "counterinstitutions" that embodied the desire of disillusioned young people to build a new society that would be open and participatory rather than managed and technocratic. But the counterculture—the "Movement," as it was often called—turned out to be a short-lived experiment, flourishing only between about 1967 and 1972, and rapidly disintegrating thereafter in the face of political opposition and its own internal weaknesses. Most—although certainly not all—free schools collapsed after a short time, and most of the networks, conferences, and publications that linked them into an informal movement disappeared by the mid-1970s.

American education has become profoundly divided in the twenty-five years since the collapse of free school ideology. On one hand, the technocratic system has gained increasingly rigid control over schooling. After the publication in 1983 of *A Nation at Risk* by President Reagan's National Commission on Excellence in Education followed by a stream of similar reports, the federal government and virtually all state governments, teacher training institutions, teachers' unions, major foundations, and the mass media have all pushed strenuously for higher standards, greater accountability, more "time on task," and more impressive academic results so that young people are (supposedly) better prepared to contribute to the corporate economy. Public education has been defined as a weapon in global economic competition and young people have literally been referred to as "intellectual capital"; consequently the management of human experience in schools has become ever tighter. "Social promotions" are no longer allowed, so that children who fail to meet standards are forced into summer programs or made to repeat grades. Disruptive behavior is managed with powerful psychoactive drugs such as Ritalin, or by shunting "at risk" youths into "alternative" schools, which some critics have called "soft jails." The radical education critique of the 1960s, it would appear, has been thoroughly and decisively repudiated. Yet at the same time, thousands of families, refusing to view their children as "intellectual capital," are removing them from this system and sending them to charter schools, progressive schools, Montessori schools, Waldorf schools, Afrocentric schools, religious schools—or teaching them at home and in their communities. Numerous activists call for state-funded voucher plans, and some have set up privately funded programs to support parents in paying independent school tuition. There are calls for complete school choice and even the "separation of school and state." I believe that the history of the free school movement sheds light on the confusion and controversy surrounding American education in recent years, for many of these divisive issues stem from cultural stresses that became dramatically apparent in the late 1960s.

HISTORICAL PRECEDENTS

The free school movement reflected an unprecedented outpouring of educational dissent, but it did have roots in earlier efforts to redefine the mission of schooling. Some radical critics and free school activists recognized their ancestors and sought to learn from them, while many others seem to have been quite oblivious to those who came before them. From an historical standpoint, earlier examples of educational dissent demonstrate that certain stress points have long existed in American culture, and even if later waves of protest have seemed to "reinvent the wheel" without awareness of earlier attempts, their efforts make historical sense. For example, I find a fundamental cultural divide in attitudes toward industrialization and capitalism. From the early nineteenth century to the present, mainstream American culture has welcomed the continuing evolution and expansion of the industrial (and later corporate) economy as a potent vehicle of prosperity, personal opportunity, national power, and "progress" while a small but vocal minority of Americans have mistrusted the concentration of economic and political power, and the rise of inequality and exploitation, which tend to accompany capitalist expansion.[1] Clearly the corporate industrial state has prevailed over these objections, and so education has come to be defined as preparation for employment, citizenship, and consumerism in a vast economic enterprise. Misgivings about capitalist beliefs and values have therefore often given rise to educational dissent. The free school movement fit into this long-established pattern.

In the early nineteenth century, before mass public schooling was established, European romanticism and American Transcendentalism provided the basis for a handful of schools that might later be labeled as "progressive" or "holistic"; among other things, these schools rejected prevailing practices such as rote memorization and corporal punishment. The most notable were schools organized in Pennsylvania, Kentucky, and Indiana between 1809 and 1826 by Joseph Neef, a disciple of the Swiss romantic educator J. H. Pestalozzi (who in turn had been deeply inspired by Rousseau's emphasis on the natural unfolding of the child's personality), and schools attempted by A. Bronson Alcott in Connecticut and Massachusetts in the 1820s and 1830s; Alcott was a philosophical idealist intoxicated by his readings of British and German romantic thinkers. Both of these educators explored early precursors of "countercultural" lifestyles of the 1960s, with Neef involved in the socialist New Harmony community and Alcott engaged in a series of social experiments. Their educational ideas were clearly radical for their time, and their schools were all short-lived. In his journal, Alcott recorded a telling encounter with Horace Mann at a Teachers' Institute Mann had organized. "The Secretary of Education deemed it unsafe to introduce me to the teachers, and, on pressing my desire to give them the benefit of my experience as an educator, I was informed that my political opinions were esteemed hostile to the existence of the State." Alcott was not primarily a political activist but a moralist, a social critic who opposed the materialism and greed that he saw giving rise to a more centralized economy. Since he defined education as the cultivation of each child's spiritual essence rather than (like Mann) the preparation of young people for the emerging industrial economy, his romantic critique was seen as a barrier to the kind of economic progress that the Whig politician Mann envisioned.[2]

Neef and Alcott, in their opposition to the rising culture of materialism and capitalism, left a legacy of educational dissent that later generations would rediscover in the form of progressive education and the free school movement. But romanticism and Transcendentalism were swept aside by a culture that was more interested in Manifest Destiny and preoccupied with slavery, sectionalism, and civil war. During the later nineteenth century—the so-called gilded age—American society was concerned with industrial development, the continued expansion of territory and wealth, the assimilation of immigrants, and a confrontational relationship between capital and labor that led to mass protests, strikes, and violence. The prevailing view of education was well expressed by William Torrey Harris, an influential school leader and U.S. commissioner of education, who argued that schooling must discipline young people according to the needs of an industrial society; he especially emphasized the need for punctuality, order, precision, and obedience. The outstanding exception to this trend was Francis W. Parker, a public school leader, teacher educator, and author who vigorously advocated a "new" education during the late nineteenth and early twentieth centuries. Parker had gone to Germany to study the holistic pedagogy of Pestalozzi and Froebel, and his innovative practices formed the nucleus of what would come to be known as "progressive" education. In the 1890s, social reformers becoming alarmed by the excesses of industrialism and desperate living conditions of urban immigrants began to fashion a "progressive" critique of social institutions, including education. Pediatrician Joseph Mayer Rice created a "sensation" with his reports on urban schools in the *Forum* magazine in 1891 and 1892, which became a book, *The Public School System of the United States*, in 1893.[3]

During the following years, educators and social activists introduced reforms in public schools and inaugurated independent schools, such as John Dewey's Laboratory School at the University of Chicago, to explore the practicality of radical innovation. In *Schools of Tomorrow* (1915), Dewey and his daughter Evelyn profiled some of these schools and explained their philosophy, which was grounded in the view "that education is not something to be forced upon children and youth from without, but is the growth of capacities with which human beings are endowed at birth. . . . The first years of learning proceed rapidly and securely before children go to school, because that learning is so closely related with the motives that are furnished by their own powers and the needs that are dictated by their own conditions."[4] This is the "organic" learning, the emphasis on relevance to immediate life, that free school ideology would emphasize fifty years later, and John Dewey acknowledged its origins in Rousseau's thought. It was, indeed, a radical alternative to the conventional understanding of education. But in this particular book—indeed, in most of his early educational writings—Dewey failed to develop an explicit critique of the culture at large which had in fact defined education as "something to be forced upon children." Parker, too, had challenged authoritarian educational practices, but did not link these practices to authoritarian elements of the wider society. Progressive education thus took on a "child-centered" quality that was pedagogically challenging but politically quietist. However, a later generation of progressive educators, building on Dewey's more mature writings on education and democracy as well as the latent radicalism of organic pedagogy, developed the "social reconstructionist" wing of progressive education. Foreshadowing Jonathan Kozol's critique of apolitical free schools, George A. Counts in his 1932 treatise *Dare the School Build a New Social Order?* called child-centered progressive educators "romantic sentimentalists" who wanted to protect children from harsh realities.

The progressive education movement, with both its romantic and reconstructionist strands, became the most significant effort before the mid-twentieth century to practice education in liberating, personalist terms. After World War II, although progressive ideals informed various school reform efforts and models, from nongraded (multiage) classrooms to integrated or "core" curricula to cooperative learning approaches, such reforms were often isolated and short-lived in the face of strong political and philosophical demands for "basics" and "standards"; consequently, "progressive education" as a vibrant, coherent movement declined significantly. Still, groups of scholars and educators in the progressive tradition (most recently, the National Coalition of Education Activists and the *Rethinking Schools* network) have sought to revive its legacy, a legacy that stood behind the free school impulse in significant, if often implicit, ways.[5]

An even more direct philosophical ancestor of free schools was the anarchist "modern school" movement of the early twentieth century. The first of these was founded in Spain in 1901 by Francisco Ferrer, a radical anti-monarchist in the tradition of European anarchists Bakunin, Stirner, Godwin, Kropotkin, and Tolstoy. Joel Spring has traced the libertarian critique of state schooling to eighteenth-century English liberals such as Joseph Priestly and Erasmus Darwin, and identified its primary goal as "a nonauthoritarian society in which people will be free to determine the type of economic and political organizations they want based on the goals of individual pleasure and happiness"—an objective that clearly resonates with the language and ideals of 1960s radicals and free schoolers. State-regulated schooling, according to the anarchist analysis, perpetuates the power of a ruling class by limiting or prohibiting genuinely free thought. Like the earlier anarchists, Ferrer argued that established educational systems are dominated by the interests of state, church, and elites. "The children must learn to obey, to believe, and to think according to the prevailing social dogmas. . . . There is no question of promoting the spontaneous development of the child's faculties, or encouraging it to seek freely the satisfaction of its physical, intellectual, and moral needs." After Ferrer was executed in 1909 (allegedly for promoting violent riots, but more likely because he was an effective anarchist voice), radicals in the freethinking enclave of New York's Greenwich Village (a circle that included Emma Goldman, Upton Sinclair, Lincoln Steffens, Eugene O'Neill, and Max Eastman, among others) formed a Francisco Ferrer Association and opened a school based on his model. Between 1911 and the 1950s, about twenty of these schools were founded around the United States, many supported by clusters of radical, working-class immigrants. In these schools, "personal relationships were the most important thing. People were allowed to develop their own potentialities." In anarchist thought and practice, the freedom of self-expression was an inherently political act, and these lively radical schools represented an early critique of technocratic society. Until the more widespread revolt against technocracy took place in the 1960s, however, anarchist education constituted only a marginal, ephemeral outburst of countercultural energy.[6]

THE RISE OF THE FREE SCHOOL MOVEMENT

The 1960s provided a cultural climate in which the romantic/libertarian tradition could finally, after more than a century of struggling in obscurity, grow into a grassroots educational rebellion. A few free schools were organized in the mid-1960s, primarily by educators who had been inspired by Neill's *Summerhill*, but also by scattered groups of campus radicals or other activists responding to local conditions. For example, after his discouraging experience as a Boston public school teacher, Jonathan Kozol joined with a group of inner-city parents to form the New School for Children in 1966. "We were very much aware of doing something different," he recalled. There was "no literature to turn to." Significantly, many in the 1960s generation did not turn to the progressive education literature; perhaps it seemed antiquated, not urgent enough for the challenges facing American culture at the time. A new literature was emerging, more critical of social institutions such as public schooling, and more directly concerned with pressing issues such as alienation and racism. The books of Friedenberg, Neill, Goodman, and Holt found enthusiastic readers. In 1966 a group of teachers, social workers, and civil rights and peace activists in Toronto founded *This Magazine is About Schools*, which would become an enduring and important forum for radical educational ideas (it claimed 7,000 readers in 1968). The movement started to gather momentum around 1967 and 1968, and then, according to Kozol, "all in a rush around the winter of 1969 and spring of 1970, each of us began to be aware of one another."[7]

The free school movement took place because the young generation's rebellion against technocracy, along with African Americans' courageous struggle for justice, opened unprecedented possibilities of cultural dissent. For many, participation in a free school was a concrete, immediate, even exhilarating opportunity to change social conditions that were becoming perceived as oppressive and alienating. Bill Ayers, who was to become famous (or infamous) as a leader of the radical Weatherman (later, the Weather Underground) faction (and who, today, is a widely respected educational scholar), recounted his involvement in the Children's Community in Ann Arbor. In 1965, at the age of 20, he was already acutely sensitive to issues of injustice and was involved in civil rights and anti-war activities. When he heard about the school while in jail after a draft protest, he recalled,

> It resonated with me as part of the spirit of the day. An alternative school was like a food coop or work coop or living communally. It was a romantic idea. I was in a romantic frame of mind. It was that feeling of liberation, anti-establishment, we're birthing something new, and the old is hopelessly bad and backwards. But also, we had labored and toiled around the issue of civil rights, integration in particular. Here I was in a school for the first time in my life where black and white staff and kids were mixed together in a way that seemed entirely natural and humane and stood as a big banner against the degradation of everything we'd been fighting against. I felt that the school was part of the insurgency against the old . . . ; it was a place to enact the radical politics on the ground.[8]

In this passage Ayers succinctly reflects the dual nature of the free school phenomenon. A free school was at once "romantic"—an existential, countercultural rebellion against established authority, the exciting opportunity to create "something new"—*and* "a place to enact the radical politics." In saying that "the old is hopelessly bad and backwards," Ayers and others of his generation were not simply seeking escape from authority for the sheer thrill of self-indulgence; rather, they were reacting against specific cultural limitations and social injustices that produced an uncomfortable experience of alienation. Through their activism they sought to create positive alternatives to the old, unsatisfactory system. Ayers, for example, said that he and his colleagues were influenced by Myles Horton's model of education for social change (which Horton had developed at the Highlander Folk School in Tennessee, a multiracial center for adult learning that effectively empowered a generation of union activists and civil rights leaders). They often called their school a "freedom school," like those established in the South during Freedom Summer (1964), also influenced by Horton. Probably most people who became involved in free schools had similar concerns. One former parent and teacher recalled that "we were not just talking about a school, some of us were talking about the world, others were working to change their own lives. We were talking about social structures and social change, about the way the world might work. Some of us wanted to change the whole world starting in that little place."[9]

Those attracted to teaching in free schools were primarily young people; Graubard found that 69 percent of these teachers were under 30 years old. Empowered by the civil rights and free speech movements, young teachers rebelled against the bureaucratic restrictions they experienced in public education. Len Solo recounted that his involvement was triggered when he was asked to resign from a presumably progressive public high school. His principal had told him "In spite of my admonitions, you continue to act like an individual" and criticized him "for getting too close to the students." Kozol had chafed at similar restraints. The young generation—the dissident portion of it, at least—was by then proclaiming that acting like an individual and having authentic relationships with other persons were exactly what people needed to do regain their freedom and dignity from the oppression of technocratic society. Free schools offered opportunities to do so. One school founder reflected that "We loved the thought of forming this community of ideas, with like-minded people. Starting a school gave us a sense of connection in an impersonal, disconnected world." This teacher, and according to Solo, many others, were at least as concerned with "seeking answers to our own questions" as they were with the task of teaching young people.[10]

On the other hand, many free schools came into being as a result of students' needs or explicit demands. In some cases, this appears to have prodded their parents to become associated with educational ideas entirely foreign to them. John Holt believed that a "substantial" number of free school parents "were not really committed to any libertarian view of childhood but thought 'my kid is doing badly in regular school and if I let him go someplace where he can wear dirty blue jeans, run around and have a little fun, then he will buckle down and do his regular school work, and he'll get back onto that 'Ivy League Express' or whatever express they want him to be on." Jerry Friedberg confirmed this suspicion, observing that while his school in New York was "committed to a radically libertarian approach, . . . we knew that most parents who were likely to come initially would not come because they wanted that approach. They would come because they knew the public schools are crap and because they need some alternative. Any alternative that's anywhere half decent they will grab. That's exactly what happened." He reported that the teachers sought to educate parents about the school's philosophy, but said that many parents still did not understand or fully accept it, and this led to problems.[11]

Given that many free schools were established by idealistic young people who were generally more radical than most of their students' parents, this sort of friction was more or less inevitable. However, there is little evidence in the literature suggesting that free school activists assumed that parents would be adversaries. Believing that they were on the leading edge of a social revolution that would bring about more democracy, more freedom, more compassionate and humane interpersonal relations, they seem to have expected, or hoped at least, that parents would appreciate them for helping to liberate their children. Most of the school brochures and flyers did not contain any flaming social critique but simply sought to demonstrate to parents that free schools were great places for their children. In the context of the later 1960s and early 1970s, many liberal parents were, in fact, receptive to this message, even if they did not subscribe to New Left or countercultural ideologies.

Some schools, in fact, were successful in engaging parents' interest and support. One school in Massachusetts was started in 1968 by thirty young people "who wanted a real education based *on their own needs*. . . . The parents went along, but not without some major adjustments in their own thinking. A community of people formed that tried to learn about freedom and education by immersing themselves in it."[12] Besides becoming involved directly in schools, many people in the late 1960s were exploring issues of freedom and education through reading books by Neill, Goodman, Holt, Kozol, Herbert Kohl, and others. Most of these authors were invited to teach seminars at major universities (such as one on Non-Authoritarian Teaching at the University of California, Berkeley, in 1968 and 1969, and a popular course Holt taught at Harvard), and discussion groups and free university classes appeared in numerous settings. A group of radical Berkeley teachers (including Kohl), meeting after school hours, founded Other Ways—a pioneer publicly funded alternative school. Momentum began to build, and by 1969, a new educational phenomenon was blossoming.

Accounts of these schools are fairly consistent in their portrayal of pedagogical practices and daily life for students and teachers. It is not my purpose here to attempt a thorough sociological study, but the evidence seems to suggest that most free schools did faithfully implement many of the ideas expressed in the radical education literature. They allowed children extensive, sometimes unlimited time for free play, and provided art materials, woodshops, gardens, and other environments that invited purposeful, creative activities without formal requirements; teachers were present as guides and mentors but did not, for the most part, expect particular results. Children were rarely, if ever, segregated according to age or ability, and mixed freely in large and small group activities or spent quiet time on their own as they chose. Most, if not all, of the schools refused to grade students' work.

"Curriculum" was replaced by open-ended learning determined by students' as well as teachers' personal interests. Claudia Berman, writing about the School Around Us in Maine, reflected that the "curriculum is real life. . . . It is not required or contrived. It does not come from the top down and is not put upon anyone. It is built from the interests, desires, and needs of the learning community of students and teachers." Berman indicated that the subjects of learning were often influenced by current events, holidays, the seasons, and an ongoing interest in the natural environment.[13] Many other accounts of free schools in the 1960s and 1970s reported that the spontaneous "curriculum" frequently revolved around the social and political turmoil of the time (particularly, of course, for older children and teens): people wanted to discuss racial conflict, women's liberation, sexuality, Vietnam and American foreign policy, and theories of psychology and human development that addressed alienation and the impersonal institutions of modern society (existentialist and Beat writers, and interpreters of Asian religion such as Alan Watts, were very popular). Virtually all the schools encouraged self-expression through arts, crafts, poetry, and creative writing.

Usually, the time devoted to learning activities was fluid and flexible. Some schools, loosening the iron grip of curriculum entirely, placed no requirements on children's use of time, and while a few of these schools (the Sudbury Valley School in Massachusetts, in particular) turned this freedom into a successful pedagogical practice by encouraging each student's personal responsibility for one's own learning, others experienced periods of "chaos" in which unregulated behavior was clearly not productive. These schools used various techniques, including having students draw up daily personal schedules or learning contracts, to balance freedom with some educational structure. Allen Graubard reported that at one school, once the children "knew in advance what their choices were and had to spend at least a few minutes thinking seriously about how they would like to spend their time, they usually decided that they would like to participate in at least some of the offered activities." This sort of planning also allowed teachers to coordinate lessons rather than responding to random individual requests. But nearly all free schoolers valued organic planning over fixed, formal scheduling. According to Berman, "classes and projects, whether individual, large- or small-group, have a life of their own. They start because of the children's interest and enthusiasm and continue until the subject matter is fully explored to the developmentally appropriate level, until the students' interest and enthusiasm dissipates, or the project is complete." Classes were scheduled for topics that attracted interest, but attendance was rarely required. Herb Snitzer related an incident that captures the pedagogical spirit of the free school: after the season's first snowfall, some of the younger students wanted to go sledding rather than attend their math group, and Snitzer went along with them. "Numbers can wait," he reasoned. "Firsts are firsts, after all, occur but once and ought not to go uncelebrated. . . . They are also part of the present, urgent, meant-to-be-lived now."[14]

Virtually all of these schools sought, in one way or another, to build a sense of community among the people involved. This task had two broad dimensions—emotional and organizational. The adults tried to step outside the conventional teaching role to become mentors and friends to their students. George Dennison, describing the tone that staff members established in the first weeks of the First Street School's existence, commented that "it seemed like a family gathering, or a picnic, or perhaps a clubhouse of some sort. . . . And we launched out immediately on the business of *losing time*. That is to say, we got to know the children really well, held long conversations with them, not on school topics, but on whatever occupied their minds: details of family life, neighborhood events, personal worries and personal interests." It was important for the children to get to know each other, so they "played a great deal among themselves, and we went on many outings."[15] This description probably applied to the community life of nearly all free schools. Personal issues—problems at home, fights with other children, relationships, and one's private dreams and aspirations—were as much a part of daily conversation as any academic subject. Some schools arranged specific mechanisms, such as all-school council meetings held regularly or called on the spot, to deal with conflict or other community problems.

The literature often reveals (or implies) that many of the young adults involved in running free schools were themselves struggling with personal issues of identity, emotional confusion, anger, or conflict (complicated by their rebellious relationship to the troubled society of the time), and the caring, healing environment they sought to create was as much for themselves as for their students. Indeed, the environment itself demanded attention to one's emotional life in a way that professional teaching roles prohibited. "Working closely with the kids," wrote Chris Mercogliano of the Albany Free School, "inevitably brought teachers face-to-face with their own unresolved childhood issues. Many of us had grown up in dysfunctional families ourselves. . . . All of us felt extremely challenged by the intimate depth and the emotional content of the relationships in the school—children with children, children with adults, adults with adults."[16] At this school and apparently in others, staff members formed their own therapeutic encounter group that met weekly to work through their issues. On the other hand, this intense intimacy proved to be overwhelming for many people, and unresolved conflicts and emotional outbursts seem to have contributed to the early demise of a number of free schools.

The schools also built community by practicing participatory governance. Although some schools (including many of the successful ones) were guided by decisive, visionary leaders, virtually all of them sought to involve the entire staff, and the entire group of students (and in some cases parents), in discussions and decision-making processes. Clearly, rule by consensus (or even by majority) is far "messier" and more challenging than delegating authority to administrators with well-defined responsibilities, and probably all free schools struggled at one time or another with unresolved disagreements. Again, many schools seem to have collapsed under the weight of these conflicts. But the literature expresses free schoolers' fervent desire to make participatory democracy work for themselves and their students.

Free schools used many sorts of inexpensive spaces—rented rooms in churches, storefronts, and homes. Graubard stated that "the key to space use in free schools is improvisation and ingenuity. . . . As in curriculum and governance, participation is an important factor. Often, the setting up and transformation of the physical space is one of the major tasks of the staff, students, and parents; and doing this work is considered an important part of the educational process itself."[17] Many students spent significant amounts of time outside their schools, exploring the life of their cities or traveling to other places.

"Discipline," as it is understood in conventional schooling, was not a typical problem in free schools, for students' behavior was not regulated and suppressed. These schools tolerated a wide range of behavior: like other havens for the counterculture, free schools in the late 1960s and early 1970s were places to experiment with the elements of the "hippie" lifestyle—long hair and flamboyant clothing, beads and message-bearing buttons, marijuana and sometimes other drugs, informal and irreverent language, folk and rock music, and open sexuality. Students, along with staff members, frequently participated in anti-war protests. To impose a code of behavior on the community was disdained as "laying a trip" on people; the counterculture, above all, sought freedom from artificial restraint on spontaneity. Students themselves often participated in determining school rules, and these were generally concerned with protecting individuals' rights and keeping the environment relatively safe. A student who violated such rules would generally not be punished, but approached by an adult mentor in conversation or confronted by a school council meeting or student court. The written accounts give the impression that free schools had far more trouble with adults' disagreements (with each other and with the larger society) than with young people's rebellious energies. Neill and his followers seem to have been correct on this point: when organic energies are not repressed but given a supportive, caring community environment, growing human beings do, to a great extent, learn the art of self-regulation.[18]

Such was the educational environment that several thousand young people experienced for a few years, during a time of cultural upheaval. The emergence and actual extent of the free school movement has never been adequately documented—and may never be entirely described with precision. In his recent study, Tate Hausman concluded that "there is no conceivable way to accurately count the number of free schools. . . . Free schools came and went very quickly, flashed in the pan before they could be counted. Free schools were sometimes lonely institutions that intentionally isolated themselves; they did not want to be counted, they wanted to be counted out."[19] Nevertheless, various observers did attempt to gauge the extent of the movement. Sociologist Frank Lindenfeld, who started a Summerhill-inspired school, reported that there were over 800 free schools in existence in 1973. The *New Schools Exchange Newsletter* stated that there were over 1,000 nonpublic alternative schools in 1974–75, and a press release issued by the National Coalition of Alternative Community Schools in 1976 claimed the existence of 2,000 such schools. Solo estimated that the Teacher Drop-Out Center identified about 2,500 different schools, but admitted that it was difficult to make an accurate count, and difficult to strictly distinguish "free" schools from other types of progressive alternatives. Allen Graubard, in a 1971 study, did try to make this distinction and did not count preschools, more conventional progressive schools, or publicly funded alternatives; consequently his own systematic survey found only about 200 schools that he considered to be true free schools. Sifting through the available evidence, Hausman estimated that fewer than 35 free schools were started between 1964 and 1967, about 30 appeared in 1968 and over 50 more in 1969, 120 new schools emerged in 1970 and

100 more in 1971. His graph shows a dramatic decline after that. Stuart Rosenfeld estimated that at its peak, the free school movement served about 10,000 students, or one-quarter of one percent of the school population in the United States.[20]

Perhaps one can place these numbers in perspective by considering other measures of the reach of "counterinstitutions." The *New York Times*, in December 1970, identified nearly 2,000 communes across the United States, and Jane Lichtman estimated that there were 150 free university programs in 1971. Terry H. Anderson claimed that in 1970 there were 600 underground newspapers with a circulation of about 5 million.[21] Whatever the exact number of free schools, they were clearly a vibrant and visible part of a grassroots movement that involved a significant number of (mostly young) people. Even so, the counterculture never attracted more than a small minority of Americans. Perhaps because of its flamboyance, its novelty, and, ultimately, the seriousness and wide sweep of its critique of existing institutions, the counterculture—including the free school movement—made an impression on the culture at large well out of proportion to its actual scope. This consideration helps explain the paradox that despite the small size and rapid decline of the free school phenomenon, it introduced ideas that seeded later, more widespread reforms, including public alternative schools, charter schools, and homeschooling. As well, it is important to keep in mind that many thousands of students, educators, and citizens who did not actually take part in free schools did read some portion of the free school literature, and in recent years I have often met liberal parents and public school teachers who fondly recall reading *Summerhill* or Holt's writings.

Among the newsletters, clearinghouses, and advocacy groups that began to appear around 1968–69 were *The Teacher Paper* (Portland, Oregon), *Centerpeace* (Cambridge, Mass.), *New School News* (Chicago, published by American Friends Service Committee), the Bay Area Radical Teachers' Organizing Committee (San Francisco), the *Red Pencil* (published by a radical teachers' group in Boston), *Outside the Net* (Lansing, Mich.), and *Communications on Alternatives* (New York). Dave Lehman estimated that at least eighteen different publications served the free/alternative school movement. A major step took place when Len Solo and Stan Barondes founded the Teacher Drop-Out Center (TDOC) at the University of Massachusetts, Amherst, in 1969; almost immediately, Solo reported years later, "the avalanche of mail that we received was incredible," and during that year the number of identifiable free schools tripled. TDOC helped hundreds of teachers find jobs in free schools and published a newsletter linking radical educators around the country. It later became the Teacher Information Center and continued until December 1977.[22]

A Conference on New Schools was held at a well-established progressive school in Menlo Park, California (the Peninsula School), in March 1969, attracting more than 200 people representing fifty schools. This led to the founding, a month later, of the *New Schools Exchange Newsletter* by Harvey Haber. Along with TDOC, this publication became a nucleus of the free school movement, and it provided a platform for discussions about education and social change. Under a series of editorial collectives (which included Kat Marin, Bill Harwood, and Dave Lehman), it moved to Ohio in 1973 and to Arkansas in 1974 before disbanding, after 140 issues, in February 1978. One observer claimed that *NSEN* reached a peak circulation of 6,000 in 1971–72; by February 1973 it had dropped to 3,000. In 1971, the Summerhill Society, which published a regular bulletin, reported that its membership had reached an all time high of 800.[23]

Collections of free school literature contain scattered reports of various other conferences and gatherings that helped define the movement, including the following events. In April 1970, between 1,000 and 3,000 people (the estimates differ), including John Holt, George Dennison, Michael Rossman, and other notables, attended a Conference on Alternatives in Education at Zaca Lake, California, near Santa Barbara. It appears that this gathering, more than any other single event, signaled to free school participants that they were part of a nationwide network of radical educators with common beliefs and goals. Allen Graubard called it "the Woodstock of free schools" and recalled how people drove from all across the United States "in their old school buses" to the isolated campground. In October 1970, a North Country Festival for Alternatives in Education was held at Macalester College, St. Paul, Minnesota, helping to establish the Twin Cities as a major center for radical educational reform, both public and "free." In April 1971, 250 folks camped out at an Alternative Education Conference in Ocala, Florida, while several hundred others (including Neil Postman, Goodman, Holt, Kozol, and Rossman) attended a Konference (*sic*) on Alternatives at Fordham University, New York City. At this event, a "radical caucus" formed in response to Postman's charge that free schoolers were "copping out" and should be working to change public education. In turn, the caucus angrily accused the famous writers—particularly Holt, oddly enough—of profiting off the movement, but this controversy appears to have died out fairly quickly. In February 1972, the Center for New Schools held a conference in Woodstock, Illinois, on "decision-making in alternative schools."[24]

About 300 to 400 people gathered in New Orleans in April 1972, where tensions within the free school movement broke into the open. According to Bill Harwood, "The romantic folks, characterized by the

California contingent, were at odds with the folks who were working in urban areas with poor kids and concentrating on survival skills. . . . Detested by both were the folks who were working within the established system." Harwood wrote that this meeting put an end to the notion of a unified free school movement. Indeed, as Hausman's survey indicated, the momentum supporting the rise of a free school movement began to decline around 1972. A local newspaper article featuring the success of one school in Indiana opened by saying that "alternative schools are on the wane nationwide." The article cited no source or statistics, but the perception itself was significant, coming only a year or two after many felt that an educational revolution was in the making. This perception was reflected in the tone of several free school publications I surveyed; a sense of excitement, a belief that the numbers of free schools was growing exponentially, gave way to a sense of doubt and confusion. Paul Goodman died. John Holt gave up on the possibility of reforming schools and joined Ivan Illich in calling for "deschooling"—a shift of emphasis that left many education radicals feeling abandoned. Although a few important books appeared in 1972 and shortly after (including Steve Bhaerman and Joel Denker's *No Particular Place to Go*, Herb Snitzer and Doris Ransohoff's *Today is For Children—Numbers Can Wait*, and Neil Postman and Charles Weingartner's *The School Book*) there was not another title that moved readers as *Summerhill*, *Growing Up Absurd*, or *The Lives of Children* had done only a few years earlier. Except for an "Alternative Learning Festival" in St. Louis in May 1972 (which seems to have marked a shift from the free school movement to a growing interest in public school alternatives), I have found no evidence of major gatherings of radical educators for several years after the New Orleans conference.[25]

Many schools, including Lewis-Wadhams, one of the pioneer free schools, closed in the mid-1970s. A letter from founder Herb Snitzer cited the changing social climate in the United States a decade after the Free Speech and anti-war movements: "Today, the climate for alternative approaches is clouded," he concluded. Joe Nathan wrote that the national media, which had given a great deal of attention to radical education critics, free schools, and innovative educational approaches (attention which helped legitimate these ideas and fuel the rise of the free school movement), simply grew "bored" with alternatives by 1974; aside from the change in climate, which diminished interest in radical education, these ideas were no longer news.[26]

Why did the movement decline so rapidly? A high proportion of the radical schools closed after only a year or two of operation, or even less. It was often difficult to start, let alone maintain, a free school. One group in Salt Lake City wrote that "a citizen's committee has been formed against us. They think Summerhill is immoral and that we're communists." One politically active free school in New Haven, Connecticut (draft resisters, Weathermen, and Black Panthers taught there), was regularly visited by FBI agents in trench coats, or sometimes poorly disguised as hippies, and the students learned how to pretend they were doing "real" education by pulling out textbooks when these visitors arrived; once they even included an agent in their democratic school meeting and candidly discussed his purpose there. Even when opposition was not so well organized or ideologically focused, there are many stories in the literature of harassment by public officials, including school administrators and fire and health inspectors. Aside from the possibility that many of these schools, with their highly informal, laid-back attitudes and "hippie" appearance (with all the disorder that implied), were in fact in violation of codes, those reporting the inspections were convinced that officials were particularly overzealous in their enforcement efforts when it came to alternative schools. "Indeed," writes Hausman, "a few journals and authors I read insinuated that local officials constituted the most significant threat to their survival (though rarely, free schoolers claimed, did the authorities succeed)."[27]

Without public funding or, in most cases, wealthy backers, free schools were difficult to maintain financially. A "New Nation Seed Fund" was established in Philadelphia to raise money for alternative schools. Although its appeals were signed by most of the well-known authors on radical education, it does not appear that the Fund achieved much success. At many schools, supplies and furnishings were often sparse or scavenged, and salaries were meager. One teacher told Hausman, "You know, we were very counterculture and we didn't think money mattered at all. To ask to get paid was unheard of." Hausman added that "in about half the free schools I encountered, money had never been available. These schools had always operated in the red. . . . Many free schools survived on [energy and idealism] and self sacrifice alone—for two or three years. At that point, reality started to set in." Financial difficulties apparently put a number of schools out of business.[28]

Another problem, however, arose from free school ideology itself. Because of their resistance to authority, and their desire to involve the entire school community in decision-making processes leading to consensus, governing these schools was frequently experienced as an "arduous" task demanding endless negotiation and conflict resolution. Although free school ideology was committed to participatory democracy, which was, as we saw earlier, successfully practiced in a number of schools, it is quite evident that the rejection of conventional forms of governance produced destructive conflict and unmanageable chaos in many free schools. A few typical examples illustrate how passions ran high in these schools. A school in Washington state reported "a difficult first year with much dissention among community members over how the school was being run." A school in New Mexico was split between parents and teachers who wanted some pedagogical structure and others who wanted virtually none; in a charged atmosphere, one new faculty member was able to "stir up the parents who were anxious about organic learning": they sought to replace consensus decision making with a director and parent board, and this drove staff members committed to "free school philosophy" out of the school. Frank Lindenfeld reported that his school in Los Angeles, Summerhill West, had suffered from a serious split between those who truly believed in the Summerhill philosophy and those who did not. Terrence E. Deal commented that "The counterculture ideology abhors organization, routinization, and bureaucracy, and as a result decision making in the alternative schools was participatory, consensual, cumbersome, burdensome, and ineffective." Many schools, Deal wrote, went through a "euphoric" stage of rebellion, when organization was unimportant, but as they tried to sustain themselves they plunged into a stage of "psychic upheaval," by which he meant "a normless, listless, confused reaction to the lack of formal feedback for the learning activities of the first stage. . . . Teachers became overworked, but unable to make needed changes since their proposals were modified or aborted by the consensual decision-making process."[29]

Deal, who, at the time he wrote this, was involved in public alternative schools, held that nonauthoritarian schools could survive the governance crisis only by finding some compromise between their countercultural ideology and some formal structure in which roles, goals, and authority were clarified. Ann Swidler, writing as a social scientist on "the dilemmas of social control," also found the egalitarian consensus model unrealistic. But many free schoolers themselves, although they were aware of the problems of participatory democracy, remained committed to it, and one should not evaluate the governance problem in an entirely negative light. Free school participants believed that the difficulty of participatory democracy was an inherent element of the growth process—a necessary step in evolving from a hierarchical society to one that is truly free. One book, a manual for free schoolers called *Rasberry Exercises,* considered the sorts of issues raised in nonauthoritarian learning environments—How much structure is appropriate? Without rules, how are conflicts worked out?—and encouraged participants in these schools to work through them, for in their solution lay the beginnings of a new society. As Swidler acknowledged, free schools abolished authority "not simply to educate children better but to create a new sort of human being and a new model of cooperative social life." She called their goal a "utopian determination to change the entire structure of human relations by changing the structure of schooling."[30]

Due to the existing "structure of human relations," changing the "structure of schooling" was not easy. At a forum on starting new schools sponsored by the Summerhill Society, one participant observed that "the idea of freedom as practiced in Summerhill is a brand new one in our culture. I think it's a very difficult one to get hold of, for me and for every adult that I've talked to." In a letter to *New Schools Exchange Newsletter*, Herb Snitzer acknowledged that "the mortality rate of free schools . . . is frightening" but he blamed society at large rather than free school idealism; he complained "how difficult it is to find adults who are loose enough and straight enough within themselves to sustain a living process through which the games and masks are not only uncovered but stay down." Similarly, a Colorado school stated on a job opening form for the TDOC that "schools such as ours are exciting places to work, and also exhausting—the pace is fast. You really find out who you are—and so does everybody else. Perhaps a little like an encounter group—every aspect of your personality comes careening out sooner or later." While most professional educators—indeed, most people in general—would be horrified at the prospect of "every aspect" of their personalities being exposed in public, the counterculture saw this encounter group quality as a hallmark of authenticity. One can say in retrospect that this faith was "utopian" if it really expected communities or organizations to operate at all effectively while everyone's emotions were exploding on every side. Swidler argued that such an open-ended role for teachers invited rapid burnout, devalued their own knowledge and skills, and could make them so "uncertain about their own role in the educational process" that they would have trouble following through on even their own libertarian goals.[31]

But those who chose to follow this path valued authenticity over efficiency and were determined to build a society that would support this value. Commenting on alternative college programs, Judson Jerome remarked that even though radicals' faith in human nature had run head on into "the otherworldly depths of human disorganization," and they had found that "human relationships with no holds barred, no protective artificialities, no institutional havens" are extremely difficult to maintain, they continued to seek these relationships because they were *real*. Authenticity was the supreme value. Despite the obstacles, free schoolers sought to build a participatory democracy for future generations. Jerry Mintz, an alternative school founder in the 1960s who has remained one of the leading activists in the movement to the present, has observed and frequently commented that while adults, raised in a hierarchical and competitive society, do find it very difficult to practice democratic decision making, the arts of dialogue and consensus come naturally to young people who attend democratic schools. If adults can somehow manage to keep these schools intact, even if imperfectly, the next generation will, it is believed, be far more capable of practicing democracy in education and, presumably, other institutions as well.[32]

Some free school people did make one concession, however, and admitted that in order to work each school might need to be somewhat exclusive. Bonnie Barrett Stretch, one of the first journalists to write about the free school movement, reported that most of the schools did go through a trying process of discovering how difficult it was to implement their ideology of freedom; in particular, she commented, many upper-middle-class parents experienced considerable anxiety when they realized how free the free schools actually were. She concluded that ideological agreement was necessary. "Parents and teachers who have worked out their ideas together, who have similar goals, who know what they want for their children and why, have a better chance of keeping their school alive." But ideological consensus requires a certain degree of exclusivity, of privatization, which violates the democratic values free schoolers professed. Lindenfeld concluded that "a degree of lack of democracy is essential in the process of selection of who is to become a member of the school to allow us to have more democracy within it." As Jerry Friedberg put it, his school was not an "organic" community because it did not reflect complete agreement on common values, and conflicts between parents and staff were emotionally draining. Like Lindenfeld, Friedberg suggested that in order to thrive a school should be controlled by its committed staff and not by parents.[33]

There clearly is an irreconcilable tension between the desire for "organic" community and the existence of a pluralistic democracy. Free school ideology did not, and probably could not, adequately solve this dilemma. Since the radical educators were such a tiny minority among the American public, there is no way that their practices could have prevailed in public schools (this is why many young teachers abandoned public education), so they felt justified in establishing detached enclaves where public policy would, for the most part, leave them alone. By doing so, they set a precedent for more isolationist elements in modern society, such as religious conservatives who seek to be left alone by the powers of secular culture and who homeschool their children for this reason. Yet since free schoolers sought to advance participatory democracy and social change, their flight to isolated, exclusive enclaves was as ironic as it was necessary! This dilemma has attracted the interest of social democratic theorists in the Deweyan tradition, whose critique of educational privatization will be considered in the following chapter.

The rapid decline of the free school movement and its ideals was not entirely due to finances or internal "dilemmas of social control." By 1972–73, the moral urgency of the counterculture had largely disintegrated, and it was quite clear that no massive revolution was in store. Hausman concluded that "more than any other factor, the decline of the Movement in the early 1970s caused the decline of the free school movement." In May 1972, a letter from a reader of *Centerpeace* reflected this perception poignantly. "We that have cried for Kennedy, King, Malcolm X, etc. etc., we who have marched for integration, peace, draft resistance—and on and on: We are discouraged, tired, and we want to get on with living our lives. I admire those people who are still actively fighting, maybe it is possible to effect a minor/major revolution. But a lot of it still seems to be some groovy powerless people holding rap sessions." Writing in *Edcentric* in May 1973, Eric Davin lamented that "the system, it seems, is much more stable than any of us gave it credit for being" and cautioned against any desire for rapid social change. He recognized that "the historical trend is towards greater centralization of the economy, the state and all its subsidiary institutions—of which schools are one"—an observation that has been amply confirmed by developments in the past twenty-five years. Even so, this sober recognition came as a shock to many radicals. Summing up his study of the "years of hope," Todd Gitlin commented, "Who could have expected a reformation without a counter-reformation? . . . Still, the force of the recoil was extraordinary." In a similar vein, educational theorist/historian Ira Shor reflected that while, at the end of the 1960s, "a great historical change was in the offing . . . the walls of Jericho seemed to be crumbling, . . . the decline of these Utopian hopes was as breathtaking as their sudden arrival."[34]

FRAGMENTATION OF FREE SCHOOL IDEOLOGY

In the early 1970s, with the decline of the counterculture, the end of the Vietnam War, and a more conservative, career-oriented educational discourse being generated by the Nixon administration, the free school movement largely lost its identity as a coherent social movement; the growth of free schools subsided dramatically between 1972 and 1973. Even so, the educational ideas that it had championed did not simply disappear. The radical pedagogy of Neill, Goodman, Holt, Kozol, Dennison, and their peers had found concrete expression in free schools, but when these schools proved to be so difficult to sustain, this pedagogy went on to influence other forms of educational practice. Free school ideology appears to have split into three distinct (in some ways opposing) camps: a much reduced, less visible, but still active group of "organic" community-based schools; a professional movement for public alternative schools; and a grassroots movement for homeschooling.

The nature of this split sheds some light on an issue that has repeatedly come up in this study—the tension between the existential and the explicitly political dimensions of free school ideology. So long as the counterculture—the "Movement" or the "revolution"—appeared to be a viable force for changing American society, these dimensions were complementary. As Dennison so clearly put it, in the context of the counterculture, to live according to values of authenticity, freedom, and spontaneity was perceived to be a culture-changing act, and therefore inherently political. But when, in the 1970s, American politics stabilized and hippie fashions, rock music, natural foods, and other trappings of the counterculture were transformed into commercial commodities, the tension between consciousness and politics, between personal wholeness and social change, developed into a split, and radical pedagogy was largely divided into its constituent elements. The desire for alternatives in education was not so explicitly a political act, and could be accommodated by the dominant culture as private choice of values or lifestyle. Tate Hausman comments that "people who sought alternative education for their children or communities no longer had the same cultural framework that encouraged them to create free schools." Even further, with the decline of the counterculture, free school ideology itself lost much of its appeal. Hausman quotes one teacher who said that "they couldn't just be hippies anymore, like in the sixties, talking about children's freedom. Because society changed, and that rhetoric just wouldn't fly anymore."[35]

By the mid-1970s, the term "free schools" was replaced by "alternative schools," even among the remaining group of small, fiercely independent schools. The new term was less suggestive of countercultural lifestyles or radical politics, and was adopted as well by innovators in public education. During the height of the free school movement, recalled one participant, "we were all involved in politics and saw the school as an extension of our activism." But this activism gradually softened, and although "alternative" schools have, since the mid-1970s, continued to provide educational havens for various cultural and political dissidents, they are not as distinctly oppositional as were the free schools of the 1960s. A small number of activists have tried to keep the momentum going, although it would seem that the "conservative restoration" of the 1970s and 1980s made their efforts increasingly marginal. In May 1973, *New School News* in Chicago sponsored a Festival of Educational Alternatives, which gave rise to the Alternative Schools Network (ASN). In 1976, ASN held a conference in Chicago,

"Education for Change," which was attended by over 1,000 people, the most since Zaca Lake. Ivan Illich and Jonathan Kozol addressed the gathering, and participants agreed to form a National Coalition of Alternative Community Schools (NCACS). Bill Harwood, quoted earlier, saw this gathering as evidence of "considerable maturation" that had taken place since the 1972 New Orleans conference. Indeed, NCACS seemed to rekindle the activist idealism of the previous decade. An early brochure stated that "the coalition is committed to creating an egalitarian society by actively working against racism, sexism, ageism, and all forms of social, political, and economic oppression." NCACS became active after a meeting in Ann Arbor in June 1978, and by the next year it claimed 250 members (many of which were individuals, not schools). But in the following years, in a hostile cultural climate, NCACS declined in size, influence, and activism. Although it continued to hold conferences and produce various publications and directories, maintaining the legacy of the free school movement, it become a small informal network keeping its several dozen member schools (not all of them "free" schools) in contact with each other. These schools do in fact offer several hundred young people alternatives to the conventional school system, and this may well be a contribution to "creating an egalitarian society," but NCACS has not been a major force "actively work[ing] against . . . all forms of social, political, and economic oppression."[36] Recently, however, activists in NCACS are working to change that and reclaim the organization's mission; they hope to reignite the vitality of the free school movement.

Educators who sought to implement progressive, humanistic reforms in *public* schools were far more successful—at least for a few years. It is important to clarify the relationship between the free school movement and the rise of "open" education, "schools of choice," and other public alternatives. Free school ideology was explicitly countercultural and sought to replace the existing institutions of modern society with a radically decentralized, personalistic, communal form of society. Open education valued democracy and individuality, and in this sense it was congruent with free school ideology, but its goals were far more modest: it was concerned primarily with humanizing forms of instruction and learning within the existing system of public schools. Many liberal educators hoped, as Don Glines put it, that "through learning we could eliminate the social ills of our society"; this faith in education as a nonpolitical solution to social problems is deeply engrained in the American democratic myth, and I previously discussed how John Holt, for one, rejected it. While most educators who led public alternative schools were politically liberal—they supported civil rights and programs to fight poverty—they were not often "utopian" or "romantic" dissidents who believed that an entirely new culture should or could be fashioned. Many times, they explicitly distanced themselves from free school radicals. "The social revolutionaries have not been given a platform here," declared the editors of a *Phi Delta Kappan* special issue on public alternative schools.[37]

In that particular issue, Robert D. Barr defined the notion of "alternative" schools as meaning that because different students learn in different ways, they need various kinds of learning environments, and he emphasized that "free schools are not for everybody; they may be best for only a small percentage of people"; in a later, important work on public alternative schools, Terrence E. Deal and Robert R. Nolan made these same points. This definition sidestepped the reason that free schools existed at all: free schoolers were not trying to provide a better learning environment to promote academic and career success but were explicitly questioning whether such instrumental learning should be the central priority of education at all. Liberals, who answered to a much larger and more moderate constituency—the public at large—could not belittle the importance of academics even had they wanted to do so. Addressing a 1971 conference that helped launch the public alternative school movement, Mario Fantini claimed that 60 percent of the public *were* satisfied with the educational system (despite all the turmoil of the 1960s), and he explained that since free schools and vouchers threatened public education as such, the system itself ought to provide choices for students who needed them. When Fantini described his notion of "public schools of choice" in a 1974 article in *Today's Education*, he made it clear that while public education needed to be responsive to the diverse needs of students, all schools must share common goals: "mastery of the basic skills, nurturing of physical and emotional development, vocational and avocational preparation. . . . Our public schools are necessarily talent development centers, linking talent to economic careers." Of course, this is *precisely* what the counterculture found so repugnant in mass education! Because they rejected this package of goals, Fantini observed that free schools "are the most difficult to legitimize under a public school framework," and in a later work, he pointed out that most Americans were turned off by "hippy type" schools and excessive permissiveness.[38]

Don Glines, who has worked for substantive public school reform for the past fifty years, recalled this issue in more colorful terms. With a grant from the federal Experimental Schools Program, Minneapolis set up diverse public alternative schools in 1971, including a public free school, and Glines remembered that it attracted "hippies, flower girls, beards, beads, braided hair . . . dirty clothes with holes, unbathed youths, profanity, bare feet, 'don't tell me what to do' kids. . . . Many of us who led the 'alternatives' effort were just as radical, just as concerned with *deschooling*, just as concerned with civil rights, free speech, Vietnam, et. al.," but did not adopt a visibly anti-authoritarian lifestyle. When Glines gave a speech at the 1970 Macalester conference, wearing his customary bow tie, "you could see the disbelief. Who the h___ is this guy? He's not one of us." But, Glines said, he gave the most radical speech at the conference and received a standing ovation. A parent in attendance, who later became mayor of St. Paul, told Glines that he had made radical public school change respectable.[39] It may well be that only the "dirty" appearance and "profanity" of disaffected youths kept free schools from being respectable in the eyes of some apparently quite progressive people. However, if my understanding of the counterculture is correct, the appearance and behavior of these "hippies" held an ideological meaning: they represented a complete rejection of the values of technocracy. Free school ideology, while it did not explicitly or necessarily condone dirtiness or profanity, did insist that for a new culture, a new consciousness, to emerge, people had to reject the indoctrination and prevailing norms of existing institutions, and this created opportunities for outbursts of antisocial behavior (recall Kenneth Cmiel's comment in Chapter One on the decline of civility in the counterculture). A. S. Neill had insisted that by freedom he did not mean "license" where one's behavior affected the rights of others, but Summerhill and most free schools did permit a wide range of experimentation and self-expression—a much wider range than public schools could tolerate. Consequently, when the counterculture declined, it took free schools down with it, but the more respectable public alternative schools thrived, at least for a while.

The ideological divide between free schools and public alternatives was highlighted in a debate in *New Schools Exchange Newsletter* in March 1973. Robert Barr argued that "If we ever hope to liberate anything more than a romantic few, we must address ourselves to the task of reforming public education." Barr exemplified the liberal, progressive attitude toward education; in his writings he recognized the diversity of American culture and sought to provide options to address diverse needs, and he did believe, unlike more traditional and conservative school leaders, that education should aim to "liberate" individuals. (Explaining the formation of a national organization for public alternative schools, another educator expressed the liberal conscience, writing that "the monolithic system is not responsive to the needs of many—the poor, the dropout, the culturally or racially different.") But in a pithily titled rebuttal, "On Combatting Liberalism," Eric Davin insisted that public schools could not reproduce the "face-to-face" community life of free schools. "Free schools are only accountable to the people who run them—the parents, the kids, the teachers. The kind of alternatives the liberals want are accountable to the *existing* structure of professionals, administrators and bureaucrats—to the ruling class. . . . Those who control the public schools may introduce 'alternatives'—but only as a means of retaining their control over restless students." Davin charged that liberals like Barr did not fully understand the roots of student dissent; they did not acknowledge that schooling essentially serves the status quo, maintaining class inequality by fitting people into social roles. Liberals, Davin pointed out, still believed in meritocracy. "They created the schools as we know them and used them as an excuse for not dealing simply and *directly* with the political, economic and social inequalities of our society." Here was the key point: public school alternatives "deradicalize educational protest." Free schools, by their very existence, sought to challenge the status quo and its inequalities. Free school ideology did not share the American faith that social problems could be solved indirectly through better education, but insisted upon a fundamental renovation of society itself, which included (and was not limited to) the replacement of mass schooling by more intimate, responsive, participatory forms of teaching and learning.[40]

The relationship between free schools and public alternatives was complicated by the role that the free school movement—particularly the popular books of Holt, Kozol, Neill, Kohl, and the rest—had played in exposing the authoritarian, technocratic, and often racist nature of mass public schooling, thus making the desire for substantial change more legitimate if not urgent. It may have been true, as Fantini said, that 60 percent of the public still supported public education, but this meant that 40 percent had serious reservations. Was the glass half full or half empty? Vernon Smith, another early advocate of public alternative schools, observed in 1971 that "Never has a nation had less faith in its schools." As I explained in Chapter One, scholars such as Peter Lewis and David Tyack and Elisabeth Hansot recognized that the cultural dissent of the 1960s cracked open the monolithic system of public education and legitimated the notion of pedagogical diversity and school choice. The free schools did open new horizons for educational reform, even if they could not be replicated entirely in public education: Solo stated that some public school reformers did view free schools as models for change, while Fantini, as well as Kozol, in a later edition of his *Free Schools* (significantly, retitled *Alternative Schools: A Guide for Educators and Parents*), claimed that the free school movement had in fact provoked transformation within public education. If we believe these three men who were so deeply involved in the events of the time, it seems that in a significant way the free school movement may have cleared the ground for the rise of alternative public schools in the early

1970s. I have no tangible evidence to support this conjecture, but as I try to understand why notions of "open education" and "public schools of choice" gained significant support at that particular time (during the Nixon administration and a cultural backlash against radicalism), perhaps one could say that at least the free school rebellion prepared the culture to accept educational reforms that in any other age would have appeared unacceptably radical, but in the 1970s came as a welcome alternative to a truly threatening ideology.[41]

Still, open education and other progressive reforms in public schools had a history of their own, completely independent of free school ideology. Barr, seeking to distance public alternatives from the free school movement, emphasized this different history and argued (unlike Solo) that the alternatives movement was *not* significantly influenced by free schools. It is true that for the most part the philosophical roots of open education lay elsewhere. In a brochure from the early 1970s, the teacher training program at Pacific Oaks College reminded the radical generation that it had been promoting open classroom methods since 1945. Throughout the 1960s, progressive educators such as J. Lloyd Trump, John Goodlad, Vito Perrone, and Don Glines were attempting to implement many of the same major reforms that Dewey, Kilpatrick, Bode, Washburne, and others had struggled to achieve during the first half of the century. For example, Trump's 1959 book, *Images of the Future: A New Approach to the Secondary School,* called for flexible schedules, more group discussion, and more independent learning; he insisted that schools should accommodate individual differences and encourage critical thinking and intellectual inquiry. Well before the radical education critique was heard, and during a time that the nation had repudiated progressive education in order to outperform the Soviet Union, Trump's approach attained some success. A 1961 article in *Time* magazine claimed that the "Trump Plan" was being used in 1,000 schools, and a few years later he was a major figure in the Model Schools Project. Glines was an innovative administrator in Arizona, Missouri, and South Dakota in the early and mid-1960s who inspired systemic change everywhere he went; in 1968 he transformed the public Wilson Campus School at Mankato State University, Minnesota, into a renowned model of open education. "Our motto was 'if schools are to be significantly better, they must be significantly different,'" he recalled. "With our early successes, we thought we really could change public education."[42]

Another wave of progressive thinking augmented, and in fact overshadowed, these efforts. In 1967, Joseph Featherstone's articles in the *New Republic*, collected into a volume entitled *Schools Where Children Learn*, introduced Americans to the open classrooms of the British infant schools, a humanistic approach inspired more by Jean Piaget's developmentalist psychology than by any ideological agenda, and similar in style to American child-centered progressive schools. American educators imported the method enthusiastically, and the years 1970 and 1971 saw the publication of Charles Silberman's highly influential book *Crisis in the Classroom* and articles in *Newsweek*, the *Wall Street Journal, Saturday Review*, and other mainstream periodicals that touted substantive pedagogical reform cleansed of the radical, countercultural agenda that was integral to free school ideology. For the next several years, numerous innovations were attempted in public schools, supported by major foundations and even, for a brief time, by the federal government. Timothy W. Young reported that public high schools in Newton, Massachusetts, and Portland, Oregon, had adopted "open" education as early as 1967 and 1969, respectively, and he estimated that over 1,000 public alternative schools were opened by 1975. Barr put the number at 1,250, and pointed out that state education departments and teacher training programs were supporting the movement.[43] In the early 1970s the National Alternative Schools Program was established at the University of Massachusetts (with a federal grant) and began publishing the newsletter *Applesauce*, and the International Consortium on Options in Public Education was launched at Indiana University and began publishing *Changing Schools;* supported by foundation grants, 10,000 free copies were sent out in 1972–73. Over 1,000 people attended the First International Conference on Options in Public Education in Minneapolis in October 1973, and a *Journal of Open Education* began publication that year. The Educational Development Center (EDC) near Boston, where John Holt had been affiliated for a time, also helped public school leaders and teachers implement progressive models. This is not an exhaustive account of the organizations or government programs involved in school reform, but it does convey the sense that significant, progressive reform was widely supported in the early 1970s.

However, this support was not wide, or deep, enough to sustain a systemic change of American education. A fundamental shift began taking place in the later 1970s, transforming many, if not most, "alternative schools" from sites for experimentation and innovation into safety valves—refuges for disaffected or unsuccessful students that allowed the majority of schools to function more smoothly without dissent. As early as 1975, a former state school superintendent told a conference that "there was not a groundswell of support for efforts to reform education, that alternative education is viewed by many as a dumping ground for students who don't fit the conventional schools." By 1978, alternative educators themselves observed that public alternative schools, despite demonstrating success with students, were in trouble. "The back to basics thrust seems to have grown into a movement of its own, often in opposition to alternative schools. Indeed, in many respects the future of alternative schools appears gloomy."[44]

The future, it has since turned out, was not entirely gloomy, although it has become politically complex. Public alternative schools were joined in the 1980s by urban magnet schools, which sought to achieve racial integration by providing specialized learning environments (e.g., schools for performing arts) that could attract interested students across lines of race, class, and ethnicity. In the 1990s, the notion of school choice received substantial political support, albeit primarily from conservatives who see competition and, ultimately, privatization, as solutions to the problems of a still largely monolithic system, and the rapid proliferation of charter schools is one result. While subject to state-mandated standards, many of these publicly funded, independently managed schools are organized by progressive and other humanistically inclined educators, hence they function much like the public alternatives advocated in the early 1970s. Here again is the paradox that liberal (if not radical) innovation is made possible by a conservative agenda of privatization. Today, educational options (highly traditional as well as progressive ones) are available to many thousands of young people in communities across the country. Quite simply, the notion of "alternative education" is legitimate and commonplace in a way that was inconceivable before the 1960s.

However, in the big picture the liberal reform agenda was as unsuccessful as the free school movement. The "back to basics thrust" became the dominant national and state policy during the Reagan and Bush administrations: the publication of *A Nation at Risk* by the federal government in 1983 followed by the reports of several elite foundations and commissions solidly recommitted the American educational agenda to serving traditional goals of prescribed intellectual discipline, economic growth, social efficiency, and cultural uniformity. State legislatures mandated school reform, but not the sort of reform that progressive educators believed would make any difference. A leading alternative educator of the 1980s remarked that "school people, ever anxious to look like they're engaged in systemic change when they aren't, have effectively sapped the term 'alternative' of most any useful denotation. School districts and, in some cases, whole states have warped the term, alternative, to mean schools for particular, usually difficult clientele. Most often, these 'alternatives' have become places to send kids whose behavior has become a constant, embarrassing reminder that *today's conventional schools, particularly its secondary schools, are fundamentally flawed enterprises.*"[45]

The failure of both radical and liberal school reform explains the success of the third branch of the free school legacy: the homeschooling movement. In 1970, Ivan Illich's *Deschooling Society* attacked the "myth of institutionalized values" and argued that schools *as such* diminish the experience of learning and therefore inhibit genuine development of self or community. "Once we have learned to need school," Illich proclaimed, "all our activities tend to take the shape of client relationships to other specialized institutions. Once the self-taught man or woman has been discredited, all nonprofessional activity is rendered suspect. . . . In fact learning is the human activity which least needs manipulation by others. Most learning is not the result of instruction. It is rather the result of unhampered participation in a meaningful setting." Illich's critique of technocracy was not far off Paul Goodman's; his definition of learning was almost identical to the notion of "organic" learning that nearly all free school participants followed. But Illich took one step beyond free school ideology by suggesting that any institution set aside for the specific purpose of education abstracted people from direct life in the community. Even free schools, he said, did not sufficiently free people from the technocratic assumption that self-development must occur in specially designed and administered places. "Many self-styled revolutionaries are victims of school. They see even 'liberation' as the product of an institutional process. Only liberating oneself from school will dispel such illusions. The discovery that most learning requires no teaching can be neither manipulated nor planned. Each of us is personally responsible for his or her own deschooling, and only we have the power to do it."[46]

Many free schoolers, and certainly nearly all progressive reformers of public education, rejected this line of thinking. But a few other radical educators were reaching similar conclusions. Jerry Friedberg commented that while free schools were a step toward a more organic lifestyle, they were not a "substitute for rich family and community life." Most significantly, John Holt, who had been an early supporter and key facilitator (I hesitate to say "leader") of the emerging free school movement, was starting to think this way himself, and he welcomed Illich's bold critique. In 1970 he visited Illich at his radical think tank, Center for Intercultural Documentation (CIDOC) in Cuernavaca, Mexico, and in the following years gave presentations there himself. By 1977, Holt had become a leading advocate and, again, facilitator, of an incipient deschooling movement, when he began publication of the newsletter *Growing Without Schooling*. Holt had come to see, as he put it, "that the movement for school reform was mostly a fad and an illusion. Very few people, inside the schools or out, were willing to support or even tolerate giving more freedom, choice, and self-direction to children." Those who did make a sincere effort found the task exhausting, and Holt simply asked one parent who had written for help, "Look, do you really want to run a school? Or do you just want a decent situation for your own kids?"[47]

This was, indeed, a critical question, and it reflected the change in temper between the late 1960s and the mid-1970s. Free school ideology sought revolutionary cultural change, and saw participation in counterinstitutions, as difficult a commitment as this was, as being an important part of the change process. For the brief period (roughly 1967–70) that the counterculture seemed to be growing rapidly into a dynamic force for cultural renewal, it was possible to believe that this effort would bear fruit. It was reasonable to feel that increasing numbers of citizens, educators, and parents were rejecting traditional assumptions about schools and joining a mass movement for freedom and relevance in education. But with the rise of the conservative restoration, the "silent majority's" repudiation of countercultural values made the free school movement feel more like a quixotic and doomed enterprise. By 1973, the former dean of the Harvard School of Education, Theodore Sizer (who would later become the leading public school reformer in the nation), recognized that "Americans are bored with being told that their educational system is a mess. They have been lectured so often, and with such passion, that one would expect them to be up in arms by now, outraged at what is happening to their young. Not so: their reaction has been disinterest and annoyance. . . . Most Americans are fundamentally satisfied with schools as they are. . . . They want their schools to be conservative, traditional, not the engines of social reform which many critics would have them become." For those who still held radical ideals about children's learning, the question shifted from "How do we bring about an educational revolution?" to "How can I save my children from the grasp of an unresponsive system?" The resistance of the dominant culture turned a budding movement for participatory democracy into a private search for freedom. If technocracy could not be overcome, it had to be avoided.[48]

The activism of the 1960s was participatory, local, and self-initiated; those who sought to change their lives or change the system did not wait for permission or leadership from experts or bureaucrats. This climate of activism made homeschooling conceivable. Len Solo commented in his 1972 study that the educational experimentation that arose during the free school (and, I would add, free university) period, which included learning exchanges and informal apprenticeship networks, was a significant step toward the deschooling of society. Illich's—and eventually Holt's—critique may have faulted free schools for continuing to institutionalize the learning process, but clearly the free school and free university movements took major strides toward deinstitutionalizing learning. Just as the literature of radical educational critique and free school ideology created an opening in the monolithic system for public school choice, it blazed the trail for deschooling. Ironically, though, a movement that began with the intention of promoting greater democracy and radical cultural change evolved, in part, into an archconservative enclave attracting religious fundamentalists, free market libertarians, and reclusive survivalists. The countercultural impulse does still exist in segments of the homeschooling movement, but it has been overshadowed by elements that are entirely hostile to social democracy. Larger forces in American culture thwarted the radical vision of free school/deschooling ideology and used its decentralist impulses to fuel an antithetical vision. In order to understand the paradoxical legacy of the free school movement, it is useful to explore more deeply the relationship between the radical education critique of the 1960s and the Deweyan social democratic view of education, a task I take up in the following chapter.

CHAPTER 5

Education and Democracy

Free school ideology poses a disconcerting dilemma to progressive educators. The liberal democratic theory of education suggested by Thomas Jefferson and carefully articulated by John Dewey a century ago rests upon the premise that education is a *public* endeavor whose ultimate purpose is the preparation of thoughtful, engaged citizens in a democratic community. According to this view, whether or not schools are operated directly by the state, the democratic public has a compelling interest in providing learning opportunities to all citizens that will enable them to reach beyond their private desires and parochial prejudices in order to take part in a common public life. The educators who were involved in the free school movement were passionately committed to building a more democratic community, but they came to believe that public schooling, as it had been developed, was not the appropriate means to this goal. They concluded that in a mass technocratic culture, the "public" had become a mechanical abstraction and was actually a stubborn barrier to the development of participatory democracy. Their radicalism was not foreign to the Jeffersonian ideal but sought to *reclaim* it in a society where political and economic power had become overly centralized. As Paul Goodman argued early in the 1960s, progressive education (by which he, like Dewey, meant an education for democratic participation in the community) could not be practiced in a mechanical, alienating society in the same form that it might have been practiced in a more organic, local-scale culture. A democratic education could not be entrusted to the mass institutions of the corporate state. But if that were the case, who would be responsible for educating the next generation of citizens—small, self-selected groups of visionaries and activists? Families in the privacy of their own homes? Weren't these responses as parochial and undemocratic as any elitist or sectarian forms of schooling? What does education for democracy mean in a mass, overly centralized society?

This chapter considers the democratic vision of progressive education and the extent to which this vision was shared by those in the free school movement. I examine how and why free school ideology diverged from the liberal social democratic commitment to public education, and consider the implications of this division. In this study I have been sympathetic to the radical educational critique of the 1960s: I believe it makes a great deal of sense given the turbulent historical context and the obviously deeply felt experiences of disillusionment and alienation that turned so many young people and idealistic educators away from mainstream social institutions. Nevertheless, the rebellion against liberalism contained an implicit contradiction: since the counterculture could not build a new, organic society, dissenters' flight from existing public institutions weakened the position of progressive (social democratic) forces within the mainstream culture. In abandoning the "public" (however justified they may have been in doing so), they may have helped spawn an agenda of privatization that swept American culture in the 1980s and 1990s. In education, this has meant the abandonment of public schools and the proliferation of privatization schemes such as vouchers, choice plans, charter schools, and homeschooling. Social democrats are deeply disturbed by these developments, and if these are unintended consequences of countercultural ideology, they must not be overlooked. In the end, however, the radicals' most poignant question remains: How can a liberal democracy be nurtured in a technocratic world?

GROUNDING IN THE PROGRESSIVE TRADITION

Few free school theorists, besides Paul Goodman and George Dennison, credited John Dewey as a significant influence on their thinking. Even so, Dewey's democratic theory of education provided the implicit background for many of their ideas. During his sixty-year career as the preeminent liberal philosopher in the United States, Dewey had sought to define education far more broadly than the transmission of knowledge within school classrooms. He argued that education is a fundamental cultural activity: the communication of experiences, ideas, and perspectives that shape and enlarge the common understandings of a society as a whole. A society that narrows the scope of education cannot be democratic, he reasoned, because it does not enable citizens to expand their limited or parochial experiences into intelligent understanding necessary for social participation. "Progressive" education, as Dewey conceived it, sought to involve young people, indeed all people, as active and inquisitive citizens in the affairs of their community.

This interest in participatory democracy provided a platform for New Left thinkers such as C. Wright Mills; it offered a legitimate conceptual alternative to the technocratic mind-set that had come to predominate in the social sciences and political theory by the 1950s. Rather than an "end of ideology" in a well-managed corporate state, Dewey (like Jefferson) envisioned a dynamic social and political discourse that perpetually renewed or reconstructed the foundations of a democratic culture. Dewey's liberalism was not the "corporate" or "managerial" liberalism that young radicals saw in the Democratic politics of the post-war era, and it invited critique of those politics.

It makes sense, then, that looking back, observers such as Lawrence Cremin, Len Solo, Terrence E. Deal and Robert R. Nolan, and the editors of a 1981 directory of alternative schools all believed that the free school movement had important roots in Deweyan progressive education. But roots do not mean direct influence, and some commentators overstated the case. Neil Postman and Charles Weingartner claimed that "In intellectual terms, the present school reform movement is simply a replay of what Dewey started seventy-five years ago. . . . It is sufficient to say that his spirit hovers over all school criticism." Stuart Rosenfeld commented that "free schools were to become change agents for the reintroduction of progressive education" into public discourse about schools. But these judgments are a little too facile; the free school movement was not "simply a replay" of Dewey's work; it introduced more radical elements relevant to social conditions of the post–World War II era. Postman and Weingartner sought to downplay these elements because they were attempting to support the emerging public alternative school movement. Had he still been alive, Dewey himself might have approved of this reconstruction of progressivism, as Paul Goodman suggested, but in important ways free school ideology departed from the progressive tradition as it was understood by many of Dewey's students and followers. It is necessary to approach Dewey's complex and prolific work in several layers in order to establish specific points of agreement and disagreement between his ideas and free school thought.[1]

Dewey's emphasis on *experience* formed a fundamental point of contact between progressive education and the radical critique of the 1960s. Throughout his work Dewey vigorously dissented from the dominant Western philosophical traditions of materialism and idealism, which both maintain (in complementary ways) that there is some pure realm of "reality," some essential Being, that is formed without human participation and is therefore reliably stable if not eternal. Dewey insisted, on the contrary, that the world is fundamentally characterized by "incompleteness and precariousness" as much as by the "finished and the fixed" and therefore "involves us in the necessity of choice and active struggle." Reality assumes diverse *meanings* according to the intention and quality of our engagement with the world—we know reality, not directly and purely, but in terms of its *relationship* to our needs, aims, prior encounters, and culturally shaped habits. In other words, we know it only through *experience* rather than in some absolute objective sense. Our active participation in an incomplete world helps shape it and leads to particular consequences that we can judge to be useful or harmful, good or evil. These qualities do not reside in "reality" but in our dynamic relationship to the environment. Furthermore, according to Dewey, because the meanings of reality are always contingent on changing life situations, our knowledge is never complete or final. "For in any object of primary experience there are always potentialities which are not explicit; any object that is overt is charged with possible consequences that are hidden; the most overt act has factors which are not explicit. Strain thought as far as we may and not all consequences can be foreseen or made an express or known part of reflection and decision."[2]

In Dewey's thought, then, the world is essentially fluid, interrelated, and organic (responsive and evolving) rather than deterministic or mechanical. This worldview has important social and political implications, which are expressed in a "progressive" liberal understanding of social change: once it is acknowledged that human effort and intelligence create meaning rather than simply reflect a fixed reality or predetermined destiny, it must be recognized that people are responsible to engage in "active struggle" to shape social reality in ways that enhance the quality of life for the community as a whole. Dewey strongly emphasized that more possibilities are opened for fruitful and nourishing experience when our efforts are collaborative rather then merely self-interested, and guided by reflective intelligence and inquiry rather than dogma, tradition, or superstitious ritual. He advocated participatory democracy because he saw it as an active collaboration among people to fashion social meaning that would enrich, enliven, and "reconstruct" (continually deepen and expand) their experience.

In *Democracy and Education* Dewey explained that authoritarian forms of society, which owe their power to dogmatic views of reality, produce isolation, stagnation, "mechanical" relationships between persons, and "formal institutionalizing of life," while democratic societies are essentially based upon an exchange of communication and perspectives leading to enlargement and enrichment of experience.[3] Critics of technocracy in the 1950s and 1960s made very much the same argument. So again, when free school writers spoke in these terms, they covered intellectual terrain that Dewey had already surveyed, usually without acknowledging his contribution. It is not clear how many free school writers had read *Democracy and Education*, so the direct influence is hard to determine, but it seems legitimate to claim that Dewey provided a serious philosophical voice to the normally "romantic" critique of technocracy, giving free school ideology an intellectual heritage that it would otherwise have lacked. By not explicitly grounding their ideology in Dewey's careful articulation of a philosophy of experience in democratic society, free school writers often came across as intellectually unrooted and overly polemical (George Dennison being a notable exception), but the point is that the ideas themselves are not intrinsically incoherent.

Dewey described the relationship between the fundamental character of a society and the form of education it would be likely to adopt. An authoritarian society, concerned primarily with imposing a uniform view of reality on its population, will choose educational methods that aim only to transmit "knowledge" as this has been defined by tradition and by those with the most cultural influence. (In a mass consumer society, this includes large corporations and the communications media they control.) In such a system, the student is expected to learn the curriculum as it is presented, to be a passive, unquestioning recipient of correct knowledge. Throughout his career, beginning with his earliest works on education in the 1890s, Dewey insisted that education for a democratic society must, in contrast, involve an active collaboration among learners to make sense of the world according to their experience. Education for a democratic society is most explicitly *not* a mechanical transfer of information but the development of skills of inquiry, reflection, critique, and communication. In an essay for the progressive journal *Social Frontier* in 1937, for example, Dewey stated that education for a democratic society requires "the active participation, the interest, reflection, and understanding of those taught." He continued: "Democracy also means voluntary choice, based on an intelligence that is the outcome of free association and communication with others. It means a way of living together in which mutual and free consultation rule instead of force . . . in order that each individual may become what he, and he alone, is capable of becoming." This is an important passage and it is fully congruent with any of the radical education texts of the 1960s or early 1970s, for it emphasizes the pursuit of authenticity (personal development according to each individual's unique identity) and insists that "free association" rather than imposed social structure enables democratic habits of mind to thrive.[4]

Consequently, when schooling attempts to inculcate a predetermined curriculum or set of values on young people it implicitly reinforces forms of social organization that are not democratic. Dewey consistently attacked conventional understandings of education that emphasize the authority of curriculum or subject matter, where "facts are torn away from their original place in experience and rearranged with reference to some general principle" (that is, they are made abstract). Rather, he argued that "no prescribed and ready-made scheme can possibly determine the exact subject-matter that will best promote the educative growth of every individual young person" because it is only in each individual's experience, in one's thoughtful and purposeful engagement with the world, that intelligence is truly expanded. "Abandon the notion of subject-matter as something fixed and ready-made in itself, outside the child's experience; cease thinking of the child's experience as also something hard and fast; see it as something fluent, embryonic, vital; and we realize that the child and the curriculum are simply two limits which define a single process." For Dewey, this single process was an organic relationship between learner and world. Rather than treating knowledge as abstract, objective, and removed from the child's life experience, progressive education sought to maintain the immediacy of the learning process, the direct relevance of education to the learner's actual life situation. Education, he stated in "My Pedagogic Creed" (1897) and repeated in later writings, "is a process of living and not a preparation for future living." Although free school ideology did not acknowledge that Dewey had blazed this theoretical trail seventy years earlier, it wholly shared this understanding that education is rooted in the present life experience of the learner, and school practices isolated from life experience do not qualify as genuine education.[5]

Dewey's educational theory preceded the radical critics in another important sense as well. As Dewey biographer Robert Westbrook put it, he explicitly viewed schools as "agencies of social reform rather than agencies of social reproduction" and sought above all to make education an instrument for the further development of democratic values. In taking this position, Dewey was as radical in the early twentieth century as Paul Goodman or John Holt were in the 1960s. Indeed, he was fighting the same battle against the rise of technocracy. Educational historian Herbert Kliebard commented that "it is likely that what Dewey saw as the basic function of education, the development of the kind of intelligence that would lead to a command of the conditions of one's life and ultimately to social progress, was not what most people saw as the major requirement of a modern industrial society. The appeal of a stable social order with each person efficiently fulfilling his or her appointed tasks was far more compelling. John Dewey, the quintessential American philosopher, may, paradoxically, have been out of step, in at least some significant respects, with dominant American values." To the extent that he was, in fact, out of step, resisting the growing use of education for vocational sorting and class differentiation, he provided a model of educational dissent that radicals in the 1960s would replicate, if not consciously emulate.[6]

Significantly, Dewey's vision of social renewal through education evolved during his career as he faced many of the same issues that challenged the free school advocates. Westbrook pointed out that during the early phase of Dewey's career (which coincided with the optimistic "Progressive" era before the First World War), Dewey held a fairly "naïve estimate of the place of the school in social reconstruction," believing that democratic forms of education could instill habits of collaborative social life in the young generation that they would bring to their participation in society as adults. Later in his life, after the Progressive agenda was repudiated by a resurgence of conservatism and materialism in the 1920s, he recognized that radical social change would require more substantive political and economic transformation. By the 1930s, "Dewey now more openly acknowledged that schools were inextricably tied to prevailing structures of power and therefore extremely difficult to transform into agencies of democratic reform." He joined with the social reconstructionist circle at Teachers College who were placing education within a more radical social democratic agenda, and although his rhetoric was not as strident as many of theirs (George Counts, for example, called for schools to "indoctrinate" young people in democratic values), his critique clearly took on a political edge that it had previously lacked, as in a typical passage from 1934: "In a world that has so largely engaged in a mad and often brutally harsh race for material gain by means of ruthless competition, it behooves the school to make ceaseless and intelligently organized effort to develop above all else the will for co-operation and the spirit which sees in every other individual one who has an equal right to share in the cultural and material fruits of collective human invention, industry, skill and knowledge." In a book published in 1935, Dewey stated explicitly that "the educational task cannot be accomplished merely by working upon men's minds, without action that effects actual changes in institutions." Even if Dewey was not widely acknowledged as a hero by the 1960s counterculture, he was, indeed, similarly envisioning an egalitarian, open society in which authentic human relationships could thrive. He still believed that education could help create such a society, so long as it was part of a larger movement for social change.[7]

What if this movement failed, though? What if, as in fact happened in the 1950s, the culture at large were to become indifferent or hostile to "progressive" ideals and insist that schools perform their traditional task of "social reproduction"—or, as occurred in the 1960s, implement piecemeal "progressive" reforms in public schools without substantially altering the mission or structure of the system as a whole? What if educational reformers were to find themselves fighting an increasingly hopeless battle to make public schools agencies of participatory democracy? I suggest that the shift from Deweyan progressive education to free school ideology was a response to just these scenarios. In one sense the free school movement was a radical extension of Dewey's ideas, an attempt to adapt the practices of progressive education to a time that seemed to demand more desperate measures. Just as Dewey himself saw education in a more political context after the 1920s, Paul Goodman, George Dennison, and their peers adapted progressive education to the social and economic climate of their time. Lawrence Cremin and other writers are partially correct to claim that free school ideas, even when not explicitly grounded in the Deweyan position, were intellectually related to it. Nevertheless, it is also true that the radical critics took progressive thinking into territory where other faithful students of Dewey in the 1960s and early 1970s refused to venture, and it is critical to understand why these paths diverged.

THE RADICAL RESPONSE TO TECHNOCRACY

Free school ideology formed part of a countercultural uprising that arose out of radical disenchantment with American society. In general, those who were attracted to free schools were discouraged about the possibility of reform or alienated from public institutions to a greater degree than those who continued to work for progressive education within public schools. The difference between radical and progressive educators in the 1960s was not deeply ideological, but reflected different assessments of, or temperamental responses to, American culture in the 1960s. As Allen Graubard noted at the time, most of those drawn to free schools held "the kind of egalitarian, anti-elitist views that in America have been strongly supportive of the public school system, at least in its ideal form. The fact that an increasing number of people with this perspective now find themselves founding their own schools in direct philosophical confrontation with the public school (a very different situation from traditional private schools) is a sign of a profound and growing disillusionment with the public school system." In other words, the radical critics and free school participants shared important elements of the Deweyan vision of democratic education, but had come to feel that American society was too deeply flawed, too corrupt, too hierarchically managed to support this vision in public schools. Joseph Kirschner has emphasized the distrust of social institutions that emerged in the 1960s: "Gone was a belief that public schools could shape a virtuous citizenry. Instead, feelings of powerlessness and meaninglessness came to predominate." This is a significant observation: it is not simply that radical democrats found themselves losing political battles that they might, through the medium of public dialogue and persuasion, at a later time win, but that they no longer perceived the possibility of achieving political success. The existing system was so alien to their ideals that

they experienced it as *meaningless*, and so oblivious to their concerns that they felt *powerless*. It is entirely understandable that they would give up on the reform of social institutions and retreat to "counterinstitutions" where they might experience both meaning and empowerment.[8]

Arguably, one might understand the radicals as romantic idealists who avoided any long-term effort to achieve social reform incrementally because they refused to compromise or lacked tenacity. Progressives who continued to labor for public school reform would then be seen as "realists." Perhaps. Phenomenologically, however, the radicals' sense of discouragement does not appear unreasonable. As the extent and influence of the technocratic system became apparent in the 1960s, the democratic vision of Jefferson and Dewey seemed increasingly remote. It was not clear that public schools could reclaim this vision, and if they could not, the radicals reasoned, they were not worth saving. John Holt weighed the actual quality of young people's learning experience against the liberal commitment to the abstract principle of public schooling, and concluded by 1970 that "if a school seems not only bad but unwilling to change, immovable, a teacher who works there will probably not only be wasting his time, but in spite of his good intentions will, as much as anyone else in the school, be doing more harm than good to his students." He argued that those who insisted on reforming public schools despite the obvious resistance "seem to me to make a stronger commitment to the system than to the children." For Holt, of course, that was a mistake.

Another free school activist commented that loyalty to the system compromised teachers as well: "I noticed that teachers who remained in the school system for a few years came to resemble the system rather than the other way around." Those who fled the system to participate in free schools were simply not willing to sacrifice the lives of children, or their own ideals, to a system they experienced as damaging. Paul Goodman captured the essential reason for abandoning public education when he wrote that "John Dewey used to hope, naively, that the schools could be a community somewhat better than society and serve as a lever for social change. In fact, our schools reflect our society closely, except that they *emphasize* many of its worst features." Even Susan Douglas Franzosa, a Deweyan social democrat who disapproved of Holt's "libertarian" advocacy of deschooling, acknowledged that the public schools had so far failed to live up to Dewey's hopes.[9]

Radical educators in the 1960s concluded that if they were to work for participatory democracy, it would have to be outside this stagnant and repressive system. A 1970 editorial in the Summerhill Society *Bulletin* argued that "It hardly needs to be pointed out that some libertarian teachers are doing their damndest to radically reform the public school system from within. But at best, as we all sadly realize, such attempts are highly problematical. The existing setup is too rigid, the existing bureaucracy is too unresponsive, the existing structure is too big and unwieldy to allow for widespread *basic* change. . . . No, the opening of small antiauthoritarian schools, the maintenance of parallel institutions to the existing institutions, still seems the best way for Summerhillians." A great deal of evidence supported this perception. In 1970, for instance, a book by journalist Henry S. Resnik reported on the determined efforts that Superintendent Mark Shedd and his allies had made to "humanize" the public schools of Philadelphia in the late 1960s. Resnik called these efforts "a full-fledged assault on the old guard" and described how truly radical Shedd's ideas were. Here was a serious attempt to introduce principles of democracy and student-focused learning into public education. (Indeed, Allen Graubard observed in a 1971 report that Philadelphia had no free schools because so many options existed in the public system.) Yet Shedd was ultimately defeated because conservative political forces discredited his "permissiveness." Resnik reflected that "I had never expected that these values would flourish without opposition but the strife I encountered in Philadelphia was so much greater than anything I anticipated that for a while it dazed me. . . . The system was bigger than the sum of its parts. . . . To confront it was to invite a degree of frustration no one could stand for long." Surely the radical educators who fled public education for free schools had experienced this frustration, and they could not stand it for long. "The atmosphere at school was choking us to death and we wanted out," wrote Steve Bhaerman and Joel Denker. "We acted out of necessity—we had no other options." Resnik's wording is reminiscent of comments that others made in the early 1970s: those working for major social change had expected opposition—they were not naïve—but they were overwhelmed by its force. They found that the mainstream culture was not willing to surrender its authority over education, and that traditional ideas about schooling, teaching, and learning were strongly established. As Dewey scholar Robert Westbrook wryly commented, "The schools simply are not an independent locomotive of social transformation sitting idly on a siding, readily available for democratic engineers who would take the controls."[10]

Free school ideology reflected the belief that radical educational reform was *fundamentally incompatible* with the purposes and operation of public school systems. In *Freedom and Beyond*, John Holt explained his loss of faith in school reform. "Even if the schools give up the idea that they should be preparing children for society as it is, and try instead to prepare them to live in or make a better society, they will not be allowed to go very far in that direction." If one is convinced that this is, in fact, the case, then the progressive education agenda for public schools is rather hopeless. The radical critics had come to believe that it was *futile* to try to democratize public education. The system *by its very nature* was resistant to any serious effort in this direction.

During the early 1970s Jonathan Kozol expressed this argument more forcefully than any other writer in the movement. He wrote in *Free Schools* that public alternative schools "cannot, for reasons of immediate operation, finance and survival, raise serious doubts about the indoctrinational and custodial function of the public education apparatus." In a 1971 essay, "Look, This System is Not Working," he claimed that "public school was never in business to produce Thoreau. It is in business to produce a man like Richard Nixon and, even worse, a population like the one which could elect him. . . . An interlocking network of industrial, political, and academic interests does not exist to subsidize the demolition of its methods. . . . If innovation is profound, it is subversive. If it is subversive, it is incompatible with the prime responsibility of public school." In an article published in *New Schools Exchange Newsletter* in 1973, Kozol turned loose his fiercest rhetoric. "School serves the state; the interest of the state is identified, for reasons of survival, with the interests of industrial dominion. The school exists to turn out manageable workers, obedient consumers, manipulable voters and if need be, willing killers. . . . Is it conceivable that public schools can serve at once the function of indoctrinating agent and the function of invigorating counterfoil? I find this quite improbable and view with reservations of the deepest kind such genteel changes as may appear to offer broader liberties to captive children. The only forms of educational innovation that are serious and worth consideration in this nation in the year of 1972 are those which constitute direct rebellion, explicit confrontation or totally independent ventures." As late as 1975, Kozol was still making this argument. "School is in business to produce reliable people, manageable people, unprovocative people," he wrote. "School does not exist to foster ethics or upheaval. It exists to stabilize the status quo. It exists to train a population which is subject to the power of such instruments of mass-persuasion as the social order has at hand."[11]

Eventually, with the decline of the free school movement (and his own reservations about how seriously they were addressing issues of poverty and inequality), Kozol changed course dramatically and began to defend public education as the only realistic vehicle for educating marginalized and poor communities—provided that society could be goaded politically to make educational opportunities more equal.[12] But twenty years after he wrote these passages castigating public schooling, Kozol graphically documented that little had occurred to justify his renewed faith in public education, for it was instrumental in promoting "savage inequalities" in American society. Rather than being an agency for social democracy, public schooling was "a battlefield on which a class and racial war is being acted out." Kozol did not see evidence of progress but believed that "social policy has been turned back almost one hundred years." Public schools had not improved but, at least for the poor, had declined even further: "Filth and disrepair were worse than anything I'd seen in 1964." In the 1990s, education for democracy was still a distant dream, as "children in one set of schools are educated to be governors; children in the other set of schools are trained for being governed." Children of the privileged "learn to shut from mind the possibility that they are winners in an unfair race, and they seldom let themselves lose sleep about the losers." Kozol has continued to advocate the fight to democratize public education rather than abandon it, but his bleak portrayal would seem to confirm what the radical educators of the 1960s (including himself) discovered to their horror—that the venerated common schools were in large measure *hostile* to the democratic values that progressives hold dear.[13]

The same might be said about the work of educational scholars known as "critical theorists" (who, like Kozol, have been profoundly influenced by Paulo Freire) who have been arguing along these lines since the mid-1980s. Two of the leading figures in this group, Peter McLaren and Henry A. Giroux, summarized their position in this way: "In general, critical educational theorists maintain that the cultural politics of the schools historically and currently inculcate a meritocratic, professional ideology, rationalizing the knowledge industry into class-divided tiers; reproduce inequality, racism, and sexism; and fragment democratic social relations through an emphasis on competitiveness, androcentrism, logocentrism, and cultural ethnocentrism."[14] Unlike free school and deschooling activists, critical theorists contend that public schools are unique "cultural arenas" in which social democrats can wage the struggle against this dominant agenda, and the point of their critique, like that of the reconstructionist progressives of the 1930s (including Dewey), is to urge advocates of democracy to engage in this struggle wholeheartedly. Nevertheless, their analysis of public schooling is also discouraging, and may be interpreted as further confirmation that 1960s-era school dissenters were quite realistic (precisely not "romantic") in their assessment of the public school system. Given that public education serves a dominant cultural agenda that is largely hostile to ideals of egalitarian, participatory democracy, it is enormously difficult to bring about significant, lasting reforms. So the question that moved Holt and his peers to give up the struggle was simply this: For how long should parents subject their children to a regime of competitiveness, racism, ethnocentrism, and the other evils McLaren and Giroux identify, if no change is in sight and alternatives are possible?

The counterculture formulated a holistic critique of American culture, an analysis of the interrelated institutions, beliefs, and underlying worldview of the society. The free school movement reflected an understanding that school reform alone could not achieve a democratic culture, and indeed would be impossible to accomplish in any substantive sense, because the society *as a whole* was plagued by problems of inequality, racism, militarism, an overly competitive materialism, and the like. The radicals did not perceive public schools as open cultural arenas but as the most resistant of social institutions. As Allen Graubard put it, "My firm view is that attempts at truly humanizing the public schools must run up against the fundamental social realities—the sickness of American society." Liberal reformers like Charles Silberman, he said, ignored the underlying social and political ills that make schools what they are. The radical critics recognized that schooling serves a specific function in a technocratic society—the managing and harnessing of human energies to serve the efficient operation of social institutions. Introducing "humanistic" reforms into such an institution was absurd so long as the society continued to use that institution for technocratic purposes. In 1965 Edgar Z. Friedenberg had written that "Any major change in the social function of the schools must come from a corresponding change in the relationship of the school to society; and the society, itself, is too contemptuous of human dignity to seek, or perhaps even to tolerate, such a change."[15]

Given the perception that American society was "sick" and unable to tolerate democratic social change, it did not make sense to work for reform in public education. Writing in 1970, Peter Marin claimed that the free school movement was a political movement (and not simply an educational reform effort) because it was a deliberate attempt to undermine a culture that was "tattered, shredded—a hoax of the highest order. . . . By leaving existing institutions we have escaped nothing. We have instead come face to face with history." Marin warned that building a new society, even surviving while dissidents waited for it to emerge, "will be far more difficult than we have yet imagined" because the existing society was becoming more repressive.[16] This statement suggests that those who joined the free school movement had found their own cultural arena in which to battle the forces of technocracy and injustice. I conclude, then, that the educational radicals of the 1960s were not abandoning the ideal of democratic common schools, but recognizing—quite realistically, in my view—that American society was not committed to this ideal and was not likely to become committed to it any time soon. In the unusual context of the student revolt and counterculture of the 1960s, they had reason to believe that the democratic ideal *could* be practiced in alternative institutions, from which it might eventually spread to society as a whole.

In the mid-1970s, as the counterculture faded and the free school movement declined, liberal reformers stepped forward, believing that the opportunity had at last opened to make meaningful change in public education through "schools of choice" and public alternatives. From the free school perspective, however, these efforts "co-opted" the radical critique, softening it and making it palatable to the middle class while losing its essential meaning. Eric Davin, whose fiery essay "On Combatting Liberalism" I have already considered in this context, commented that Establishment liberals had already taken over the Montessori and progressive education movements, and now were doing the same to free schools. In an even angrier draft of this essay that was not published, he charged that liberals benefited from class stratification and would not accept major social change that threatened their privileges. "They continue with their minor adjustments so that nothing will get out of hand and *really* threaten the status quo," he wrote. Introducing reforms in public education did not "*deal with or question the class structure and function of the schools!*"[17]

Several articles in a 1976 issue of *Edcentric* similarly attacked the notion of alternative public schools. One writer charged that "The mythology of schooling is not being confronted in any fundamental way. Bureaucrats develop new programs that seem more enlightened while they retain control over students, and the social order pretends that its institutions are responsive." Again, one might ask whether these are the words of a "romantic" radical who could not be satisfied by incremental reforms, however positive, or of a perceptive critic who realized that so long as the institution itself remained intact and in the service of a tightly managed society, such reforms were illusory. Although many students have enjoyed more open learning environments in public alternative schools since the 1970s, the evidence seems to suggest that in the big picture, these reforms are insignificant in comparison to the increasing standardization and top-down control of American education. Stuart Rosenfeld, among others, has concluded that it was "impossible" to transfer free school ideas, which were essentially a political critique of American society, into public education. "Rather than embrace the entire concept of free schools, they [liberal reformers] tried once again to make schools run more efficiently. . . . [The free school] was a move to reassert the importance of the individual over the impersonal nature of the organization. . . . Public schools that attempted to emulate this participatory model ran into the inherent constraints of bureaucratic organization. . . . Public school administrators, used to being in command of their world of schools, were not about to relinquish any real control to lay people." Consequently, argued Rosenfeld, public school reformers only succeeded in "dissipating" the vital core of the free school critique—its insistence on decentralized, participatory forms of learning. Free school ideology justified its abandonment of public schooling on the basis that its radical educational and political ideals would not, indeed *could not*, be faithfully practiced within the system. Thousands of people turned to free schools because they were convinced that their ideas would only encounter solid opposition in public schools and required entirely new institutions, *free* institutions, in order to be realized.[18]

THE SOCIAL DEMOCRATIC PERSPECTIVE

Free school activists may have made a realistic tactical choice in abandoning public education. However, many theorists of progressive education, including radical social critics (such as McLaren, Giroux, and other critical theorists) who have expressed an equal degree of outrage over the function and operation of public schools, contend that education in a democratic society is a public endeavor and cannot be surrendered to the private sphere without seriously jeopardizing the health of a democratic community. If the society and its schools are failing to uphold democratic principles, the solution is not to retreat to small disconnected islands of protest, but to work vigorously for social change so that institutions do begin to reflect these principles. Significantly influenced by Dewey's writing on democracy and education, progressives believe that education plays a vital role in advancing democratic values, and for this reason must not be left entirely to private initiatives. During the presidency of Ronald Reagan, when the public sphere came under assault by an ascendant neoliberal agenda of privatization, progressive theorists plaintively reasserted their faith in the public search for a common good. Although directed against the ideology of aggressive laissez-faire capitalism (a conservatism that Holt and other radicals likewise rejected), by implication their writings challenged radical educators' decision to abandon public schools.

Political scientist Amy Gutmann presented this case in her 1987 book, *Democratic Education*. In a democratic society, she argued, the goal of education must be "conscious social reproduction," by which she meant "the cultivation of the virtues, knowledge, and skills necessary for political participation." A democratic community reaches decisions, and makes progress, through the interaction of different perspectives and interests in the public sphere. Democratic participation means negotiation with others in order to arrive at mutually beneficial ends—it does *not* mean that every separate group can achieve all its goals independently of every other group. In a statement that directly challenges free school ideology, she wrote that "We cannot simply translate our own moral ideals of education, however objective they are, into public policy." Although this "separation between a moral and a political ideal of education is often hard to accept," it *must* be accepted for a democratic society to exist. There must be a common social understanding that transcends differences between groups, and it is the function of education to cultivate this sense of community, this commitment to a common purpose. Progressive educators Linda Darling-Hammond and Jacqueline Ancess have written more recently that "The capacity to achieve associations beyond those of any narrow group is required for the development of democracy, the expansion of knowledge, and the search for truth." According to this view, when free school people found that they could run their enclaves of dissent most effectively by excluding those who questioned their countercultural ideology, *they actually contributed to the breakdown of democratic community life.* By holding so tenaciously to their own moral ideals, they diminished the possibility of dialogue and "conscious social reproduction" on a larger scale.[19]

Richard Battistoni, also writing during the Reagan years, similarly emphasized that education should reflect a deliberative democratic process rather than the self-selected values of numerous disparate groups. "Of all the agents of political education in American society, the school is the only one that can be significantly manipulated by political practice. Unlike the family or other more private institutions in society, a discussion of problems in the schools as they affect citizen education can be the object of public policy debate and reform." For the social democrat, education is primarily concerned with citizenship in a democratic culture and *should* be "manipulated by political practice," because only in this way can it rise above narrow conceptions of the good life or the good society. Citizenship is not the same as consumer choice: it means intelligent and open-minded participation in the affairs of the community, not the right to select whatever goods one happens to desire. Unlike the capitalist economy, the institution of public education is intended to bring citizens together to pursue their common interests. David Tyack and Elizabeth Hansot made this clear when they pointed out that "decision-making in education can provide a forum for discussing the kind of future we want as a society, not just as individuals. Such arenas for public discourse and action are hard to find." Public schools, they wrote, "offer a potential for community of purpose that is unparalleled in our society." Indeed, "public education has represented the only commitment by which American society has guaranteed to serve the needs and interests of all its citizens."[20]

While the free school radicals chose to abandon a system they felt powerless to change, many social democrats insist that it is essential to remain in the system and continue struggling for democratic values even if success does not come easily. In a democratic culture, they maintain, *it is the struggle itself that matters*. Dewey opened *Democracy and Education* by arguing that social life depends on an exchange of ideas and perspectives. "To be a recipient of a communication is to have an enlarged and changed experience," he wrote. "One shares in what another has thought and felt and in so far, meagerly or amply, has his own attitude modified." A society that facilitates communication, then, is an educative society, according to Dewey, and the democratic political process, which allows the widest possible range of perspectives to be aired and considered, is the most educative form of social life; the effort to reconcile these different perspectives in the search for a common good fuels critical intelligence and public dialogue. "In a healthy democracy," commented Tyack and Hansot, "values and interests are always in tension," and this tension leads to creative solutions to social problems, to progress and "reconstruction," to use one of Dewey's favorite terms. The contest of different perspectives produces a more dynamic and open society, widening and enriching the life experience of the individuals involved. Consequently, theorists of democratic education welcome political struggles over education and see them as "a particularly important source of social progress because they have the potential for educating so many citizens." The retreat to private forms of education does not educate the society; withdrawal from public dialogue may preserve one's cherished point of view but at the expense of expanded meaning and social progress.[21]

The social democratic position attempts to counter what it views as excessive individualism in American culture. Progressive theorists recognize the tension between "liberal" or "private" democracy, with an emphasis on personal freedom and the pursuit of self-interest, and a "public" or "republican" vision of democracy, which links freedom to social responsibility; it is the tension between the atomistic worldview of John Locke and Adam Smith, and a more holistic notion of community found in the writings of John Dewey. Indeed, Dewey addressed this problem explicitly (particularly in *Individualism Old and New* and *Liberalism & Social Action*), and progressives have continued to emphasize "an ethic of care and responsibility, not only for oneself as an isolated individual, but for one's fellow citizens as co-builders and co-benefactors of the public good." Robert Westbrook, for instance, cited a survey which showed that high school students believed that "the main characteristic of democracy was that it leaves the citizen alone"; he insisted, on the contrary, that democracy "does not leave citizens alone; it brings them together to deliberate on and act in their common interests." John Goodlad, a leading progressive educator of the past forty years, has spoken of a "*democracy of the human spirit* that transcends all individuality and binds humankind—somewhere a place for all of us, together." A democratic education, he declared, must "reach for some higher and more universal meaning of human existence" than the parochial meanings provided by religious and philosophical sects.[22]

The progressive critique of individualism not only represents a moral position but suggests a specific understanding of human nature. Dewey's conception of human development reflected the social psychology of George Herbert Mead and other theorists of the early twentieth century who emphasized the cultural sources of human behavior and intelligence. In part, this emphasis represented a break from two forms of conservatism—dogmatic theological ideas about the meaning of human life, as well as a biological (genetic) reductionism which at the time was fueling a popular eugenics movement. To believe in the efficacy of social reconstruction, one had to believe that behavior and intelligence were malleable rather than divinely ordered or genetically determined, that they were largely shaped by social forces that could be deliberately directed or redirected. Dewey, in fact, argued strenuously throughout his writings that consciousness, habit, intelligence, and education could not be understood properly apart from their *social* meaning. "The process of mental development is essentially a social process," he stated flatly. Experience is not programmed by destiny or biology, nor does it arise spontaneously within the individual, but it represents an organic *interaction* between person and environment, particularly the social environment. Although Dewey's theory of experience recognized individuality and personal authenticity, he also linked the individual inseparably to the social realm, and saw a dynamic balance between them. Child-centered educators have tended to emphasize the private, interior qualities of experience, but most of Dewey's serious students have recognized the importance he placed on the social context of individual identity. Goodlad, for example, stated that "There can be no definition and development of self apart from culture." Dennis Carlson, interpreting progressive education in the language of postmodernism, expanded the idea further, writing that "individual subjectivities are constructed within dominant discourses of power and knowledge." This line of thought reverses the classical liberal view (of Locke and Smith) that individual identity is primary and social reality only arises out of voluntary collaboration of self-determining, self-interested individuals. In the social democratic view, the political, economic, and ideological forces that shape culture provide the materials of personal consciousness itself; individuals are not entirely autonomous or self-forming. Benjamin Barber, an important democratic theorist, explicitly states that "We are born dependent, embedded in family and community; we have to learn how to sculpt our individuality from common clay." Given this premise, the social democrat insists that individuals are bound up in "political and social relations" and "cannot 'change their lives' without changing the context within which they live." Social change does not follow from an accumulation of personal decisions, but requires concerted effort in the public sphere to alter social forces.[23]

Education is vital for strengthening this public sphere, because ultimately, the "discourses of power and knowledge" are shaped by epistemological assumptions, which if not deliberately considered are rooted in traditions, superstitions, economic interests, or brute force (e.g., the severe punishment of heretics and dissidents in numerous societies). The social democratic perspective, reflecting its origins in Enlightenment thought, argues that *reason* enables people to transcend their passions, conflicts, and prejudices. Since reason is, presumably, universal, it provides an effective basis—the *only* effective basis—for common understandings. Dewey stressed this point strongly; he held that judgment not guided by intelligence is likely to be ineffective and detrimental, and that an essential goal of education is the cultivation of this intelligence. He explained repeatedly that the scientific method—the empirical analysis of concrete problems—is the most useful form of intelligence, compared to theoretical speculation or mystical insight. Dewey thus carried on an Enlightenment tradition that had influenced democratic thinkers since Jefferson—the belief that society could and should be ruled by reason. The democratic state, as propounded by the founding fathers of the United States, was an expression of universal human rights conceived and guaranteed by the use of reason. As David T. Sehr has explained, "Jefferson envisioned a highly interactive relationship between government and citizens. The government should work purposefully to educate the public's ability to reason; and the citizens, in turn, would apply reason in the numerous aspects of their participation in government."[24]

In the 1960s, the counterculture reached the conclusion that reason alone is not a trustworthy basis for a meaningful culture; as Theodore Roszak explained, the revolution in consciousness began with the realization that a modern state ruled by abstraction, objectivity, logic, and order produced, in the end, a soulless technocracy. Jefferson had not anticipated the extent to which a utilitarian, scientistic intelligence, divorced from democratic commitments, could sterilize reason. Nevertheless, modern social democrats have insisted that a democratic culture needs more, not less, critical intelligence, and so the free schoolers' often excessive deemphasis of logic, scientific method, and academic accomplishment in favor of emotional wholeness and personal insight violated one of Dewey's own most essential teachings.

While it is true that Dewey's theory of experience, with its critique of overabstractness and authoritarian forms of knowledge, provided a starting point for radical as well as social democratic educational thinking, the radicals interpreted this theory as a recipe for *personal* liberation where Dewey himself, and his closest followers (such as Barber, Goodlad, Gutmann), were primarily interested in promoting a more rational *social* order. In the 1930s Dewey sought to correct what he believed was an overemphasis on individual freedom by the "child-centered" progressive educators, and his clear statement of this position in *Experience and Education* (1938) endures as a social democratic critique of libertarian education. "When external control is rejected," he cautioned, "the problem becomes that of finding the factors of control that are inherent within experience." By "factors of control," Dewey meant the rational evaluation of our activities in light of desirable ends, and we only know what is "desirable" in a social context. It is not enough, argued Dewey, simply to enjoy freedom: experience is only educative, enriching, and productive when it is guided by critical intelligence toward meaningful—that is, socially relevant—purposes. "There is no intellectual growth without some reconstruction, some remaking, of impulses and desires" on the basis of reflection and judgment, which link experiences purposively rather than simply feed impulses and desires. Consequently, "the greater maturity of experience which should belong to the adult as educator puts him in a position to evaluate each experience of the young in a way which the one having the less mature experience cannot do. . . . Guidance given by the teacher to the exercise of the pupils' intelligence is an aid to freedom, not a restriction upon it."[25]

In the social democratic view, then, education is a deliberate ordering of experience, according to intelligent judgments that aim to serve the greatest good of the community as a whole. When experience is random or haphazard, it is not truly educative, and does not contribute to social reconstruction. If the educator does not carefully structure the learning environment, Dewey wrote, "then the young are left at the mercy of all the unorganized and casual forces of the modern social environment that inevitably play upon them as long as they live." Battistoni seconded this position: "Only by coming into contact with the community's life and history in some kind of structured manner can individuals make the choices and decisions necessary to becoming full persons *and* citizens, able to carry on the community's projects and purposes into the future. . . . Should there be a complete absence of conscious citizenship training in schools, the young will be 'socialized' by society in general and by the communications media, whose view of politics is laced with cynicism and disdain. . . . In the absence of schools taking a direct and systematic role, we will see only further political withdrawal and despair." Sehr further emphasized this point: "For most people, critical reading of mass-media messages and the political and social world around them does not come naturally. Just as students must develop the skill to read literature or legal texts critically, all citizens must develop their ability to read critically mass-media messages."[26]

Benjamin Barber has argued that democracy itself "is not a natural form of association; it is an extraordinary and rare contrivance of cultivated imagination." Entirely in agreement with the Jefferson–Dewey position that democratic society rests on deliberate education, Barber emphasizes that the cultivation of democracy is a *developmental* process requiring careful tending. Humans "are born neither wise nor literate nor responsible—nor are they born free." Turning second-graders free, he commented, does not teach them liberty. Young people "need protection from their own not yet mature selves, achieved by exposing them to the reality of limits, the necessity of discipline, the benefits of deferred gratification . . . precisely because they are not yet the educated women and men the process seeks to produce." In short, it takes time, experience, and deliberate guidance to acquire reason, and it is a democratic society's most important responsibility to support an education that provides these conditions to all its future citizens.[27]

These different interpretations of experience—the radicals' emphasis on personal liberation versus the social democrats' concern for rational collaborative discourse—reflect an underlying disagreement over the relationship between the individual and the common good. If democracy or critical intelligence does not "come naturally," who then has the authority to instill these values in young people? Who, indeed, has the right to define what is critical or reasonable? Social democratic theory holds that the community at large, acting through the medium of the state, is responsible for pursuing a deliberate common vision that transcends private or parochial interests. Gutmann justified this position by commenting, "History suggests that without state provision or regulation of education, children will be taught neither mutual respect among persons nor rational deliberation among ways of life."[28] The free school radicals saw it differently: they believed that mutual respect could best be cultivated, and that democracy would in fact "come naturally," that is, emerge organically, in intimate, caring communities. To them, the monolithic state is hardly the institution to teach human relations, and they did not believe that a common good needs to be upheld, much less manufactured, by impersonal social institutions. They feared that personal creativity, spontaneity, self-expression, and, above all, authenticity—which they saw as vital elements of a whole and meaningful life—are too readily sacrificed to the claims of modern complex society. Ultimately, with their trust in organic processes and the honest expression of emotional needs, they did not believe that "rational deliberation" was the sole means for evaluating "ways of life." As was so evident in Holt's writings, free school ideology maintained that participatory democracy naturally emerged from the unhampered striving of individuals for meaning and purpose.

Social democrats, however, tend to consider this a "romantic" attitude on the part of the counterculture, and they emphasize the more "realistic" view that a society is not governed by organic processes but by the competition or collaboration of various political interests. If those striving for democratic values do not enter the fray and constitute one of these interests, then other values will more easily prevail. (This was the basis for Jonathan Kozol's complaint [see note 12] that Holtian free schoolers had encouraged the right wing agenda.) Most progressive democrats are not willing to surrender public schools because they do not see any other educational agency that transcends private interests and addresses this larger context. Robin Barrow's critique of radical educational thought was grounded on this realist premise. He observed that "until fairly recently, the hope has been that schooling on a national scale and well carried out would be the means for providing the freedom, justice, equality and happiness desired by the radicals too. The radicals represent one kind of reaction to the growing feeling that that hope was misplaced. However, even if it is clear that the dream has not materialized, it is not clear that the whole idea was absurd. It is clear only that we have not been very successful." The struggle is not yet over, and abandoning it is a mistake.[29]

Most social democrats have argued that "romantic" responses to modern culture provide no effective solution to widespread social problems such as poverty, inequality, and racism. Even as Kozol was voicing his withering critique of public education in the early 1970s, he argued just as strenuously (in his book *Free Schools* and various articles) that child-centered free schools represented an escape from these problems rather than a serious engagement with them. Despite its sympathies with the civil rights movement, the free school movement expressed the concerns of its largely white, middle-class constituency and did not win the support of other segments of the population. Even in a strictly educational sense, critics such as Ann Swidler, Lisa Delpit, and others have maintained that children of marginalized social groups tend to need more, not less, academic rigor in order to acquire skills that more privileged youths acquire in their family and peer relationships, if they are to compete with them for scarce educational and economic advantages. The free school movement did not successfully address this concern. One participant reported that all the free schools he knew had tried to attract minority students, but found that "a lot of these people have just spent years getting their kids into public school, and they're afraid to take them out of the public school and put them into this 'hippy' school." Jane Lichtman made a similar observation in her book on free universities: "The alienated white intellectuals" who started one such program "spoke to a few other alienated white intellectuals. The ghetto poor never came; they wanted to get into the system rather than to change it." From the social democratic point of view, this failure to address the concrete educational needs of poor and minority people reflected a major flaw in the free school approach. How could these marginal "counterinstitutions" be contributing to a more participatory democracy in any meaningful way when they failed to involve the great majority of Americans in their endeavor? Advocates of public alternative schools in the early 1970s frequently stated that they, unlike the radicals and "hippies," were working to improve education for *all* young people.[30]

DILEMMAS OF DEMOCRATIC LIFE

The disagreement between progressive and free school positions boils down to their conceptions of the proper relationship between individual and collective. Taken to extremes, these positions are incompatible: a fervent commitment to social reconstructionism may well tend to breed a technocratic program of social engineering by liberal experts—including a determined defense of public schooling that overlooks its inherent flaws—while a "romantic" view of the self-created individual encourages escape from the clutches of society, into detached islands of freedom and privacy such as Summerhill or the nuclear family. The more balanced writers on both sides (Dewey and Dennison come to mind), however, have presented a holistic vision that recognizes the importance of *both* personal authenticity *and* collective responsibility. For these theorists, meaning arises from a complex interaction between person and environment. On one hand, a deep sense of meaning, and the actual quality of life experience, cannot be specified for all persons on a mass scale: the decentralist, "human scale" perspective that John Holt so well represented recognizes that there simply cannot be a unified set of "needs and interests" among all the citizens of a massive diverse nation such as the United States, and that the attempt to achieve such unification leads to technocracy or, worse, to fascism.

On the other hand, democracy requires a sense of commonality. Dewey and other social democratic theorists have insisted that even allowing for much diversity of cultural, religious, and philosophical values, a democratic society cannot thrive without a shared commitment to open communication, mutual respect, and willingness to collaborate. The common good is not something tangible or specific, not a prescription of particular values or life choices—rather, it is a sense of "public space" that fosters cooperation despite differences. The insistence on personal freedom, on the right to be left alone by the state, may well be necessary as a corrective to authoritarian tendencies in government, but it may also lead to the fragmentation of society into competing, even hostile, factions and subcultures. And it does not address problems of inequality or economic oppression. Where there is no commitment to a common good, to the welfare of all in the larger community, then inequality and injustice have freer rein and tend to grow worse as individuals engage in unchecked competition for personal success.

Free school ideology, and the counterculture in general, struggled with the tension inherent in this holistic vision of society. James Miller, discussing the New Left's ideal of participatory democracy, commented that a philosophy "which emphasizes the virtue of community and face-to-face relations uneasily coexists with one that emphasizes equality, social justice, and universal civil rights." The one addresses personal, existential concerns, while the other requires impersonal state power to enforce abstract rights. One is primarily organic, open to spontaneity and emotional expression, while the other strives to be rational and objective. Tocqueville recognized this tension, too, over a century and a half ago. He celebrated voluntary associations of citizens, seeing that these fostered cooperation and bonds of mutual interest in a society that was otherwise highly individualistic; he wrote that education ought, in fact, to cultivate this "art of associating together." Yet the power of the state is another matter, "for a government can only dictate strict rules, the opinions which it favors are rigidly enforced, and it is never easy to discriminate between its advice and its commands."[31] How does a democratic society integrate the personal, voluntary, and organic with the universal and abstract? A holistic vision must include both elements, but the tension between them threatens to undermine the vision itself.

Nowhere is this more evident than in education, for this is where the interface between person and society, individual and collective, is most explicit and deliberate. Through its system and methods of education, a society defines its preferred balance between the organic and the organized, between spontaneity and social control, between voluntary association and "strict rules" of social and economic conduct. Social democratic theory maintains that a nation can find an appropriate balance through a system of schools provided by the state. Free school ideology, however, raised the disturbing objection that the modern state—the vast complex of political authority and powerful economic interests—is *unable* to achieve a balance that in any meaningful way protects the autonomy of individual persons. Although they were equally committed to a democratic agenda of social justice, the radical educators came to believe that public education is a dangerous enemy of the democratic vision. However, few progressive theorists have been persuaded by this argument; they are acutely aware that in the years since the decline of the counterculture, it is the resurgent Right that has led the attack on public schools and promoted privatization and homeschooling. Progressives, like Gutmann, Goodlad, Battistoni, Barber, and (ironically) Kozol, have heroically defended the common school as the last bastion of social democracy, the last remaining "public space" to stand against the onslaught of greed, global corporate power, and right wing resistance to movements for social justice.[32]

However, at least one progressive theorist, Constitutional law scholar Stephen Arons, has argued that public education may in fact be more of an obstacle to participatory democracy than an essential vehicle for it. Arons has studied the numerous court battles that have taken place over public schooling, especially during the past fifty years, and concluded that the effort to inculcate shared cultural values through state education has led, instead, to more intense mistrust, conflict, and cultural fragmentation. The problem, he says, is that public schooling is essentially "a compulsory encounter between government-approved values and individual belief." The specific content of these values is not the point for Arons (indeed, they vary historically and by region or community). Rather, he argues, in a Constitutional democracy that welcomes tremendous diversity of cultural, religious, and intellectual values, for a public institution to represent any majority's set of values infringes on the minority's freedom of conscience (or, as often happens, a particularly strong or elite minority infringes on the intellectual freedom of the majority). This produces "a system of schools so overloaded with unnecessary conflict that it weakens both community and education." If we take seriously the American tradition of civil liberties and Constitutional democracy, then education is "primarily an individual journey whose goals arise from each individual's family and community life," not from political mandates. Following Tocqueville, and contrary to many progressive education theorists of recent years, Arons argues that democracy is more endangered by coercive government action than by the exercise of individual conscience or proliferation of diverse voluntary associations.[33]

This analysis supports my contention that free school ideology ought to be reconsidered, that it is not merely a "romantic" vision or an accomplice to the libertarian Right. I believe that it represents a serious expression of a "politics of meaning" that could make the progressive agenda more relevant to the problems of our time. Although Arons dissents from the social democratic faith in public education, he fully accepts the Deweyan principle that a democratic society requires a common public space where cultural, ethnic, religious, moral, and philosophical differences can be shared and discussed respectfully. Like the free schoolers, however, he observes that public schools, as they are administered in a centrally organized modern society, do not effectively provide such a sphere. Radical critics, as Joel Spring has well summarized, point out that all institutionalized forms of education represent an explicit effort to socialize the young generation, to shape the minds, attitudes, and identities of children and teens in one form or another.[34] These are high stakes indeed, and so long as factions within a society disagree strongly over which of these forms are proper, they will contest desperately for control over schools. In actual practice, the political struggle over school policy has *not* served to educate the public or expand democratic dialogue, but to polarize religious and ideological subcultures and aggravate political conflicts.

Social democrats may be convinced that secular, critical reason, multicultural awareness, and civil liberties (such as freedom of expression and sexuality) are essential to a truly democratic culture and should therefore comprise the core of an education for democracy, but by insisting upon these values in public schooling, they have in fact helped drive a substantial portion of the American population *out* of constructive public dialogue. As Michael Lerner has pointed out in his notion of the "politics of meaning," most liberal and progressive theorists have failed to recognize the extent to which people in modern society need to identify with firm moral and spiritual values that transcend political or institutional fixes to social problems. Living in accordance with such values (even when they are fundamentalist rather than progressive in content) provides a sense of meaning, of existential *authenticity*, that is not easily found in secular politics. The difficult balance that a modern democratic society must attain is to enable diverse groups of people to find existential security in their chosen values while encouraging them to collaborate in the public sphere with those who hold other values. The public sphere, then, cannot be defined by any one set of values over all others, except for bedrock Constitutional principles of fairness, justice, and equal rights. Arons emphasizes this point throughout his book, stating at one point that "communities that are forged by government coercion are just that, forgeries. They are repressive. They convert community from something to be desired into something to be feared." Holt also emphasized that genuine community arises from voluntary collaboration, because he believed that individuals are willing to participate in communal endeavors only when they feel secure in the values and purposes they have chosen for their lives.[35]

This argument serves to remind social democrats that the existential, moral, and spiritual dimensions of human life are intensely personal and not, as some of Dewey's statements (and those of many of his followers) would suggest, ultimately social; concern for the integrity of these realms of experience cannot be dismissed as merely "romantic." When presented in a balanced, holistic way, this argument does not endorse a Lockean/libertarian view of society made up of atomistic individuals who cooperate grudgingly only to advance their self-interest, because it holds that personal authenticity does give rise to genuine community, in the form of voluntary association that Tocqueville observed and celebrated. On the other hand, the problem with free school ideology arises when its emphasis on personal liberation is not tempered by recognition of any larger context. If social democrats have defined the individual too narrowly as a creature of social forces (wholly derived from "common clay"), radicals like A. S. Neill and *his* enthusiasts have overreacted, portraying human development one-dimensionally as a process of personal rebellion against oppressive social restraint, insidious conditioning, and even reason itself. Dennison, in *The Lives of Children*, and Dewey, in *Experience and Education*, have presented a dynamic balance, recognizing that experience is generated by an organic relationship between person and world, and that the educator, having the benefit of more extensive and mature experience, can help young people reflect and expand upon the meaning of their own experience without imposing socially sanctioned definitions upon it. Again, the voluntary association or authentic relationship between adult and child, teacher and learner—which free school literature so frequently emphasized—represents at its best an organic meeting of person and world, freedom and discipline, natural impulses and rational deliberation.

One conclusion, then, is that education may *not* be the proper arena in which to make a valiant stand for the liberal democratic state. If the educational process is most essentially a fluid and organic encounter between persons, if it is, as Arons writes, concerned with the "realms of intellect and spirit" that the Constitution safeguards from political manipulation, then the Enlightenment project of training citizens for democratic participation cannot work in a mass, standardized, technocratic culture. It might work in villages, or in face-to-face communities where government is actually participatory, but when it is imposed on a population en masse then it becomes indoctrination and it will engender resistance. Holt commented that "the idea that a school (or any place else) can be responsive to and democratically controlled by a 'community' of 20,000 or more persons is an absurdity. . . . Community control of large school systems . . . means that the schools will be run by the loudest shouters and the cleverest schemers, the ones who learn best how to manipulate the machinery of control."[36]

Contemporary social democrats defend public schooling because they fear it is the last remaining public space in a highly privatized society—but education conceived as an organic human relationship is not, at heart, a public endeavor. As Holt and several historians have suggested, Americans have too readily viewed schooling as a panacea to solve social problems that demand hard political choices. If the nation needs public spaces for democratic discourse, then *adult* citizens must create opportunities to come together to discuss their differences and work toward a common good, rather than turn this responsibility over to teachers and schoolchildren. Conflicts over schooling have not effectively educated the public for democracy, but divided the public ever more bitterly. The advocates of free schools maintained that their intimate communities, in which people voluntarily and collaboratively associated to address the essential human task of rearing children, effectively nourished the Jeffersonian vision of participatory democracy. Free schools gave adults as well as young people the experience of face-to-face democracy and practice in the "art of associating together"—sometimes more than they bargained for! That these communities were philosophically exclusive would constitute a problem for democratic society if the free school movement became a permanent subculture entirely isolated from public discourse, like certain religious sects. I believe, however, that the radicals intended to engage in public debate about the meaning of education; they wanted their schools to serve more as exemplary models than as detached islands. They hoped to demonstrate that participatory democracy could work in face-to-face community settings and they invited American society to follow their example. It was the dominant cultural ideology—technocracy—that prevented any genuine exchange of perspectives about the purpose of education.

The recent literature of "postmodern" critique, which is concerned with the overconcentration of cultural influence ("hegemony") within powerful elites, raises similar questions about these dilemmas of democracy. Postmodern theory recognizes a multiplicity of identities even within a common culture, and opposes efforts to subsume these identities under a single privileged cultural standard. Dennis Carlson has examined the progressive education tradition from this perspective and found that "progressivism in the modernist twentieth century was associated with the centralization and bureaucratization of decision making in the state and a tendency to make the decision-making process less visible and more technical and professional." Dewey, of course, was no advocate of bureaucratization, but in a technocratic society, one in which public institutions become increasingly remote from personal or even local control, the powerful institutions of the state become too massive, too blunt, to carry out the ideals of participatory democracy. To the extent that social democrats have viewed state institutions as agencies of progressive values, they have risked turning their agenda of social reconstruction into a program of social engineering. This is precisely why Paul Goodman and other radicals of the 1960s sought to reinvent the progressive agenda for the new technocratic era. This is why the 1960s counterculture specifically dissented from "managerial" liberalism, and why free school writers like Eric Davin and Jonathan Kozol (for a time) strongly distinguished their radical ideals from what they perceived as mere administrative adjustments that public school reformers proposed. The call by Illich and Holt to "deschool" society entirely was a logical extension of this critique. Postmodern theory has picked up this thread of dissent. Carlson, while still viewing education as a vital public function in a democratic society, recognizes that schools may not be able to "construct a 'public' curriculum that has broad-based support," and suggests that a democratic society must build public spaces besides schools—"sites in the community in which various affinity groups and social movements could monitor state policy, formulate their own positions, and be represented in an ongoing dialogue with other social movements over state policy."[37]

Free school ideology pointed toward this vision of society. However, in the heady context of the rising counterculture, radicals did not often think through the ambiguous political connotations of their celebration of personal freedom. They understood freedom, emotional wholeness, and existential authenticity as vital preconditions for building a culture in which such dialogue and cooperation could take place. But shorn of this countercultural vision, and lacking the social democratic emphasis on the importance of public space, radical educational ideas did provide viable seeds for the conservative libertarian assault on public education. Free school ideology did not celebrate individualism in an atomistic sense, as Holt's remarks on Adam Smith clearly demonstrate, but the withdrawal from public education into free schools and homeschooling blazed a trail for those who truly do understand democracy as personal sovereignty and unfettered freedom of private choice. Just as Deweyan progressivism became problematic in the rising technocracy of the 1950s, potentially a recipe for social engineering, free school ideals were co-opted by the conservative restoration of the 1970s and 1980s. The rampant individualism that grew rapidly in the post-1960s era was not the product of countercultural existentialism alone, but also of the dominant cultural values of competition, materialism, and consumerism that commodified many of the ideals of the 1960s. So long as this culture remains dominant, those who subscribe to radical educational ideals cannot afford to ignore the progressives' urgent call for a "democracy of the human spirit" to complement their search for personal authenticity.

CHAPTER 6

Free Schools and Technocracy: Some Reflections

What is the historical significance of the free school movement? The eruption of widespread educational dissent in the 1960s marked a turning point in the history of American schooling. If, as David Tyack and Elisabeth Hansot suggested, public education represented an "established church" in American society for much of the nineteenth and twentieth centuries, then the radical education critique might be considered the early stirrings of a reformation. When thousands of educators, students, and parents began to question the methods, structures, and even the defining mission of public education, they blazed a trail that other dissatisfied citizens, representing various ideological agendas, would soon follow.

Since the 1960s, political conflict over education has become increasingly polarized. On one side, reform efforts from magnet and charter schools to more radical approaches such as homeschooling, independent alternative schools, and voucher plans have challenged the hegemony of the "one best system." On the other hand, the counterrevolution that took place during the presidencies of Richard Nixon and Ronald Reagan (the so-called conservative restoration provoked by the upheavals of the 1960s) instituted a powerful educational agenda of "basics," standards, competition, accountability, and faithful service to the corporate economy. Radical educational dissent may well have provoked these competing efforts toward both the decentralization and standardization of American education. Just as the civil rights movement shattered the nation's indifference to racial injustice, free school ideology disturbed a widespread complacency about conventional educational assumptions. Quite suddenly, definitions of schooling, teaching, and learning were "up for grabs," and various factions of American society, from corporate executives to Christian fundamentalists, from free market libertarians to advocates of multiculturalism, intensified their efforts to redefine education on their terms.

I am not arguing that the free school movement in itself was entirely responsible for the decline of educational consensus, only that it played a role in opening a floodgate of protest and fragmentation. Political battle lines were already being drawn in the 1950s over race, religion, and pedagogy in public schools. Moreover, throughout this study I have emphasized that the small and short-lived network of radical schools was nestled in a cultural context that gave an expanded and powerful meaning to its particular pedagogical concerns. The writings of Neill, Holt, Goodman, and the rest found a popular audience because they voiced deeply felt concerns shared by a restless segment of the public at that particular moment. The appearance of an entire counterculture signaled that the fault lines of American society—in particular, differing attitudes toward the continuous spread of industrialization—were beginning to produce serious ruptures. It was inevitable that the shock waves from these ruptures would have a major impact on public schooling. The passionate, outspoken writings of the radical school critics gave those sympathetic to countercultural values a rallying point, and paradoxically provided an impetus to the counterrevolutionaries, both religious and secular, to protect *their* ideologies from subversion.

In strictly intellectual terms, many of these books were somewhat less than compelling; indeed, they were often marred by inconsistencies and rhetorical overkill, as Robin Barrow so clearly pointed out. It is not difficult to identify flaws in free school ideology, or in the undisciplined ways that many youthful idealists, hippies, draft resisters, and other radical seekers put this ideology into practice. If one starts with these flaws it certainly makes sense to interpret the free school movement as an extremely small, inconsequential outburst of romantic energies—the product of a brief and unusually chaotic period in the history of American culture. Perhaps this explains why most educational historians and other scholars, when they have not ignored the free school movement altogether, have largely considered it to be a quixotic aberration, irrelevant to the concerns of public education discourse and policy, and why even progressive educators have rejected the radical premises of free school ideology and maintained their faith in the democratic mission of public schooling.

Even scholars who have taken the free school movement seriously, such as sociologist Ann Swidler, have tended to downplay its cultural meaning. Swidler interpreted the free school phenomenon in functional terms that minimized its significance: she hypothesized that the emergence of small, marginal schools for radical educators and rebellious youths could be explained by one of three sociological categories—"rebellion cooptation" (the schools provided isolated enclaves where protest would not threaten the system), "educational upgrading" (the schools allowed for open-ended pedagogical practices that served the children of intellectuals but not the needs of most learners), or a "postindustrial model" of learning (in which the new "knowledge elites" could exercise their creativity). Swidler was not especially impressed by the ideals that free school people explicitly proclaimed; she was offended by the "political arrogance" of the New Left and claimed that dissidents' selfish interest in autonomy, freedom, and creativity for themselves accounted for the content of free school ideology.[1]

A cultural historical perspective needs to take free school ideology more seriously. Although it is useful to examine the possible economic and social class overtones of this ideology, these factors by no means explain the phenomenological meaning of the radical educational critique. Rather, it is necessary to account for the moral vision that lay at the heart of radical educational thought. The free school movement was motivated and sustained by strongly held ideals about the nature of the good life and the just society. Free schoolers, and the New Left as a whole, would appear "arrogant" because they were passionate moralists, condemning with a "prophetic voice" what they perceived as injustice and bad faith in society at large. From a cultural historical perspective, it is important to understand why a group of young people took this position, arrogantly or not. Those who articulated or followed free school ideology were searching for a greater degree of authenticity and meaning in their lives. While it may certainly be true, from a strictly sociological perspective, that such an endeavor largely reflected the particular concerns of a privileged social class, the moral content of this existential search cannot be entirely explained on these terms. Elites do not normally seek the overthrow of the system that gives them their status, and if anything is clear about what free schools meant to those who participated in them, it is that they were vehicles for escaping, and ideally overthrowing, the existing social order. The social democratic perspective may be correct to point out that free schools siphoned off a great deal of moral energy that could have been directed constructively within the system to attempt to change it (this was Neil Postman's explicit charge at the 1971 "Konference on Alternatives"), but it is simply not the case that free schools were established in order to co-opt radical dissent or advance the interests of elite intellectuals. Quite the opposite. The radicals did not think in functional but in moral terms. They sought liberation from social forces and institutions that they believed diminished human life for all people in modern culture.

It seems that their moral intensity was part of the reason for the radicals' failure to build a lasting movement for educational change. To a large extent free school ideology defined itself in opposition to prevailing educational and social practices; its positive vision was obscured by a relentless, sometimes desperate effort to become disentangled from old ways of thinking. Reflecting an awareness of this fact, a 1975 letter to

New Schools Exchange Newsletter complained that the correspondent's free school in Indiana "has too often merely been a defensive reaction to the public schools . . . as opposed to being a community with a conscious and positive purpose." Len Solo believed that this was a major problem in the alternative school movement and he pointed it out in several writings. In a 1973 article in *Centerpeace* he asserted that many free schools were chaotic, even "positively pernicious places" for children because so many of the adults in the movement, in rebellion against the system, were still trying to figure out their own lives. In another paper he charged that many of the schools "seem concerned with the development of feelings such as love, yet they also encourage hatred: of parents, straight schools, the straight society, the Establishment, the System. It is tough to learn to love in a world busy hating." Even several years later he charged that many in the free school movement had "fled the 'oppressive' public schools out of weakness, not out of strength" and actually did not know "how to be constructively and creatively with themselves and with children" after becoming free. Similarly, George Dennison told of a visit to one Summerhill-inspired school at which the director treated students and staff "less as people than as events in his own protracted crusade against middle-class America. The faculty, too, consisted of True Believers." Any moralistic crusade, even one seeking liberation and authenticity, contains the danger of lapsing into fundamentalism, and in many cases the free school movement did not avoid this danger.[2]

Solo pointed out that many free school enthusiasts were so determined to reject authority that in many cases they celebrated freedom excessively, apparently believing that any guidance by adults constituted "laying a trip" on children. The most popular writers in the movement, Neill in particular and Holt—depending on how one reads his work—seemed to endorse this attitude. To the extent that a critic takes this belief as representative of radical pedagogy, free school ideology can indeed appear hopelessly "romantic" in the pejorative sense. Even Joel Spring, in his sympathetic portrayal of libertarian educational thought, recognized that radical educators' desire for freedom could become counterproductive. He commented that "when freedom to learn results in no learning, free school advocates are presented with a major dilemma. . . . Giving a child freedom *not* to learn can result in restricting the child's future freedom and happiness." As Dewey emphasized, children's spontaneous interests may or may not lead to productive educational experiences because they do not necessarily make connections to the world at large, which they do not yet know well. "Meaningful use of freedom of choice," Spring observed, "requires some knowledge of what choice one has." Free school ideology, in many cases, did not acknowledge this point, and this was a major weakness in the movement. A few of the radical education writers did recognize that the value of freedom lies in opening possibilities for authentic relationships between adult mentors and the young, and in an educational context such relationships draw upon the more mature and balanced experience of adults to guide young people. As Dennison explained so well, the task of dismantling impersonal, hierarchical structures did not mean the abolition of all structure or the disappearance of the "natural authority" of adults in the lives of children. Jonathan Kozol made this point in his 1982 revised version of *Free Schools,* commenting that the schools which survived after the early 1970s tended to be those that did not pursue an extreme anti-authoritarian agenda. Jane Lichtman reported the gradual discovery by free university folks "that both people and organizations need at least a little structure."[3]

Despite these occasional realizations, free schoolers' near-desperate search for freedom and authenticity often gave rise to rhetoric that was messianic, ahistorical, and anti-intellectual. More sober scholars, even those sympathetic to elements of the radical critique, pointed to this rhetoric as a glaring flaw in the free school agenda.[4] Clearly, cultural change depends on enormously complex factors, rooted in vast social and historical forces, and it was naively optimistic to believe that a marginal group of radicals could replace the existing system of education, let alone overturn the social order. Yet the fearless rhetoric of free school ideology is understandable in its historical context. Many participants in "counterinstitutions" in the years between 1967 and 1972 believed that a cultural revolution, based upon a compelling moral vision of a post-technocratic society, was actually emerging. For a time it was not totally unreasonable to believe that industrial society had become obsolete and was beginning to decline if not unravel. Still, it did become clear, before very long, that the revolution existed only in the imaginations of a few thousand restless young people, and it is significant that this vision primarily appealed to the young—those who did not yet have a stable stake in society and who could afford to condemn it from the outside. Furthermore, although free schools attracted some professional, young, but relatively mature educators who had become disillusioned with the school system (such as Len Solo himself), they also provided convenient "hangouts" for migrating young adults who showed little commitment to a career or community. Solo has pointed out that running a school is enormously demanding work (he himself has worked fourteen hours a day as a public alternative school principal for the past twenty-five years), and in his view many in the free school movement did not understand this. "They were on their own trips, and they were trying to free themselves from whatever shackles they thought they had in their lives. They didn't understand that freedom comes through immersion in something."[5] Again, Lichtman reported a similar phenomenon within the free universities, which attracted many transient young people who believed in participatory democracy but rarely stayed around long enough to actually participate.

Nevertheless, the meaning of the free school movement is deeper and more complex than its obvious flaws. Free schools represented an alternative vision of the definition of education in modern culture, a vision that did not die when most of these schools collapsed by the early 1970s. As Ann Swidler did acknowledge, although the emergence of free schools did not immediately "herald the dawning of a new age," the movement did embody "important new social forces," and these forces have continued to influence educational discourse.[6] The free school movement challenged the hegemony of public education in American culture and opened new possibilities for alternative schools and the homeschooling movement. The rapid spread of charter schools during the 1990s, for example, might not have been possible without the insistence by 1960s radicals that schools serve diverse educational needs. (To be sure, as I acknowledged earlier, charter schools do not often reflect progressive political or educational ideals; nevertheless, their popularity is a significant indicator that many Americans no longer revere, or even fully trust, a monolithic, "one size fits all" school system.) Perhaps one of the most significant consequences of the civil rights movement and youth counterculture was an enlarged appreciation in American society for the diversity of ethnic, religious, gender, and racial identities. If American culture is no longer universally celebrated as a "melting pot" in which human differences are blurred by conformity to some prescribed ideal, then public education cannot indefinitely be expected to mold the nation's young people into a single, preconceived image. The "important new social forces" that Swidler mentioned have not yet triumphed over technocracy, but they offer an alternative that continues to challenge the centralization of cultural power.

Despite its flaws, I am convinced that the radical educational critique for the most part represented a sincere attempt to humanize the impersonal tendencies of modern society. The assertion by dissidents in the 1960s that the rise of technocratic values threatened individual authenticity and participatory democracy was an urgent warning to our culture that remains relevant today. The moral vision that motivated countercultural endeavors, the belief that economic productivity and material prosperity cannot substitute for existential meaning, seems altogether lost in our postmodern gilded age, but prophetic voices continue to declare it. "Modern industrial society," one spiritual leader has recently written, "often strikes me as being like a huge self-propelled machine. Instead of human beings in charge, each individual is a tiny, insignificant component with no choice but to move when the machine moves." This statement was not made by a disgruntled young radical in the 1960s, but by a distinguished observer from an entirely different culture: His Holiness the Dalai Lama, in 1999.[7] The social world produced by the modernist complex of global corporations, massive government bureaucracies, university and foundation experts, the exalted role of science and technology, electronic communications and instant international transfers of capital, the pervasive entertainment/advertising/public relations industry, and the influence of the mass media strikes many morally sensitive people as being impersonal and unfeeling, coldly working to achieve its purposes, like a machine. The rebellious youths of the 1960s were among the first to question the moral and cultural consequences of this hierarchical, rationally managed system, and although their counterculture failed to endure as a viable alternative, the major points of their critique remain relevant to our time.

Clearly, the technocratic system has vastly expanded its hegemony in the decades since the counterculture declined. Virtually all of the trends that Edgar Z. Friedenberg, Paul Goodman, John Holt, and their peers identified in the 1960s have continued unabated: the centralization and consolidation of power (economic if not political, as in corporate mergers and the World Trade Organization); the substitution of mass marketing and mass identity for authentic individuality; the commodification of the natural world and human endeavors, such that everything has a market value and can be packaged for sale (the rainforests are being destroyed but we can pay to visit indoor reproductions of them). In education, the grip of technocracy is far tighter now than thirty years ago: thanks to the 1983 *Nation at Risk* report and a relentless campaign by corporate leaders and the mass media to produce "excellence" in education, federal and state governments demand ever higher degrees of accountability, greater control over the curriculum, more exact measurement of progress, and more unyielding standards. Just as Ivan Illich predicted in 1970 would happen, "pedagogical therapists . . . drug their pupils more in order to make them learn better" and police officers and retired generals have been brought into schools to enforce discipline. "High stakes" testing is now used to determine whether or not young people can pursue their life goals, based entirely on their school performance. Patrick Farenga, who took over Holt's homeschooling organization after Holt's death, has pointed out that "For the first time in American history, we have laid out before us a method for social control and employment that is set in motion by one's performance as a youth in a system one is forced to attend." This seems to be precisely what Holt feared when he warned of fascism on the rise.[8]

Although this system has been vigorously challenged by a wide range of critics (many influenced by 1960s-era dissent) as well as environmental, social justice, and decentralist organizations and publications, I find it significant that no popular movement, on the scale of the 1960s counterculture, has arisen to protest the triumph of technocratic values. Why don't millions of young people explicitly voice their disillusionment and alienation in today's corporate world, which is just as existentially sterile as the "Establishment" of thirty-five years ago, and far more pervasive? Surely several factors are involved. Perhaps most important, the resurgent Right (the conservative restoration) has worked hard, and very effectively, to discredit radical and even liberal ideals and much of the cultural legacy of the 1960s. Since the collapse of the communist Eastern bloc, multinational corporations and most political leaders in developed nations have notified the public that "There is No Alternative" to the neoliberal, Adam Smithian economic agenda of privatization and unchecked competition. This agenda treats environmental and social justice concerns as a nuisance hindering the march toward global free trade. Consequently, for example, what began as a moral crusade for racial justice and human brotherhood is now widely construed as a self-interested program of quotas and preferences. In education, as even the public alternative school people discovered to their dismay in the 1980s, the Right has effectively portrayed progressive educational ideas as lacking in rigor or even common sense—because, ultimately, they do not promise to turn out competitive workers driven by production-oriented standards. (This is not new; conservatives' hostility effectively limited the reach of progressive education throughout the twentieth century.) The conservative discourse has become so pervasive that even the supposed opponents of the Right, such as the Clinton Democrats, accept many of its basic premises. In education policy, most Democrats have signed on to the standards and accountability crusades as enthusiastically as any corporate-backed Republicans.

In addition to this overt ideological assault on the alternative worldview that arose from the 1960s counterculture, the modern technocracy benefits from more subtle means to lull the public into complacent acceptance of the system. Modern society is plagued by emotional disorders, particularly depression, which in a more holistic culture would be taken as a signal of profound existential need, but which in this culture is labeled a physiological disease and soothed with potent drugs. The consumer economy produces wave after wave of commodities that temporarily satiate individuals' hunger for meaning; how else might one explain the compulsive demand for Beanie Babies, sports cards, or Star Wars souvenirs? Above all, the relentless explosion of electronic entertainment seems to keep millions of human brains perpetually entranced. Television and film, with their increasingly violent and sexually titillating content, seductive video games and music videos, and the endless fascination with the computer's power to manipulate images, information, and reality itself appear to keep vast numbers of people obsessively engaged with fictional versions of the world. In contrast, the protesters of an earlier generation seem quaint and innocent in their earnest concern for social change. Oblivious to the seductive promise of "virtual reality" and "artificial intelligence," they spoke in old-fashioned terms about "democracy," "meaning," and "freedom."[9] In the privatized and entranced consumer culture of the present, it is difficult to imagine a resurgence of a popular movement for these values. Ironically, this state of affairs makes the countercultural critique all the more relevant to our own time.

The free school movement, like all human endeavors, contained its own flaws, excesses, and blind spots, but it represented a serious effort to turn society away from the path of sprawling technocracy toward more democratic, holistic, person-centered values. More than opposition to public schooling as such, free school ideology represented conscious, deliberate resistance to the spread of technocracy, and this essential element of the 1960s radical educational critique continues to resonate in the literature of alternative, progressive, and holistic education. Critics of the dominant educational policies of standardization and competition insist that education must serve human rather than abstract economic interests, the needs of individual learners rather than the demands of corporate employers, and children's organic styles of learning rather than behaviorist models of training and control.[10] It is true that such ideas have important roots before the 1960s in the progressive tradition of Dewey's time, but as I have argued before in this study, I believe that free school ideology moved the progressive critique to a more radical position, containing a more penetrating understanding of the increasingly technocratic nature of public schooling.

I find it strange that some of the key participants in the educational standardization movement of recent years, advocating a social engineering agenda that includes deference to professional expertise, "scientific" management, and quantitative policy analysis, have claimed to be Dewey's heirs.[11] Thanks to their efforts, many of today's radical educators, such as John Taylor Gatto (who is currently the most widely known radical critic) and many in the homeschooling movement, unfortunately view Dewey and his social democratic legacy as a major enemy of decentralization and freedom in education. Technocrats who invoke Dewey's legacy to support an agenda of social engineering do a disservice to Dewey's vision of participatory democracy, and they help drive educational dissidents, who usually hold progressive social and political values, into the camp of the libertarian Right.

Reflecting on the paradoxical legacy of the free school movement, I believe that an effective, democratic movement for educational renewal will require a New Left style of political analysis, combining a deep interest in personal freedom and existential wholeness with an acute sensitivity to issues of social justice; it must be decentralist at the same time as it helps build a public sphere where diverse citizens can join together to discuss and pursue a common good. The radical critique of the 1960s deconstructed some of the epistemological and sociological assumptions that Dewey and his contemporaries took for granted, yet the result was not to repudiate Dewey but to radicalize and update his democratic vision. A post-1960s (or postmodern) agenda of progressive education still owes a great deal to Dewey even as it navigates around his rationalist social psychology. This is evident in the particular form of postmodern progressive education that I and others have been calling "holistic" education. While in many ways it embraces Deweyan pedagogy and social responsibility, holistic education is the heir to the "consciousness revolution" that I described in Chapter One, and it goes beyond the social democratic rationalism that I described in Chapter Five. It reflects a *personalist* perspective, a search for deep and authentic meaning, for connection to the Cosmos (which many holistic theorists, myself included, frankly call *spirituality*), in contrast to many contemporary progressives' emphasis on academic achievement, professional expertise, and education conceived in political and managerial terms. A holistic theory of education, exemplifying the most balanced thinking in the free school literature, avoids both extremes of privatization and social engineering; as the European Green parties have put it, this way of thinking is "neither left nor right—it is out in front."

Resistance to technocracy, which I believe to be the key to free school ideology, may well signify the emergence of a post-industrial, even post-capitalist worldview that could ultimately, although far more slowly than the 1960s radicals envisioned, lead to profound cultural change. Writing a half century ago, Lewis Mumford declared that "culture is passing now from an ideology of the machine to an ideology of the organism and the person." Although the "ideology of the machine"—technocracy—is proving to be enduringly resilient, Mumford explained why it could not retain its hold on the human imagination indefinitely:

> We know that the mechanical world is not the real world but only an aspect of the real world, deliberately abstracted by man for the purpose of expanding his physical power and multiplying the energies he commands. We know, too, that in this overconcentration upon power

> many important elements were left out of account—especially those needed for the development of life and personality. *As an integral part of modern culture, the machine will remain as long as modern culture remains*; let me italicize that statement. But as a dominant element, wholly subduing life to the demands of mechanization, reducing the personality and the group to a mechanical unit . . . concentrating on quantity and denying quality and purpose, the machine is an enemy of human development rather than an agent. . . . Indeed, the emphasis on the impersonal, the anti-organic, the non-humanistic, the "objective" must now be counteracted by a temporary over-preoccupation, perhaps, with the organic, the subjective, the personal.[12]

The counterculture that emerged nearly twenty years after Mumford wrote this passage was indeed such a "temporary over-preoccupation." Obviously, it was not immediately successful, and whether ongoing resistance to technocracy will gradually counteract the dominance of the machine in modern life remains an open question. Whether or not a truly post-industrial culture is ever to emerge, the free school movement of 1967–72 represented a genuine effort to make it a reality.

NOTES

CHAPTER ONE

1. David Tyack and Elisabeth Hansot, "Conflict and Consensus in American Public Education," *Daedelus* Vol. 110, No. 3 (1981), 3; Joseph Kirschner, "The Shifting Roles of Family and School as Educator: A Historical Perspective," in J. van Galen and M. A. Pitman, eds., *Home Schooling: Political, Historical, and Pedagogical Perspectives* (Norwood, NJ: Ablex, 1991), 139, 154; Tyack and Hansot, "Conflict and Consensus," 15, 20.

2. Bruce J. Schulman, "Out of the Streets and into the Classroom?: The New Left and the Counterculture in U.S. History Textbooks," prepublication manuscript, 1998. Virtually all interest in the free schools, even from an historical perspective, disappeared after 1980, with a few notable exceptions: one is a doctoral dissertation on "Private Education and the Subcultures of Dissent" by Peter Lewis (1991), which demonstrates indeed that before the 1960s there were few private schools other than well-established models such as Catholic parochial schools and traditional prep schools—models that did not challenge the legitimacy of public schooling—but that after the 1960s segments of the public found it reasonable to expect greater educational choice. Lewis claims that the counterculture's attack on public education led to a "change in consciousness" that has permitted the rise of numerous alternatives. Another study is a senior thesis by Tate Hausman of Brown University, "A History of the Free School Movement" (1998), based on careful original research and extensive interviews with free school participants. Although this fifty-four-page paper does not go into the depth I am attempting here, I found Hausman's data and his interpretations to be accurate and helpful. More recently, Burton Weltman's paper "Revisiting Paul Goodman: Anarcho-Syndicalism as the American Way of Life" was published in *Educational Theory* (Vol. 50, No. 2, Spring 2000). While not concerned with the free school movement as such, this work is the first in a long while to bring attention to some of its core ideas.

3. Henry S. Resnick, *Turning On the System: War in the Philadelphia Public Schools* (New York: Pantheon, 1970), 3.

4. Todd Gitlin, *The Sixties: Years of Hope, Days of Rage*, rev. ed. (New York: Bantam, 1993), xiv, 344.

5. My interpretation of the historical meaning of 1960s-era dissent has been influenced by the writings of various scholars and participants, including primarily Mark Gerzon, *The Whole World is Watching: A Young Man Looks at Youth's Dissent* (New York: Viking, 1969); Theodore Roszak, *The Making of a Counter Culture* (Garden City, NY: Anchor/Doubleday, 1969); Allen J. Matusow, *The*

Unraveling of America: A History of Liberalism in the 1960s (New York: Harper and Row, 1984); Ronald Fraser, ed., *1968: A Student Generation in Revolt* (New York: Pantheon, 1988); Terry H. Anderson, *The Movement and the Sixties: Protest in America from Greensboro to Wounded Knee* (New York: Oxford University Press, 1995); and Gitlin, *The Sixties*.

6. Richard N. Goodwin, *Remembering America: A Voice from the Sixties* (New York: Harper & Row, 1989), 18. Paul Goodman presented his analysis of alienated youth in *Growing Up Absurd* (New York: Vintage, 1960). Historical accounts that emphasize this point include Allen J. Matusow's *The Unraveling of America*, Todd Gitlin's *The Sixties*, and especially Doug Rossinow's recent study, *The Politics of Authenticity: Liberalism, Christianity, and the New Left in America* (New York: Columbia University Press, 1998).

7. David Farber, ed., *The Sixties: From Memory to History* (Chapel Hill: University of North Carolina Press, 1994), 2–3.

8. Bonnie Barrett Stretch, "The Rise of the Free School," in Martin Carnoy, ed., *Schooling in a Corporate Society* (New York: David McKay, 1972), 222.

9. Paul Goodman, *People or Personnel: Decentralizing and the Mixed System* and *Like a Conquered Province: The Moral Ambiguity of America* (New York: Vintage, 1968), 135, 252–53.

10. Marshall McLuhan and George Leonard, "Learning in the Global Village," reprinted in Ronald Gross and Beatrice Gross, eds., *Radical School Reform* (New York: Simon and Schuster, 1969), 107.

11. Andrew Jamison and Ron Eyerman, *Seeds of the Sixties* (Berkeley: University of California Press, 1994), 5, 110.

12. Benjamin Barber, "More Frightening than Militant Tactics," in Immanuel Wallerstein and Paul Starr, eds., *The University Crisis Reader*, Volume II: *Confrontation and Counterattack* (New York: Random House, 1971), 17; Goodman, *People or Personnel*, 387.

13. Sol Cohen, *Challenging Orthodoxies: Toward a New Cultural History of Education* (New York: Peter Lang, 1999), 46–47; Schulman, "Out of the Streets," 3.

14. Raymond E. Callahan, *Education and the Cult of Efficiency* (Chicago: University of Chicago Press, 1962), 246, 247.

15. David Nasaw, *Schooled to Order: A Social History of Public Schooling in the United States* (New York: Oxford University Press, 1979), 3, 4; David Tyack, *The One Best System: A History of American Urban Education* (Cambridge, MA: Harvard University Press, 1974), 5, 6, 40.

16. Diane Ravitch, *The Troubled Crusade: American Education 1945–1980* (New York: Basic, 1983), 183, 200.

17. Herb Snitzer and Doris Ransohoff, *Today is for Children—Numbers Can Wait* (New York: Macmillan, 1972), 23, 52, 160.

18. Neil Postman and Charles Weingartner, *The School Book: For People Who Want to Know What All the Hollering is About* (New York: Delacorte, 1973), 10, 44.

19. Ann Swidler, *Organization Without Authority: Dilemmas of Social Control in Free Schools* (Cambridge, MA: Harvard University Press, 1979), 32.

20. For example, in a panoramic survey of the notion of freedom in American history, Eric Foner commented about the civil rights movement: "by challenging the received orthodoxy of the Cold War, it redirected national attention to the unfinished business of freedom at home." *The Story of American Freedom* (New York: Norton, 1998), 275.

21. James Farmer, *Lay Bare the Heart: An Autobiography of the Civil Rights Movement* (New York: Plume/New American Library, 1986), 106.

22. Myles Horton, with Herbert Kohl and Judith Kohl, *The Long Haul: An Autobiography* (New York: Doubleday, 1990).

23. King quoted in Taylor Branch, *Parting the Waters: America in the King Years 1954–63* (New York: Simon and Schuster, 1988), 139, 140.

24. Vincent Harding, *Hope and History: Why We Must Share the Story of the Movement* (Maryknoll, NY: Orbis, 1990), 7, 114–15; Farmer, *Lay Bare the Heart*, 30.

25. Goodman, *Growing Up Absurd*, 114; Edgar Z. Friedenberg, *Coming of Age in America* (New York: Random House, 1965), 11; Michael Rossman, untitled chapter in Harold Hart, ed., *Summerhill: For & Against* (New York: Hart, 1970), 144; Steve Bhaerman and Joel Denker, *No Particular Place to Go: The Making of a Free High School* (New York: Simon and Schuster, 1972), 39, 46. Daniel Hinman-Smith makes a similar point in his doctoral dissertation, "'Does the Word Freedom Have a Meaning?' The Mississippi Freedom Schools, the Berkeley Free Speech Movement, and the Search for Freedom through Education" (University of North Carolina, 1993), 265.

26. Wallerstein and Starr, *The University Crisis Reader*, 18; Jamison and Eyerman, *Seeds of the Sixties*, 180; Anderson, *The Movement and the Sixties* (cf. note 5 above), 84; Michael Rossman, *The Wedding Within the War* (Garden City, NY: Doubleday, 1971), 82.

27. Jane Lichtman, *Bring Your Own Bag: A Report on Free Universities* (Washington, DC: American Association for Higher Education, 1973), 13. King quoted in Branch, *Parting the Waters*, 276. The influence of African American student activism on SDS and other white student activists is discussed by Vincent Harding in *Hope and History*, and by James Miller in *"Democracy is in the Streets": From Port Huron to the Siege of Chicago* (New York: Simon and Schuster, 1987).

28. Interview with Len Solo, December 8, 1997; Hinman-Smith, "Does the Word Freedom Have a Meaning?"

29. Hinman-Smith, "Does the Word Freedom Have a Meaning?" 58, 16, 30, 115.

30. Mario Fantini, ed., *Alternative Education: A Source Book for Parents, Teachers, Students, and Administrators* (Garden City, NY: Anchor/Doubleday, 1976), 4; Hinman-Smith, "Does the Word Freedom Have a Meaning?" 118–21, 167–68.

31. Port Huron Statement quoted in Miller, *"Democracy is in the Streets,"* 332.

32. Alice Echols, "Nothing Distant About It: Women's Liberation and Sixties Radicalism," in Farber, ed., *The Sixties: From Memory to History*, 149–74; Rossman, untitled chapter in *Summerhill: For & Against*, 143.

33. Foner, *Story of American Freedom*, 289; Gitlin, *The Sixties*, 81, 133; Flacks quoted in Miller, "*Democracy is in the Streets*," 173; Matusow, *Unraveling of America*, 60; Goodwin, *Remembering America*, 237, 208, 219; Rossman, *Wedding Within the War*, 80.

34. Anderson, *The Movement and the Sixties*, 88; Jamison and Eyerman, *Seeds of the Sixties*.

35. Rossman, *Wedding Within the War*, 92; Paul Goodman, *Drawing the Line: The Political Essays of Paul Goodman*, ed. Taylor Stoehr (New York: Dutton, 1979), 138, 128.

36. Mario Savio quoted in Hinman-Smith, "Does the Word Freedom Have a Meaning?" 261; Rossinow, *Politics of Authenticity*, 99; Jeff Lustig, "Not Foolproof, But Foolish," in Wallerstein and Starr, *University Crisis Reader*, 49.

37. Hinman-Smith, "Does the Word Freedom Have a Meaning?" 330, 398; David Kemnitzer, "Educational Reform-Revolution," *Edcentric*, June–July 1970; Carl Davidson, "Toward a Student Syndicalist Movement, or University Reform Revisited," in Wallerstein and Starr, *University Crisis Reader*, 99, 107.

38. Barry Wood, "Free Schools and the Revolution," in Terrence E. Deal and Robert R. Nolan, eds., *Alternative Schools: Ideologies, Realities, Guidelines* (Chicago: Nelson-Hall, 1978), 39, 42.

39. SDS membership figures from Matusow, *Unraveling of America*; student leader quoted in Fraser, *1968: A Student Generation in Revolt*, 11; Paul Potter quoted in Miller, "*Democracy is in the Streets*," 232; Goodman, *People or Personnel*, 263.

40. Theodore Roszak, ed., *The Dissenting Academy* (New York: Random House, 1967), preface.

41. Jonathan Kozol, *The Night is Dark and I am Far from Home*, 2nd ed. (New York: Simon and Schuster, 1990), 18; Gross and Gross, *Radical School Reform*, 17; Bhaerman and Denker, *No Particular Place to Go*, 13, 18.

42. Timothy W. Young, *Public Alternative Education: Options and Choice for Today's Schools* (New York: Teachers College Press, 1990), 11.

43. Kenneth Cmiel, "The Politics of Civility" in Farber, *The Sixties* (cf. note 7), 265, 270; Matusow, *Unraveling of America*, 335.

44. Peter Collier and David Horowitz emphasize the licentious and violent shadow side of the counterculture in *Destructive Generation: Second Thoughts About the '60s* (New York: Summit/Simon and Schuster, 1989). Rossinow mentions "predators" in *Politics of Authenticity*. Schulman's analysis is in his paper "Out of the Streets and into the Classroom?" (cf. note 2).

45. Theodore Roszak, *The Making of a Counter Culture* (cf. note 5), 54, 220, 229.

46. Rossinow, *Politics of Authenticity*, 293; Allen Graubard, *Free the Children: Radical Reform and the Free School Movement* (New York: Vintage, 1974), 369.

47. George Leonard, *Walking on the Edge of the World: A Memoir of the Sixties and Beyond* (Boston: Houghton Mifflin, 1988), 111, 167.

48. Ibid., 113.

49. The accepting attitude in free schools toward drugs and other Dionysian pursuits is evident, for example, in Snitzer and Ransohoff, *Today is*

for Children, and in Bhaerman and Denker, *No Particular Place to Go*. Neill gave his argument in *Summerhill: A Radical Approach to Child Rearing* (New York: Hart, 1960), 56–57. The Dennison quotation is from his book *The Lives of Children: The Story of the First Street School* (1969; reprint, Reading, MA: Addison Wesley, 1990), 103.

50. Gross and Gross, *Radical School Reform*, 13, 16. Postman and Weingartner made similar claims in *The School Book*.

CHAPTER TWO

1. Theodore Roszak, *The Making of a Counter Culture* (Garden City, NY: Anchor/Doubleday, 1969); Diane Divoky, *How Old Will You Be in 1984? Expressions of Student Outrage from the High School Free Press* (New York: Avon, 1969), 11; Paul Goodman, *Growing Up Absurd* (New York: Vintage, 1960), 241; Erich Fromm, untitled chapter in Harold Hart, ed., *Summerhill: For & Against* (New York: Hart, 1970), 251; Todd Gitlin, *The Sixties: Years of Hope, Days of Rage*, rev. ed. (New York: Bantam, 1993), 216; Salli Rasberry and Robert Greenway, *Rasberry Exercises: How to Start Your Own School and Make a Book* (Albion, CA: Freestone, 1970), 3.

2. Jonathan Eisen and David Steinberg, "The Student Revolt Against Liberalism," in Joseph Boskin and Robert A. Rosenstone, eds., *Seasons of Rebellion: Protest and Radicalism in Recent America* (New York: Holt, Rinehart & Winston, 1972), 195; Peter Marin, "The Open Truth and Fiery Vehemence of Youth: A Sort of Soliloquy," *The Center Magazine* Vol. 2, No. 1 (1969), 68.

3. Kathy Gross, "A Student's View of the Successes and Failures of an Alternative School," in Terrence E. Deal and Robert R. Nolan, eds., *Alternative Schools: Ideologies, Realities, Guidelines* (Chicago: Nelson-Hall, 1978), 167, 168; Robert Theobald, *An Alternative Future for America* (Chicago: Swallow, 1970), ix, x.

4. Steve Bhaerman and Joel Denker, *No Particular Place to Go: The Making of a Free High School* (New York: Simon and Schuster, 1972), 22; Robert Davis, untitled editorial, *This Magazine is About Schools* Vol. 1, No. 2 (1966), 2; Divoky, *How Old Will You Be in 1984?* 12; William K. Stevens, "Bright Milwaukee Students Find School Dull and Form Their Own," *New York Times*, February 13, 1970; Victoria Graham, "Indiana School Manages to Succeed" *Bloomington Courier-Tribune*, December 10, 1972.

5. Judson Jerome, *Culture Out of Anarchy: The Reconstruction of American Higher Learning* (New York: Herder and Herder, 1971), 6; Jane Lichtman, *Bring Your Own Bag: A Report on Free Universities* (Washington, DC: American Association for Higher Education, 1973), 15, 5.

6. Claudia Berman, *The School Around Us: 25 Years* (Kennebunkport, ME: SAU, 1994), 19–20; Deena Metzger, untitled essay in *New Schools Exchange Newsletter* #60 (1971).

7. Edgar Z. Friedenberg, *The Vanishing Adolescent* (Boston: Beacon, 1959), 13, 33, 41.

8. Edgar Z. Friedenberg, *Coming of Age in America* (New York: Random House, 1965), 177, 187, 222, 249.

9. Edgar Z. Friedenberg, *The Dignity of Youth & Other Atavisms* (Boston: Beacon, 1965), 47–48, 153, 154.

10. Jules Henry, *Culture Against Man* (New York: Random House, 1963), 4–5, 59, 291.

11. Henry J. Perkinson, *Two Hundred Years of American Educational Thought* (New York: David McKay, 1976), 283; Roszak, *The Making of a Counter Culture*, 200; Taylor Stoehr, introduction to *Drawing the Line: The Political Essays of Paul Goodman* (New York: Dutton, 1979).

12. Paul Goodman, *Growing Up Absurd* (New York: Vintage, 1960), 29, 73, 78,129.

13. Paul Goodman, *Compulsory Miseducation* and *The Community of Scholars* (New York: Vintage, 1964), 20, 23, 68.

14. Paul Goodman, *People or Personnel: Decentralizing and the Mixed System* and *Like a Conquered Province: The Moral Ambiguity of America* (New York: Vintage, 1968), 180; Goodman, *Drawing the Line*, 176.

15. Goodman, *People or Personnel*, 264; *Drawing the Line*, 234.

16. Goodman, *People or Personnel*, 279.

17. Goodman, *Compulsory Miseducation*, 40.

18. Goodman, *Growing Up Absurd*, 81–82; *People or Personnel*, 161.

19. Paul Goodman, "No Processing Whatever," in Ronald Gross and Beatrice Gross, eds., *Radical School Reform* (New York: Simon and Schuster, 1969), 99.

20. The important influence of *Summerhill* was acknowledged, for example, by Terrence E. Deal and Robert R. Nolan, *Alternative Schools* (see note 3 above), 19; by the editors of an alternative school directory, *There Ought to Be Free Choice* (Ann Arbor, MI: National Coalition of Alternative Community Schools, 1981); and by Dave Lehman, in an untitled essay in *The Unicorn* (Ithaca, NY: Alternative Schools Exchange, 1984), 9. Quotation is by Paul Dreiske in "Summerhill Revisited," the Summerhill Society *Bulletin* (January–February, 1971), 2.

21. A. S. Neill, *Summerhill: A Radical Approach to Child Rearing* (New York: Hart, 1960), 4, 162, 163–64.

22. Ibid., 243–44, 100, 102.

23. Ibid., 344.

24. A. S. Neill, foreword to Herb Snitzer and Doris Ransohoff, *Today is for Children—Numbers Can Wait* (New York: Macmillan, 1972), 15, 16.

25. Erich Fromm, foreword to *Summerhill*, xi, xiv; Fromm, untitled chapter in Harold Hart, ed., *Summerhill: For & Against* (New York: Hart, 1970), 255, 256.

26. Michael Rossman, untitled chapter in *Summerhill: For & Against*, 142; Eda J. LeShan, untitled chapter in *Summerhill: For & Against*, 138.

27. Joel Spring, *Wheels in the Head: Educational Philosophies of Authority, Freedom, and Culture from Socrates to Paulo Freire* (New York: McGraw Hill, 1994), 60–61; Neill, foreword to *Today is for Children*; Zoe Readhead, email to author, July 5, 1999. Critiques by Bettelheim and Hechinger were published in *Summerhill: For & Against.*

28. Robin Barrow, *Radical Education: A Critique of Freeschooling and Deschooling* (New York: Wiley, 1978), 2.

29. John Holt, *How Children Fail* (New York: Pitman, 1964), xiii.

30. Two informed observers, Jerry Mintz and Len Solo, indicated Holt's importance during the early phase of the free school movement. Personal interviews.

31. Holt, *How Children Fail*, 156, 157.

32. John Holt, *The Underachieving School* (New York: Pitman, 1969), 19–20; John Holt, *What Do I Do Monday?* (New York: Dutton, 1970; reprint, Portsmouth, NH: Boynton/Cook-Heinemann, 1995), 83.

33. Holt, *What Do I Do Monday?* 275; John Holt, *Freedom and Beyond* (New York: Dutton, 1972; reprint, Portsmouth, NH: Boynton/Cook-Heinemann, 1995), 223; John Holt, *A Life Worth Living: Selected Letters of John Holt,* ed. Susannah Sheffer (Columbus: Ohio State University Press, 1990), 149.

34. John Holt, preface to George Dennison, *The Lives of Children: The Story of the First Street School* (New York: Random House, 1969; reprint, Reading, MA: Addison Wesley, 1990), vii.

35. George Dennison, *The Lives of Children*, 258–59, 98.

36. Ibid., 248.

37. Susannah Sheffer, who edited a published collection of John Holt's letters as well as reprint editions of other works in this literature, cautioned that readers should keep the authors' distinctive outlooks in mind (*A Life Worth Living*, 4). My attempt to define a common educational ideology does not intend to obscure these differences, but to suggest that despite variations in outlook, the free school literature as a whole presented a philosophically coherent and consistent critique. This point contains more than historical interest: movements for alternative education in the 1980s and 1990s tended to remain isolated from each other because they emphasized their distinctiveness at the expense of their common purpose of challenging the hegemony of public education. A *holistic* interpretation of educational dissent accommodates various approaches while appreciating their shared countercultural orientation. See Ron Miller, *What Are Schools For? Holistic Education in American Culture* (Brandon, VT: Holistic Education Press, 1997).

38. Len Solo, "Some of Our Children May Live: A Study of Students in Alternative and Innovative Schools" (Ed.D. dissertation, University of Massachusetts, 1972), 7–8.

39. TDOC papers, courtesy of Len Solo. (The TDOC papers have recently been acquired by the University of Vermont library, special collection of the John Dewey Project on Progressive Education.)

40. Ann Swidler, *Organization Without Authority: Dilemmas of Social Control in Free Schools* (Cambridge, MA: Harvard University Press, 1979), 144.

41. Allen Graubard, *Free the Children: Radical Reform and the Free School Movement* (New York: Vintage, 1974), xi, 8; Theodore R. Sizer, *Places for Learning, Places for Joy: Speculations on American School Reform* (Cambridge, MA: Harvard University Press, 1973), 63–64.

42. David D. Sehr, *Education for Public Democracy* (Albany: State University of New York Press, 1997); Eric Foner, *The Story of American Freedom* (New York: Norton, 1998).

43. TDOC papers.

44. Goodman, *Drawing the Line*, 72–73.

45. Dennison, *The Lives of Children*, 246–47; Swidler, *Organization Without Authority*, 24.

46. TDOC papers; Herb Snitzer, "At the Heart of the Matter—It's a Matter of Heart," *New Schools Exchange Newsletter* #92, February 13, 1973.

47. Claire V. Korn, *Alternative American Schools: Ideals in Action* (Albany: State University of New York Press, 1991), 38; Jonathan Kozol, *Death at an Early Age: The Destruction of the Hearts and Minds of Negro Children in the Boston Public Schools* (Boston: Houghton Mifflin, 1967), 114, 117, 180.

48. Swidler, *Organization Without Authority*, 58; Snitzer and Ransohoff, *Today is for Children—Numbers Can Wait*, 45.

49. Children's Community pamphlet courtesy of Bill Ayers, California school literature, in NSE papers, Yale University.

50. Mike Williams, "Rancho Mariposa: Something New and Different in Education," *Ukiah Daily Journal*, January 27, 1971, 8, TDOC papers.

51. Holt, *A Life Worth Living*, 93; Marin, "The Open Truth" (see note 2 above), 70.

52. Interview with Jack Spicer, January 22, 1998; Goodman, *Compulsory Mis-Education*, 146, 147; John Bremer, "Some Thoughts on Education," pamphlet, School District of Philadelphia, May 1969, TDOC papers.

53. Dennison, *The Lives of Children*, 4, 113–14.

54. Solo, "Some of Our Children May Live," 132, 125–26, 134, 136.

55. Eric Davin, untitled essay, *Centerpeace* #9, March 1972, NSE papers.

56. Jerry Friedberg quoted in Solo, "Some of Our Children May Live," 167, 169.

57. Stuart Rosenfeld, "Reflections on the Legacy of the Free Schools Movement," *Phi Delta Kappan* Vol. 59 (1978), 7; Berman, *The School Around Us* (see note 6 above), 64; Chris Mercogliano, *Making it Up as We Go Along: The Story of the Albany Free School* (Portsmouth, NH: Heinemann, 1998), 6, 7.

58. Kozol, *Death at an Early Age*, 182; Richard E. Bull, *Summerhill USA* (Baltimore: Penguin, 1970).

59. *New Schools Exchange Newsletter* #65, September 30, 1971; Allen Graubard, "The Free School Movement," *Harvard Educational Review* Vol. 42, No. 3 (1972), 368; Jim Shields, "Education for Liberation," *New Schools Exchange Newsletter* #104, October 31, 1973; Summerhill Society quotation in *Inner Tooth* Vol. 1, No. 1, alternative newsletter published by The Inner College, University of Connecticut, 1970 or 1971, TDOC papers. I did not find supporting evidence for this claim. It is possible that *Inner Tooth* was a satirical publication and this story could have been a fabrication. Whether or not this was the case, the story illustrates the tension between the emphases on personal freedom and political action.

60. Jonathan Kozol, *Free Schools* (Boston: Houghton Mifflin, 1972), 58, 52, 27; Kozol, letters in *New Schools Exchange Newsletter* #65, September 30, 1971, and #98, May 15, 1973; Kozol quoted in Len Solo, *Alternative, Innovative, and Traditional Schools: Some Personal Views* (Lanham, MD: University Press of America, 1980), 29; Kozol, *Free Schools*, 11.

61. My own effort to build a holistic education movement that aims both for personal liberation and social justice has been hampered by the class bias,

or philosophical naivete, of "new age" followers who believe that a "transformation of consciousness" will lead to substantive social change. See my article, "Holistic Education in the United States: A 'New Paradigm' or a Cultural Struggle?" *Holistic Education Review* Vol. 6, No. 4 (1993), 12–18, and reprinted in my book *Caring for New Life: Essays on Holistic Education* (Brandon, VT: Foundation for Educational Renewal, 2000). David Purpel has written extensively about this issue, arguing that any "spiritual" understanding of education must include a "prophetic voice" that directly challenges injustice and suffering. See his books *The Moral and Spiritual Crisis in Education: A Curriculum for Justice and Compassion in Education* (Granby, MA: Bergin & Garvey, 1989) and *Moral Outrage in Education* (New York: Peter Lang, 1999).

62. Jonathan Kozol, letter in *Communications on Alternatives* #2, 1971.

63. Solo, *Alternative, Innovative, and Traditional Schools*, 30; Salli Rasberry and Robert Greenway, *Rasberry Exercises: How to Start Your Own School and Write a Book* (Albion, CA: Freestone, 1970), 37; Robert Greenway, untitled manuscript, NSE papers; Bhaerman and Denker, *No Particular Place to Go* (see note 4 above), 218.

64. Eric Davin, unpublished letter, October 26, 1973, NSE papers; Shields, "Education for Liberation."

65. Dennison, *The Lives of Children*, 6.

66. George Dennison letter, March 1972, NSE papers.

67. John Holt, letter in *Communications on Alternatives* #5, Spring 1972; George Dennison, untitled essay, *New Schools Exchange Newsletter* #65, September 30, 1971.

68. Rosenfeld, "Reflections on the Legacy of the Free Schools Movement," 486.

CHAPTER THREE

1. John Holt, letter in *Communications on Alternatives* #5, Spring 1972.

2. Richard S. Hootman, in an unpublished dissertation, reviewed Holt's writings and gave a fairly thorough summary of each of Holt's books. (See "The Romantic Critics of the Sixties: John Holt and Company" [Ph.D. dissertation, University of Iowa, 1976].) However, his analysis lacked historical perspective and presented Holt's ideas and proposals without adequately situating them in their cultural or intellectual context. In this study I draw upon Holt's numerous writings more selectively: rather than attempt a comprehensive review, I identify core themes that demonstrate Holt's relationship to radical politics and free school ideology. Also, I use material from Holt's letters and several obscure writings to which Hootman did not have access.

3. Interview with Susannah Sheffer, December 8, 1997.

4. John Holt, *A Life Worth Living: Selected Letters of John Holt*, ed. Susannah Sheffer (Columbus: Ohio State University Press, 1990), 17.

5. John Holt quoted in Mel Allen, "The Education of John Holt," reprint from *Yankee* magazine, December 1981, 6; *A Life Worth Living*, 27; Sheffer

interview; Peggy Hughes, "From the First 'Holt Associate,'" *Growing Without Schooling* #48, 1985.

6. Susannah Sheffer, in Holt, *A Life Worth Living*, 3, 231.

7. Sheffer interview; *A Life Worth Living*, 56–57.

8. John Holt, *Sharing Treasures: Book Reviews by John Holt*, ed. Patrick Farenga and Jane Prest Holcomb (Cambridge, MA: Holt Associates, 1990), 55; *A Life Worth Living*, 219, 276; David E. Purpel, *The Moral and Spiritual Crisis in Education: A Curriculum for Justice and Compassion in Education* (Granby, MA: Bergin & Garvey, 1989). Hootman (see note 2) pointed out Holt's tendency to cite other sources mainly to support his own ideas.

9. John Holt, letter of March 1, 1972, NSE papers; John Holt, untitled chapter in Harold Hart, ed., *Summerhill: For & Against* (New York: Hart, 1970), 97.

10. Peter Marin, review of *Freedom and Beyond* by John Holt, *Learning*, November 1972, 90.

11. *A Life Worth Living*, 24.

12. Ibid., 128, 105; John Holt, *Freedom and Beyond* (New York: Dutton, 1972; reprint, Portsmouth, NH: Boynton/Cook-Heinemann, 1995), 155, 138, 146; John Holt, *The Underachieving School* (New York: Pitman, 1969), 201; John Holt, "The Radicalizing of a Guest Teacher at Berkeley," *New York Times Magazine*, February 22, 1970, 65; *Sharing Treasures*, 58.

13. John Holt, quoted in Dave Lehman, untitled interview with Holt, *New Schools Exchange Newsletter* #113, March 15, 1974.

14. *A Life Worth Living*, 42, 235; interview with Patrick Farenga, December 8, 1997.

15. *A Life Worth Living*, 232.

16. Michael Lerner, *The Politics of Meaning* (Reading, MA: Addison Wesley, 1996), 28, 29, 7, 8.

17. John Holt, "Education and Peace," *Peace News* (London), August 26, 1966, 5; *The Underachieving School*, 130; *Freedom and Beyond*, 14, 236.

18. John Holt, *Teach Your Own: A Hopeful Path for Education* (New York: Dell, 1981), 37; *Sharing Treasures*, 12.

19. *Freedom and Beyond*, 164; *The Underachieving School*, 115; John Holt, *What Do I Do Monday?* (New York: Dutton, 1970; reprint, Portsmouth, NH: Boynton/Cook-Heinemann, 1995), 56; *A Life Worth Living*, 221.

20. *The Underachieving School*, 109; *A Life Worth Living*, 39; *What Do I Do Monday?* 82; *A Life Worth Living*, 66, 112.

21. *A Life Worth Living*, 131.

22. Allen Graubard, *Free the Children: Radical Reform and the Free School Movement* (New York: Vintage, 1974), 264; *The Underachieving School*, 75; Holt still expressed hope for public school reform in *What Do I Do Monday?*

23. Holt quoted in Graubard, *Free the Children*, 266, 267; Joseph Kirschner, "Free Schooling and the 'Fourth Great Awakening,'" *Review Journal of Philosophy and Social Science* Vol. 6 (1981).

24. John Holt, "Notes from Talks to Students," unpublished manuscript, November 23, 1971, Holt Associates files; *Freedom and Beyond*, 232; *A Life Worth Living*, 155, 195.

25. *A Life Worth Living*, 201; Nat Hentoff, review of *Freedom and Beyond* by John Holt, *Saturday Review*, July 8, 1972; Marin, review of *Freedom and Beyond.*

26. *A Life Worth Living*, 36; Sheffer, in *A Life Worth Living*, 8; *Teach Your Own*, 66, 67.

27. Mark Satin, *New Age Politics: Healing Self and Society* (New York: Delta, 1979).

28. Susan Douglas Franzosa, "The Best and Wisest Parent: A Critique of John Holt's Philosophy of Education," in Jane van Galen and Mary Anne Pitman, eds., *Home Schooling: Political, Historical, and Pedagogical Perspectives* (Norwood, NJ: Ablex, 1991); *What Do I Do Monday?* 240, *Freedom and Beyond*, 161ff.; Farenga interview; Sheffer interview.

29. John Holt, *How Children Fail* (New York: Pitman, 1964), 175.

30. John Holt, "Fundamental Reminders: We Learn for Ourselves," *Edcentric*, September 1972; *The Underachieving School*, 17.

31. *Freedom and Beyond*, 91; *What Do I Do Monday?* 27; *Teach Your Own*, 148, 149.

32. John Holt, letter in *This Magazine is About Schools* Vol. 2, No. 2 (1968), 26; *The Underachieving School*, 199, 200.

33. John Holt, untitled essay in *Growing Without Schooling* #17, 1980, 5.

34. Ibid., 5, 6.

35. *The Underachieving School*, 41; *What Do I Do Monday?* 28; *Freedom and Beyond*, 223.

36. *What Do I Do Monday?* 75, 76; *Freedom and Beyond*, 107, 167; *Teach Your Own*, 70–72.

37. Excerpts from the proceedings are taken from a photocopy of the *Congressional Record* in Holt's files at Holt Associates.

38. Hootman, "The Romantic Critics of the Sixties" (see note 2 above), 11; Neil Postman and Charles Weingartner, *The School Book: For People Who Want to Know What All the Hollering is About* (New York: Delacorte, 1973).

39. Jean Jacques Rousseau, *Emile* (1762; reprint, London: Dent, 1911), 56.

40. Franzosa, "The Best and Wisest Parent," 123.

41. Sanford W. Reitman, *The Educational Messiah Complex: American Faith in the Culturally Redemptive Power of Schooling* (Sacramento: Caddo Gap, 1992); see also Henry J. Perkinson, *The Imperfect Panacea: American Faith in Education, 1865–1965* (New York: Random House, 1968).

CHAPTER FOUR

1. In *Democracy in America*, Alexis de Tocqueville issued a prophetic warning about the rise of corporate industrialism that has largely been ignored. He observed that the new system of manufacturing "lowers the class of workmen" and "raises the class of masters" and then stated that "the manufacturing aristocracy which is growing up under our eyes is one of the harshest that ever existed in the world. . . . The friends of democracy should keep their eyes fixed firmly in this direction; for if ever a permanent inequality of conditions

and aristocracy again penetrate into the world, it may be predicted that this is the gate by which they will enter." *Democracy in America*, vol. 2, trans. Henry Reeve and Francis Bowen, ed. Phillips Bradley (1840; New York: Vintage, 1956), 169, 171.

2. Joseph Neef's *Sketch of a Plan and Method of Education* (1808; reprint, New York: Arno/New York Times, 1969) remains a classic exposition of countercultural educational thought. Much of what Neef wrote about freedom, knowledge, and experience would fit comfortably with the literature of the 1960s. See also Gerald L. Gutek, *Joseph Neef: The Americanization of Pestalozzianism* (Tuscaloosa: University of Alabama Press, 1978); Frederick Dahlstrand, *Amos Bronson Alcott: An Intellectual Biography* (East Brunswick, NJ: Associated University Presses, 1982); and Ron Miller, *What Are Schools For? Holistic Education in American Culture* (Brandon, VT: Holistic Education, 1997). Alcott quote from A. Bronson Alcott, *The Journals of Bronson Alcott*, ed. Odell Shepard (Boston: Little, Brown, 1938), 195.

3. See David Tyack, *The One Best System: A History of American Urban Education* (Cambridge, MA: Harvard University Press, 1974) and Neil G. McCluskey, *Public Schools and Moral Education: The Influence of Mann, Harris, and Dewey* (New York: Columbia University Press, 1958); Lawrence A. Cremin, *American Education: The Metropolitan Experience 1876–1980* (New York: Harper and Row, 1988), 227.

4. John Dewey and Evelyn Dewey, *Schools of Tomorrow* (New York: Dutton, 1915), 2.

5. Lawrence Cremin argued that the progressive education movement was directly connected to the free school movement, primarily due to John Dewey's influence on both. See "The Free School Movement: A Perspective," in Terrence E. Deal and Robert R. Nolan, eds., *Alternative Schools: Ideologies, Realities, Guidelines* (Chicago: Nelson-Hall, 1978). On the other hand, as Tate Hausman pointed out, the free school literature actually contains very few references to Dewey or progressive education. (I noted in the previous chapter that John Holt had not read Dewey's work at all.) Hausman, "A History of the Free School Movement" (senior thesis, Brown University, 1998). I will explore the complex relationship between Dewey and free school ideology in the following chapter. Here it is enough to say that progressive education as defined during the early years of the twentieth century was certainly in alignment with the free school movement, but did not fully address the concerns of the 1960s counterculture. In retrospect it is possible to identify intellectual consistencies, but the free school movement had a quality of its own due to its particular historical circumstances.

6. Joel Spring, *Wheels in the Head: Educational Philosophies of Authority, Freedom, and Culture from Socrates to Paulo Freire* (New York: McGraw Hill, 1994), 65. The major study of anarchist education in the early twentieth century is Paul Avrich's *The Modern School Movement: Anarchism and Education in the United States* (Princeton: Princeton University Press, 1980). Francisco Ferrer, *The Origin and Ideals of the Modern School*, trans. Joseph McCabe (New York: Putnam, 1913), 68. Quotation from Avrich, *The Modern School Movement*, 229.

7. Jonathan Kozol, *Free Schools* (Boston: Houghton Mifflin, 1972), 1, 6.

8. Interview with Bill Ayers, December 18, 1998.

9. For a moving account of Myles Horton's life and work, see *The Long Haul: An Autobiography*, by Horton with Judith Kohl and Herbert Kohl (Garden City, NY: Doubleday, 1990). Horton (1905–90) grew up in rural Appalachia, and while studying at the Union Theological Seminary in New York and the University of Chicago, found such mentors as John Dewey, Reinhold Niebuhr, and Jane Addams. He also spent time in the folk schools of Denmark, and adapted their approach to conditions in his native region. Joe Nathan (letter to author, September 21, 1999) has suggested that the citizenship schools run by Septima Clark and other African American activists in the South—encouraged by Myles Horton's support—along with street academies started in northern cities by chapters of the National Urban League, deserve more extensive treatment in any comprehensive study of the free school movement. I did not have the opportunity to research this topic thoroughly, but I agree that they represent an important dimension of the movement, demonstrating its roots in serious social activism. Quotation is from Claudia Berman, *The School Around Us: 25 Years* (Kennebunkport, ME: SAU, 1994), 32.

10. Allen Graubard, "The Free School Movement," *Harvard Educational Review* Vol. 42, No. 3 (1972); Len Solo, *Alternative, Innovative, and Traditional Schools: Some Personal Views* (Lanham, MD: University Press of America, 1980), 43; quotation from Hausman, "A History of the Free School Movement," 31.

11. Dave Lehman, untitled interview with John Holt, *New Schools Exchange Newsletter* #113, March 15, 1974; Gerald Friedberg, untitled essays, Summerhill Society *Bulletin* (June 1970 and September–October 1970).

12. Massachusetts school literature, TDOC papers.

13. Berman, *The School Around Us*, 137.

14. Allen Graubard, *Free the Children: Radical Reform and the Free School Movement* (New York: Vintage, 1974), 77; Berman, *The School Around Us*, 141; Herb Snitzer and Doris Ransohoff, *Today is for Children—Numbers Can Wait* (New York: Macmillan, 1972), 27, 28.

15. George Dennison, *The Lives of Children: The Story of the First Street School* (New York: Random House, 1969; reprint, Reading, MA: Addison Wesley, 1990), 31, 32.

16. Chris Mercogliano, *Making It Up as We Go Along: The Story of the Albany Free School* (Portsmouth, NH: Heinemann, 1998), 14.

17. Graubard, *Free the Children*, 124.

18. Mercogliano (cf. note 16) explains that numerous children who have come to the Albany Free School after experiencing failure and disciplinary action in other schools have changed their behavior dramatically in the freer atmosphere of his school. He provides compelling case studies of several children. In a more recent work, he argues that the millions of children being diagnosed with "attention deficit hyperactivity disorder" (ADHD) and sedated with psychoactive drugs because they do not conform to school discipline are not victims of any organic illness but of a ruthless system of behavior management. Again, he provides case studies of children who have thrived at the Free School after being

diagnosed with ADHD and drugged to be manageable in other environments. Chris Mercogliano, "Rid-a-Him: Or, Why Are So Many Kids Labeled and Drugged in School?" unpublished manuscript, 1999.

19. Hausman, "A History of the Free School Movement," 26. I agree with Hausman's assessment, and I have found many details of this history to be elusive. In a fairly extensive search of known collections of primary sources, I discovered only a few random samples of (or brief references to) various publications—most of them low-budget newsletters that were not collected by libraries—and brief reports of conferences usually held on campuses or campgrounds with little documentation, as well as conflicting estimates of numbers of free schools and shifting discussions about goals and methods. By pulling these scattered pieces of information together, it is at least possible to obtain a picture of a widely dispersed grassroots movement that flourished between 1969 and 1972 and continued to influence educators in some fashion well into the 1970s. For the purpose of this study, this impressionistic account will suffice, for the ideological meaning of these events is quite clear. A more thorough social history of the movement will require a far more extensive search of private collections of papers and memorabilia, and based on the evidence I have gathered I do not believe the additional details such a search might yield would affect my interpretation of the intellectual origins of the movement.

20. Frank Lindenfeld, "Easy Come, Easy Go: Growth and Turnover of Free Schools in North America," TDOC newsletter, August 1975 (reprinted from an unspecified issue of *New Schools Exchange Newsletter*); press release in NSE papers; Solo, *Alternative, Innovative, and Traditional Schools*; Stuart Rosenfeld, "Reflections on the Legacy of the Free Schools Movement," *Phi Delta Kappan* Vol. 59, No. 7 (1978).

21. Len Solo, "Some of Our Children May Live: A Study of Students in Alternative and Innovative Schools" (Ed.D. dissertation, University of Massachusetts, 1972); Jane Lichtman, *Bring Your Own Bag: A Report on Free Universities* (Washington, DC: American Association for Higher Education, 1973); Terry H. Anderson, *The Movement and the Sixties: Protest in America from Greensboro to Wounded Knee* (New York: Oxford University Press, 1995). Some researchers believe that "tens of thousands of intentional communities were created between the years 1965 and 1975," according to Daniel Bennett Greenberg in "Growing Up in Community: Children and Education Within Contemporary U.S. Intentional Communities" (Ph.D. dissertation, University of Minnesota, 1993), 17. Although this dramatic growth of communes constituted an important element of the counterculture, Greenberg points out that few of them provided sites for radical educational endeavors because most of their members were young adults with very young (if any) children, and most of the communal experiments were short-lived. Among the more stable and enduring communities that Greenberg studied in the early 1990s, more than half sent their children to public and alternative schools (such as Waldorf and Montessori schools) outside the communities—although many parents did experience conflict with the values taught in public schools. Other communities rejected public education "as a method of mass indoctrination into the dominant base values of the popular culture" and pursued homeschooling or other alternatives

within their communities (p. 75). The link between free school ideology and the intentional community movement is indirect; both reflect similar countercultural values but the free school literature has not exerted a strong influence on educational practices in communities. I reviewed issues of *Communities* magazine from 1973, 1984, and 1990 that focused on education, and found no significant references to free school literature.

22. Dave Lehman, untitled essay, *The Unicorn* Vol. 3, No. 1 (1984); interview with Len Solo, December 8, 1997; in "Some of Our Children May Live," Solo stated that TDOC as well as NSE received fifty inquiries a day.

23. Lehman, untitled essay; Jack Perron, "Alternative Publishing and Education," *Phi Delta Kappan* Vol. 54, No. 7 (1973).

24. Graubard quoted in Hausman, "A History of the Free School Movement," 23; North Country Festival described by Don Glines, letter to author, October 21, 1998.

25. Bill Harwood, untitled essay, *New Schools Exchange Newsletter* #134, June 30, 1976; Victoria Graham, "Indiana School Manages to Succeed," *Bloomington Courier-Tribune*, December 10, 1972.

26. Snitzer letter in NSE papers; Joe Nathan, "Let Us Be Extremely Frank—A Concise History of Public Alternative Schools," *New Schools Exchange Newsletter* #132, March 31, 1976.

27. *New Schools Exchange Newsletter* #23, October 25, 1969; interview with Madelin Colbert, November 13, 1998; Hausman, "A History of the Free School Movement," 33 n.

28. Hausman, "A History of the Free School Movement," 45, 46, 47.

29. Washington school document, TDOC papers; New Mexico school account in *New Schools Exchange Newsletter* #39, 1970; Frank Lindenfeld, untitled essay, Summerhill Society *Bulletin*, December 1967; Deal and Nolan, *Alternative Schools*, 119–21.

30. Ann Swidler, *Organization Without Authority: Dilemmas of Social Control in Free Schools* (Cambridge, MA: Harvard University Press, 1979), 3.

31. Unnamed author, untitled article, Summerhill Society *Bulletin*, February–April, 1970, 9; Herb Snitzer, letter to *New Schools Exchange Newsletter* #24, November 1, 1969; Colorado school document, TDOC papers; Swidler, *Organization Without Authority*, 124, 125.

32. Judson Jerome, *Culture Out of Anarchy: The Reconstruction of American Higher Learning* (New York: Herder and Herder, 1971), 133, 134; Jerry Mintz, personal communications with author, and interview of February 9, 1998.

33. Bonnie Barrett Stretch, "The Rise of the 'Free School,'" in Martin Carnoy, ed., *Schooling in a Corporate Society* (New York: David McKay, 1972), 217 (originally published in *Saturday Review*, June 20, 1970); Lindenfeld, untitled essay, 1967, 6; Friedberg, untitled essays, June and September–October 1970 (see note 11 above).

34. Hausman, "A History of the Free School Movement," 42; Todd Gitlin, *The Sixties: Years of Hope, Days of Rage*, rev. ed. (New York: Bantam, 1993), 435; Ira Shor, *Culture Wars: School and Society in the Conservative Restoration 1969–1984* (London: Routledge & Kegan Paul, 1986), 2.

35. Hausman, "A History of the Free School Movement," 44.

36. Interview with Jack Spicer, January 22, 1998; NCACS brochure, NSE papers.

37. Don Glines, letter to author, November 19, 1998; among the liberal reformers who specifically distinguished their ideas from the radical educators' critique were Charles Silberman, Roland Barth, and Ewald Nyquist; see Miller, *What Are Schools For?* 191; *Phi Delta Kappan* special issue, Vol. 54, No. 7 (1973). On the other hand, Joe Nathan, who has been active in public alternative education and charter schools for thirty years, commented upon reading a draft of this passage that "some of us *did* feel that way"—that is, that major cultural renewal, not simply educational change, was necessary.

38. Robert D. Barr, "Whatever Happened to the Free School Movement?" *Phi Delta Kappan* Vol. 54, No. 7 (1973), 456; Deal and Nolan, *Alternative Schools*; Mario Fantini, untitled article in *Changing Schools* #3, 1972; Mario Fantini, "Public Schools of Choice" (reprint of 1974 article), in Deal and Nolan, *Alternative Schools*, 50, 51, 53; Mario Fantini, ed., *Alternative Education: A Source Book for Parents, Teachers, Students, and Administrators* (Garden City, NY: Anchor/Doubleday, 1976). Again, Joe Nathan points out that some public school reformers dissented from Fantini's remarks, and some, such as Miriam Wasserman, continued to find value in the free school critique.

39. Don Glines, letter to author, October 21, 1998.

40. The exchange between Barr and Davin was published in *New Schools Exchange Newsletter* #94, March 15, 1973; quotation in parentheses from an untitled essay in *Changing Schools* #3, 1972.

41. Vernon Smith, untitled essay, *Changing Schools* #2; Solo interview, 1997; Fantini, *Alternative Education*; Jonathan Kozol, *Alternative Schools: A Guide for Educators and Parents* (New York: Continuum, 1982).

42. Barr, "Whatever Happened to the Free School Movement?" 457; Pacific Oaks College brochure, TDOC papers; William A. Shields, "J. Lloyd Trump: An Historical Perspective of an Innovator in American Education" (Ed.D. dissertation, Loyola University, Chicago, 1998); Glines letter of November 19, 1998.

43. Timothy W. Young, *Public Alternative Education: Options and Choice for Today's Schools* (New York: Teachers College Press, 1990); Robert D. Barr, untitled article in *Changing Schools* #13 (1975).

44. Michael Bakalis, in *Changing Schools* #15, 1976; untitled article in *Applesauce: A Journal for Alternative Education* Vol. 2, No. 6 (1978).

45. Thomas B. Gregory, "What Makes Alternative Schools Alternative?" *Holistic Education Review* Vol. 1, No. 2 (1988), 26.

46. Ivan Illich, *Deschooling Society* (New York: Harper and Row, 1970), 56, 68–69.

47. Friedberg, untitled essay, September–October 1970, 9; John Holt, *Teach Your Own: A Hopeful Path for Education* (New York: Dell, 1981), 4, 10.

48. Theodore R. Sizer, *Places for Learning, Places for Joy: Speculations on American School Reform* (Cambridge, MA: Harvard University Press, 1973), 1.

CHAPTER FIVE

1. Lawrence Cremin, "The Free School Movement: A Perspective," in Terrence E. Deal and Robert R. Nolan, eds., *Alternative Schools: Ideologies, Realities, Guidelines* (Chicago: Nelson-Hall, 1978); interview with Len Solo, December 8, 1997; Deal and Nolan, eds., *Alternative Schools,* 3; National Coalition of Alternative Community Schools, *There Ought to Be Free Choice* (1981–82 directory of alternative schools) (Ann Arbor, MI: Author, 1981); Neil Postman and Charles Weingartner, *The School Book: For People Who Want to Know What All the Hollering is About* (New York: Delacorte, 1973), 211; Stuart Rosenfeld, "Reflections on the Legacy of the Free Schools Movement," *Phi Delta Kappan* Vol. 59, No. 7 (1978), 487.

2. John Dewey, *Experience and Nature* (1925; New York: Dover, 1958), 51, 53, 20–21.

3. John Dewey, *Democracy and Education* (1916; paperback edition, New York: The Free Press/Macmillan, 1966), 86.

4. John Dewey, "Education and Social Change," in *The Later Works of John Dewey 1925–1953*, vol. 11 (Carbondale: Southern Illinois University Press, 1987), 415, 417.

5. John Dewey, "The Child and the Curriculum," in Reginald D. Archambault, ed., *John Dewey on Education: Selected Writings* (New York: Random House, 1964), 341; John Dewey, "The Need for a Philosophy of Education," in Archambault, *John Dewey on Education*, 9; Dewey, "The Child and the Curriculum," 344.

6. Robert B. Westbrook, *John Dewey and American Democracy* (Ithaca, NY: Cornell University Press, 1991), 109; Herbert M. Kliebard, *The Struggle for the American Curriculum, 1893–1958* (Boston: Routledge & Kegan Paul, 1986), 88.

7. Westbrook, *John Dewey and American Democracy*, 508, 509; Dewey, "The Need for a Philosophy of Education," in Archambault, *John Dewey on Education*, 13; John Dewey, *Liberalism and Social Action* (1935; paperback edition, New York: Capricorn, 1963), 61. "Can Education Share in Social Reconstruction?" (1934) was another essay expressing Dewey's more radical view of education and social change. He declared that individualism and laissez faire economics had failed to nourish either individuality or economic freedom for the majority of people and argued that schools should be allied with an agenda of "social control of economic forces." *Later Works,* vol. 9, 205–9.

8. Allen Graubard, *Free the Children: Radical Reform and the Free School Movement* (New York: Vintage, 1974), 44–45; Joseph Kirschner, "The Shifting Roles of Family and School as Educator: A Historical Perspective," in Jane van Galen and Mary Anne Pitman, eds., *Home Schooling: Political, Historical, and Pedagogical Perspectives* (Norwood, NJ: Ablex, 1991), 154.

9. John Holt, *What Do I Do Monday?* (New York: Dutton, 1970; reprint, Portsmouth, NH: Boynton/Cook-Heinemann, 1995), 272, 273; Steve Bhaerman and Joel Denker, *No Particular Place to Go: The Making of a Free High School* (New York: Simon and Schuster, 1972), 28; Paul Goodman, *Compulsory Mis-Education* and *The Community of Scholars* (New York: Vintage, 1964), 23, 24;

Susan Douglas Franzosa, "The Best and Wisest Parent: A Critique of John Holt's Philosophy of Education," in Jane van Galen and Mary Anne Pitman, eds., *Home Schooling: Political, Historical, and Pedagogical Perspectives* (Norwood, NJ: Ablex, 1991).

10. Editorial, Summerhill Society *Bulletin*, June 1970; Henry S. Resnik, *Turning On the System: War in the Philadelphia Public Schools* (New York: Pantheon, 1970), xi, xii, 99; Bhaerman and Denker, *No Particular Place to Go*, 63; Robert B. Westbrook, "Public Schooling and American Democracy," in Roger Soder, ed., *Democracy, Education, and the Schools* (San Francisco: Jossey Bass, 1996), 141.

11. John Holt, *Freedom and Beyond* (New York: Dutton, 1972; reprint, Portsmouth, NH: Boynton/Cook-Heinemann, 1995), 4; Jonathan Kozol, *Free Schools* (Boston: Houghton Mifflin, 1972), 14; Jonathan Kozol, "Look, This System is Not Working," Summerhill Society *Bulletin*, March–April 1971; Jonathan Kozol, "The Open Schoolroom: New Words for Old Deceptions," *New Schools Exchange Newsletter* #98, May 15, 1973; Jonathan Kozol, *The Night is Dark and I am Far from Home* (1975; New York: Simon and Schuster, 1990), 99, 226.

12. Kozol made this shift clear in his speech to the 1976 conference on alternative schools in Chicago and in an interview he gave at the time. He charged that those who had advocated entirely for children's freedom (he singled out Holt) "deserve to be blamed for the right wing swing which we are faced with now because we made a caricature of our vision." *New Schools Exchange Newsletter* #134, June 30, 1976; Donna Joy Newman, "Back to the Basics, Says Education's Unique Rebel," *Chicago Tribune*, June 2, 1976.

13. Jonathan Kozol, *Savage Inequalities: Children in America's Schools* (New York: Crown, 1991), 110, 4, 5, 176, 177.

14. Peter McLaren, with Henry A. Giroux, *Critical Pedagogy and Predatory Culture: Oppositional Politics in a Postmodern Era* (New York: Routledge, 1995), 30.

15. Graubard, *Free the Children*, 260; Edgar Z. Friedenberg, *Coming of Age in America* (New York: Random House, 1965), 222.

16. Peter Marin, letter in *New Schools Exchange Newsletter* #49, 1970, 7.

17. Eric Davin, unpublished manuscript, NSE papers.

18. Norman Solomon, "Alternatives and Liberation," *Edcentric* #37, February–March 1976, 8; Rosenfeld, "Reflections on the Legacy of the Free Schools Movement," 487, 488.

19. Amy Gutmann, *Democratic Education* (Princeton: Princeton University Press, 1987), 287, 12; Linda Darling-Hammond and Jacqueline Ancess, "Democracy and Access to Education," in Roger Soder, ed., *Democracy, Education, and the Schools* (San Francisco: Jossey Bass, 1996), 168.

20. Richard M. Battistoni, *Public Schooling and the Education of Democratic Citizens* (Jackson: University Press of Mississippi, 1985), 13; David Tyack and Elisabeth Hansot, "Conflict and Consensus in American Public Education," *Daedelus* Vol. 110, No. 3 (1981), 22, 23, 21.

21. Dewey, *Democracy and Education*, 5; Tyack and Hansot, "Conflict and Consensus," 20; Gutmann, *Democratic Education*, 5.

22. David T. Sehr, *Education for Public Democracy* (Albany: State University of New York Press, 1997), 5; Westbrook, "Public Schooling and American Democracy," 126; John I. Goodlad, "Democracy, Education, and Community," in Roger Soder, ed., *Democracy, Education, and the Schools* (San Francisco: Jossey Bass, 1996), 89, 92. Alan Ryan draws attention to Dewey's critique of individualism in *John Dewey and the High Tide of American Liberalism* (New York: Norton, 1995).

23. Dewey quoted in Westbrook, *John Dewey and American Democracy*, 106; Goodlad, "Democracy, Education, and Community," 93; Dennis Carlson, *Making Progress: Education and Culture in New Times* (New York: Teachers College Press, 1997), 72; Benjamin R. Barber, *An Aristocracy of Everyone: The Politics of Education and the Future of America* (New York: Ballantine, 1992), 4; Franzosa, "The Best and Wisest Parent," 133.

24. Sehr, *Education for Public Democracy*, 34–35.

25. John Dewey, *Experience and Education* (1938; reprinted edition, New York: Collier/Macmillan, 1963), 21, 64, 38, 71.

25. Dewey, "The Need for a Philosophy of Education," in Archambault, *John Dewey on Education*, 9; Battistoni, *Public Schooling and the Education of Democratic Citizens*, 141, 12; Sehr, *Education for Public Democracy*, 62. Lawrence Cremin made exactly the same point in a 1973 article, saying that "turning children loose in an unplanned and unstructured environment" was to abandon them "to the blind forces of the hucksters." "The Free School Movement: A Perspective" (see note 1), 208.

27. Barber, *An Aristocracy of Everyone*, 5, 210, 209.

28. Gutmann, *Democratic Education*, 30–31.

29. Robin Barrow, *Radical Education: A Critique of Freeschooling and Deschooling* (New York: Wiley, 1978), 179.

30. Lisa Delpit caused quite a stir in educational and academic circles when she argued that well-meaning progressive educators had not "come to terms with the concerns of poor and minority communities." Her critique applies to free school ideology although she did not specifically mention it. See *Other People's Children: Cultural Conflict in the Classroom* (New York: The New Press, 1995). Free school participant quoted in Richard E. Bull, *Summerhill USA* (Baltimore: Penguin, 1970), no page numbers. Jane Lichtman, *Bring Your Own Bag: A Report on Free Universities* (Washington, DC: American Association for Higher Education, 1973), 19.

31. James Miller, *"Democracy is in the Streets": From Port Huron to the Siege of Chicago* (New York: Simon and Schuster, 1987), 150; Tocqueville, *Democracy in America*, 316–17, 117, 118. Stephen Arons explicates Tocqueville's theory in *Short Route to Chaos: Conscience, Community, and the Reconstitution of American Schooling* (Amherst: University of Massachusetts Press, 1997), 125.

32. Critical theorists such as McLaren and Giroux, along with Michael Apple, Stanley Aronowitz, and many others whom I have not cited in this study, have also emphasized the role of public schools in the fight against the corporate/right wing privatization agenda. A national network of progressive, primarily urban public school teachers and parents, connected to the National

Coalition of Education Activists and the publication *Rethinking Schools*, have strongly defended public education as a principal means for achieving a more authentic democracy in the United States, and they strenuously oppose privatization schemes such as vouchers.

33. Stephen Arons, *Short Route to Chaos*, xv, 7, 99. Battistoni opens his argument for democratic public schooling by acknowledging the divisive court cases on education, allowing that they signal "a failure to maintain or achieve any community of meaning in the schools." Arons, unlike Battistoni, draws the conclusion that it is not desirable to attempt to create this community.

34. Joel Spring, *Wheels in the Head: Educational Philosophies of Authority, Freedom and Culture from Socrates to Paulo Freire* (New York: McGraw Hill, 1994).

35. Arons, *Short Route to Chaos*, 132. In another passage (p. 81), Arons interprets the Supreme Court's 1943 decision in *West Virginia v. Barnette* as meaning that "achieving national unity—like building communities of any size—must be a voluntary process. Common values and commitments are the products of shared life experiences, of accidents of history and moments of individual reflection, of teaching and study and the formation of conscience, all unencumbered by government coercion." John Holt stated, quite directly, that "It is time to think of American *Ways* of Life, of sharply separated and perhaps widely different cultures existing in this country in mutual respect and under the equal protection of the law." *The Underachieving School* (New York: Pitman, 1969), 123.

36. John Holt, *Sharing Treasures: Book Reviews by John Holt*, ed. Patrick Farenga and Jane Prest Holcomb (Cambridge, MA: Holt Associates, 1990), 7.

37. Carlson, *Making Progress*, 24, 114.

CHAPTER SIX

1. Ann Swider, *Organization Without Authority: Dilemmas of Social Control in Free Schools* (Cambridge, MA: Harvard University Press, 1979), 160–70.

2. Letter from Indiana in NSE papers, Yale University. Leonard Solo, "Strawberry Fields Forever: A Free School Deception?" *Centerpeace* Vol. 17 (Summer 1973); Leonard J. Solo, "Some of Our Children May Live: A Study of Students in Alternative and Innovative Schools" (Ed.D. dissertation, University of Massachusetts, 1972), 82. Len Solo, *Alternative, Innovative, and Traditional Schools: Some Personal Views* (Lanham, MD: University Press of America, 1980), 16. George Dennison, *The Lives of Children: The Story of the First Street School* (1969; reprint, Reading, MA: Addison Wesley, 1990), 105. Claire V. Korn drew attention to the problem of alternative educators being motivated more by opposition than a positive vision in *Alternative American Schools: Ideals in Action* (Albany: State University of New York Press, 1991), and Kathy Gross mentioned it in "A Student's View of the Successes and Failures of an Alternative School," in Terrence E. Deal and Robert R. Nolan, eds., *Alternative Schools: Ideologies, Realities, Guidelines* (Chicago: Nelson-Hall, 1978), 171.

3. Joel Spring, *Wheels in the Head: Educational Philosophies of Authority, Freedom, and Culture from Socrates to Paulo Freire* (New York: McGraw Hill, 1994), 76; Jonathan Kozol, *Alternative Schools: A Guide for Educators and Parents* (New York: Continuum, 1982), 7; Jane Lichtman, *Bring Your Own Bag: A Report on Free Universities* (Washington, DC: American Association for Higher Education, 1973), iii.

4. Lawrence Cremin, for example, stated that "the notoriously atheoretical, ahistorical character of the free school movement" clearly distinguished it from earlier expressions of progressive education. "The Free School Movement: A Perspective," in Terrence E. Deal and Robert R. Nolan, eds., *Alternative Schools: Ideologies, Realities, Guidelines* (Chicago: Nelson-Hall, 1978). Fred M. Hechinger, the widely read *New York Times* education writer of the period, was generally sympathetic to A. S. Neill's critique but warned that "the history of reforms is strewn with wreckage caused by kindly emotions defeated by lack of intellectual rigor." Untitled essay in *Summerhill: For & Against*, ed. Harold Hart (New York: Hart, 1970), 42. Allen Graubard recognized in *Free the Children: Radical Reform and the Free School Movement* (New York: Vintage, 1974) that free schoolers were often overly idealistic in their belief that a new culture could be "willed into existence by a small, well-meaning group of good people" and he concluded that the movement was, as a whole, unrealistically utopian—"a good dream, but a dream nonetheless" (165, 303–4).

5. Interview with Len Solo, December 8, 1997.

6. Swidler, *Organization Without Authority*, 149.

7. His Holiness the Dalai Lama, *Ethics for the New Millennium* (New York: Riverhead, 1999), 8.

8. Ivan Illich, *Deschooling Society* (New York: Harper and Row, 1970), 72. Pat Farenga, "Unschooling 2000," in Ron Miller, ed., *Educational Freedom for a Democratic Society: A Critique of National Goals, Standards and Curriculum* (Brandon, VT: Resource Center for Redesigning Education, 1995), 218. Probably the majority of the public perceives the presence of police and metal detectors, and the unconstitutional searching of students' lockers, as a necessary deterrent to violent crime in schools. Jerry Mintz, who has been active in alternative education since the mid-1960s, sees it differently, however, suggesting that violence in schools is an "armed rebellion" against an oppressive system, a desperate expression of pain and frustration (personal communication). From this perspective, bringing the police into schools is not so much about protecting students as suppressing their vital energies, just as drugging so-called hyperactive children, ostensibly to help them learn, is a means of forcing them to conform to the mechanistic routines of the system.

9. One might argue that the use of LSD and other hallucinogens was a foray into "virtual reality" as well. However, those who pursued this journey often reported a transformational experience of an *expanded* reality, a deeper knowledge of themselves in relation to the world, rather than a fictional reality programmed by clever engineers. Aldous Huxley, among others, emphasized that hallucinogens widened the "doors of perception"; computerized virtual reality, on the other hand, fools our perception and merely presents an entertaining illusion.

10. Some outstanding examples of this literature include James Moffett, *The Universal Schoolhouse: Spiritual Awakening Through Education* (San Francisco: Jossey Bass, 1994), Deborah Meier, *The Power of Their Ideas: Lessons for America from a Small School in Harlem* (Boston: Beacon, 1995), Chris Mercogliano, *Making it Up as We Go Along: The Story of the Albany Free School* (Portsmouth, NH: Heinemann, 1998), and Alfie Kohn, *The Schools Our Children Deserve: Moving Beyond Traditional Classrooms and "Tougher Standards"* (Boston: Houghton Mifflin, 1999).

11. Several years ago I wrote a critique of a volume that particularly represented the technocratic "progressive" agenda, and distinguished their social engineering approach from my own holistic perspective. The book was *Schooling for Tomorrow: Directing Reforms to Issues that Count,* edited by Thomas J. Sergiovanni and John H. Moore (Needham Heights, MA: Allyn and Bacon, 1989), and it was comprised of presentations made by twenty leading scholars and policy analysts at a 1987 conference—smack in the middle of the Reagan-era *Nation at Risk* school reform craze. It was filled with the language of statistics, management, professionalism, and utilitarian accommodation to the economic and political system. (Indeed, the authors explicitly agreed that schooling should serve the interests of the system.) See Ron Miller, "Schooling in the Modern Age: Core Assumptions Underlying the Standards Agenda," in Ron Miller, ed., *Educational Freedom for a Democratic Society*. I discussed the differences between Dewey's social democratic rationalism and the spiritual concerns of holistic education in Chapter Six of *What Are Schools For? Holistic Education and American Culture*, 3rd ed. (Brandon, VT: Holistic Education Press, 1997).

12. Lewis Mumford, "Monumentalism, Symbolism, and Style" (1948; reprinted in Lewis Mumford, *The Human Prospect*, ed. Harry T. Moore and Karl W. Deutsch [Boston: Beacon, 1955], 213, 214).

BIBLIOGRAPHY

Alcott, A. Bronson. *The Journals of Bronson Alcott.* Edited by Odell Shepard. Boston: Little, Brown, 1938.

Allen, Mel. "The Education of John Holt." Reprint from *Yankee* magazine, December 1981.

Anderson, Terry H. *The Movement and the Sixties: Protest in America from Greensboro to Wounded Knee.* New York: Oxford University Press, 1995.

Arons, Stephen. *Short Route to Chaos: Conscience, Community, and the Re-Constitution of American Schooling.* Amherst: University of Massachusetts Press, 1997.

Avrich, Paul. *The Modern School Movement: Anarchism and Education in the United States.* Princeton: Princeton University Press, 1980.

Ayers, Bill (director of The Children's Community School, Ann Arbor, mid-1960s; educational scholar at the University of Illinois at Chicago). Interviewed December 18, 1998.

Barber, Benjamin R. *An Aristocracy of Everyone: The Politics of Education and the Future of America.* New York: Ballantine, 1992.

Barr, Robert D. "Whatever Happened to the Free School Movement?" *Phi Delta Kappan* Vol. 54, No. 7 (March 1973), 454–57.

Barrow, Robin. *Radical Education: A Critique of Freeschooling and Deschooling.* New York: Wiley, 1978.

Barth, Roland S. *Open Education and the American School.* New York: Agathon, 1972.

Battistoni, Richard M. *Public Schooling and the Education of Democratic Citizens.* Jackson: University Press of Mississippi, 1985.

Berman, Claudia. *The School Around Us: 25 Years.* Kennebunkport, ME: SAU, 1994.

Bhaerman, Steve, and Joel Denker. *No Particular Place to Go: The Making of a Free High School.* New York: Simon and Schuster, 1972.

Branch, Taylor. *Parting the Waters: America in the King Years 1954–63.* New York: Simon and Schuster, 1988.

Bremer, John. "Some Thoughts on Education," pamphlet, School District of Philadelphia, May 1969, TDOC papers.

Bull, Richard E. *Summerhill USA.* Baltimore: Penguin, 1970.

Callahan, Raymond E. *Education and the Cult of Efficiency.* Chicago: University of Chicago Press, 1962.

Carlson, Dennis. *Making Progress: Education and Culture in New Times.* New York: Teachers College Press, 1997.

Cohen, Sol. *Challenging Orthodoxies: Toward a New Cultural History of Education.* New York: Peter Lang, 1999.

Colbert, Madelin (student at The Children's School, New Haven, CT). Interviewed November 13, 1998.

Collier, Peter, and David Horowitz. *Destructive Generation: Second Thoughts About the '60s*. New York: Summit/Simon and Schuster, 1989.

Counts, George C. *Dare the School Build a New Social Order?* New York: Day, 1932.

Cremin, Lawrence A. "The Free School Movement: A Perspective," in Terrence E. Deal and Robert R. Nolan, eds., *Alternative Schools: Ideologies, Realities, Guidelines*. Chicago: Nelson-Hall, 1978. (Originally published in *Notes on Education*, October 1973.)

———. *American Education: The Metropolitan Experience 1876–1980*. New York: Harper and Row, 1988.

Dahlstrand, Frederick C. *Amos Bronson Alcott: An Intellectual Biography*. East Brunswick, NJ: Associated University Presses, 1982.

Davis, Robert. Untitled editorial. *This Magazine is About Schools* Vol. 1, No. 2 (August 1966).

Deal, Terrence E., and Robert R. Nolan (editors). *Alternative Schools: Ideologies, Realities, Guidelines*. Chicago: Nelson-Hall, 1978.

Dennison, George. *The Lives of Children: The Story of the First Street School*. New York: Random House, 1969. Reissued 1990 by Addison Wesley (Reading, MA).

———. Untitled essay. *New Schools Exchange Newsletter #65*. September 30, 1971.

Dewey, John. *Democracy and Education* (1916). New York: The Free Press/Macmillan, 1966.

———. *Experience and Nature* (1925). New York: Dover, 1958.

———. "Why Have Progressive Schools?" (1933). *The Later Works of John Dewey 1925–1953*. Vol. 9, pp. 205–9. Carbondale: Southern Illinois University Press, 1986.

———. *Liberalism and Social Action* (1935). New York: Capricorn, 1963.

———. "Education and Social Change" (1937). *The Later Works of John Dewey 1925–1953*. Vol. 11. Carbondale: Southern Illinois University Press, 1987.

———. *Experience and Education* (1938). New York: Collier/Macmillan, 1963.

———. *John Dewey on Education: Selected Writings*. Edited by Reginald D. Archambault. New York: Random House, 1964.

Dewey, John, and Evelyn Dewey. *Schools of Tomorrow*. New York: Dutton, 1915.

Divoky, Diane. *How Old Will You Be in 1984? Expressions of Student Outrage from the High School Free Press*. New York: Avon, 1969.

Dreiske, Paul. "Summerhill Revisited." Summerhill Society *Bulletin* (January–February 1971).

Eisen, Jonathan, and David Steinberg. "The Student Revolt Against Liberalism," in Joseph Boskin and Robert A. Rosenstone, eds., *Seasons of Rebellion: Protest and Radicalism in Recent America*. New York: Holt, Rinehart & Winston, 1972.

Fantini, Mario. "Public Schools of Choice," in Terrence E. Deal and Robert R. Nolan, eds., *Alternative Schools: Ideologies, Realities, Guidelines*. op. cit., 1978. (Originally published in *Today's Education*, 1974.)

Fantini, Mario (editor). *Alternative Education: A Source Book for Parents, Teachers, Students, and Administrators*. Garden City, NY: Anchor/Doubleday, 1976.

Farber, David (editor). *The Sixties: From Memory to History*. Chapel Hill: University of North Carolina Press, 1994.

Farenga, Patrick (homeschooling activist and associate of John Holt; publisher of *Growing Without Schooling*). Interviewed December 8, 1997.

Farmer, James. *Lay Bare the Heart: An Autobiography of the Civil Rights Movement*. New York: Plume/New American Library, 1986.

Ferrer, Francisco. *The Origin and Ideals of the Modern School*. Translated by Joseph McCabe. New York: Putman, 1913.

Foner, Eric. *The Story of American Freedom*. New York: Norton, 1998.

Franzosa, Susan Douglas. "The Best and Wisest Parent: A Critique of John Holt's Philosophy of Education," in Jane van Galen and Mary Anne Pitman, eds., *Home Schooling: Political, Historical, and Pedagogical Perspectives*. Norwood, NJ: Ablex, 1991.

Fraser, Ronald (editor). *1968: A Student Generation in Revolt*. New York: Pantheon, 1988.

Friedberg, Gerald. Untitled essay. Summerhill Society *Bulletin*, June 1970; untitled essay, Summerhill Society *Bulletin*, September–October 1970.

Friedenberg, Edgar Z. *The Vanishing Adolescent*. Boston: Beacon, 1959.

———. *Coming of Age in America*. New York: Random House, 1965.

———. *The Dignity of Youth and Other Atavisms*. Boston: Beacon, 1965.

Gerzon, Mark. *The Whole World is Watching: A Young Man Looks at Youth's Dissent*. New York: Viking, 1969.

Gitlin, Todd. *The Sixties: Years of Hope, Days of Rage* (1987). New York: Bantam, 1993.

Glenn, Charles Leslie, Jr. *The Myth of the Common School*. Amherst: University of Massachusetts Press, 1988.

Glines, Don (radical public school reformer, popular speaker in 1960s and 1970s). Personal letters to author, October 21, 1998, and November 19, 1998.

Goodlad, John I. "Democracy, Education, and Community," in Roger Soder, ed., *Democracy, Education, and the Schools*. San Francisco: Jossey Bass, 1996.

Goodman, Paul. *Growing Up Absurd*. New York: Vintage, 1960.

———. *Compulsory Mis-Education* and *The Community of Scholars*. New York: Vintage Books, 1964.

———. *People or Personnel: Decentralizing and the Mixed System* and *Like a Conquered Province: The Moral Ambiguity of America*. New York: Vintage, 1968.

———. *Drawing the Line: The Political Essays of Paul Goodman* (1977). Edited by Taylor Stoehr. New York: Dutton, 1979.

Goodwin, Richard N. *Remembering America: A Voice from the Sixties*. New York: Harper and Row, 1989.

Graham, Victoria. "Indiana School Manages to Succeed." *Bloomington Courier-Tribune*, December 10, 1972, NSE papers.

Graubard, Allen. "The Free School Movement." *Harvard Educational Review* Vol. 42, No. 3 (August 1972), 351–73.

———. *Free the Children: Radical Reform and the Free School Movement*. New York: Vintage, 1974.

Gregory, Thomas B. "What Makes Alternative Schools Alternative?" *Holistic Education Review* Vol. 1, No. 2 (Summer 1988), 26.

Gross, Kathy. "A Student's View of the Successes and Failures of an Alternative School," in Terrence E. Deal and Robert R. Nolan, eds., *Alternative Schools: Ideologies, Realities, Guidelines*, op. cit., 1978.

Gross, Ronald, and Beatrice Gross (editors). *Radical School Reform*. New York: Simon and Schuster, 1969.

Gutek, Gerald Lee. *Joseph Neef: The Americanization of Pestalozzianism*. Tuscaloosa: University of Alabama Press, 1978.

Gutmann, Amy. *Democratic Education*. Princeton: Princeton University Press, 1987.

Harding, Vincent. *Hope and History: Why We Must Share the Story of the Movement*. Maryknoll, NY: Orbis, 1990.

Hart, Harold (editor). *Summerhill: For & Against*. New York: Hart, 1970.

Harwood, Bill. Untitled essay. *New Schools Exchange Newsletter*, #134, June 30, 1976.

Hausman, Tate. "A History of the Free School Movement." Unpublished senior thesis, Brown University, April 1998.

Henry, Jules. *Culture Against Man*. New York: Random House, 1963.

Hentoff, Nat. Review of *Freedom and Beyond* by John Holt. *Saturday Review*, July 8, 1972.

Hinman-Smith, Daniel. "'Does the Word Freedom Have a Meaning?' The Mississippi Freedom Schools, the Berkeley Free Speech Movement, and the Search for Freedom Through Education." Unpublished Ph.D. dissertation, University of North Carolina (Chapel Hill), 1993.

Hodgson, Godfrey. *America in Our Time*. Garden City, NY: Doubleday, 1976.

Holt, John. *How Children Fail*. New York: Pitman, 1964.

———. "Education and Peace." *Peace News* (London), August 26, 1966.

———. Untitled letter. *This Magazine is About Schools* Vol. 2, No. 2 (Spring 1968).

———. *The Underachieving School*. New York: Dell, 1969.

———. Testimony before the subcommittee on education, U.S. House of Representatives, December 17, 1969. *Congressional Record* excerpt, Holt papers, Holt Associates.

———. "The Radicalizing of a Guest Teacher at Berkeley." *New York Times Magazine*, February 22, 1970.

———. *What Do I Do Monday?* (1970). Portsmouth, NH: Boynton/Cook, 1995.

———. "Notes from Talks to Students." Unpublished manuscript, November 23, 1971. Holt Associates.

———. "Fundamental Reminders: We Learn for Ourselves." *Edcentric*. September 1972.

———. *Freedom and Beyond* (1972). Portsmouth, NH: Boynton/Cook, 1995.

———. Untitled essay. *Growing Without Schooling*, No. 17. Boston: Holt Associates, 1980.

———. *Teach Your Own: A Hopeful Path for Education*. New York: Dell, 1981.

———. *A Life Worth Living: Selected Letters of John Holt*. Edited by Susannah Sheffer. Columbus: Ohio State University Press, 1990.

———. *Sharing Treasures: Book Reviews by John Holt*. Edited by Patrick Farenga and Jane Prest Holcomb. Cambridge, MA: Holt Associates, 1990.

Hootman, Richard S. "The Romantic Critics of the Sixties: John Holt and Company." Unpublished Ph.D. dissertation, University of Iowa, 1976.

Horton, Myles; with Herbert Kohl and Judith Kohl. *The Long Haul: An Autobiography*. New York: Doubleday, 1990.

Hughes, Peggy. "From the First 'Holt Associate.'" *Growing Without Schooling*, No. 48. Boston: Holt Associates, 1985.

Hutchins, Robert M. "The Schools Must Stay." *The Center Magazine* Vol. 6, No. 1 (January–February 1973), 12–23.

Illich, Ivan. *Deschooling Society*. New York: Harper and Row, 1970.

Jamison, Andrew, and Ron Eyerman. *Seeds of the Sixties*. Berkeley: University of California Press, 1994.

Jerome, Judson. *Culture Out of Anarchy: The Reconstruction of American Higher Learning*. New York: Herder and Herder, 1971.

Kaestle, Carl F. *Pillars of the Republic: Common Schools and American Society, 1780–1860*. New York: Hill and Wang, 1983.

Karier, Clarence J. *The Individual, Society, and Education: A History of American Educational Ideas*. 2nd ed. Urbana: University of Illinois Press, 1986.

Katz, Michael. *The Irony of Early School Reform*. Cambridge, MA: Harvard University Press, 1968.

Kemnitzer, David. "Educational Reform-Revolution." *Edcentric*, June–July 1970.

Kirschner, Joseph. "Free Schooling and the 'Fourth Great Awakening.'" *Review Journal of Philosophy and Social Science* 6 (1981), 72–82.

———. "The Shifting Roles of Family and School as Educator: A Historical Perspective," in Jane van Galen and Mary Anne Pitman, eds., *Home Schooling: Political, Historical, and Pedagogical Perspectives*. Norwood, NJ: Ablex, 1991.

Kliebard, Herbert M. *The Struggle for the American Curriculum, 1893–1958*. Boston: Routledge & Kegan Paul, 1986.

KOA (Kommunications on Alternatives). A short-lived newsletter published in 1971–72. After issue #1, "Communications" was spelled conventionally.

Korn, Claire V. *Alternative American Schools: Ideals in Action*. Albany: State University of New York Press, 1991.

Kozol, Jonathan. *Death at an Early Age: The Destruction of the Hearts and Minds of Negro Children in the Boston Public Schools*. Boston: Houghton Mifflin, 1967.

———. "Look, This System is Not Working." Summerhill Society *Bulletin*, March–April 1971, reprinted from the *New York Times*, April 1971.

———. *Free Schools*. Boston: Houghton Mifflin, 1972.
———. "The Open Schoolroom: New Words for Old Deceptions." *New Schools Exchange Newsletter* #98, May 15, 1973.
———. *The Night is Dark and I am Far from Home* (1975). New York: Simon and Schuster, 1990.
———. *Alternative Schools: A Guide for Educators and Parents*. New York: Continuum, 1982.
———. *Savage Inequalities: Children in America's Schools*. New York: Crown, 1991.
Lehman, Dave. Untitled interview of John Holt. *New Schools Exchange Newsletter* #113, March 15, 1974.
———. Untitled essay. *The Unicorn* (Alternative Schools Exchange, Ithaca, NY) Vol. 3, No. 1 (Spring 1984).
Leonard, George. *Walking on the Edge of the World: A Memoir of the Sixties and Beyond*. Boston: Houghton Mifflin, 1988.
Lerner, Michael. *The Politics of Meaning*. Reading, MA: Addison Wesley, 1996.
Lewis, Peter Stephen. "Private Education and the Subcultures of Dissent: Alternative/Free Schools (1965–1975) and Christian Fundamentalist Schools (1965–1990)." Unpublished Ph.D. dissertation, Stanford University, 1991.
Lichtman, Jane. *Bring Your Own Bag: A Report on Free Universities*. Washington, DC: American Association for Higher Education, 1973.
Lindenfeld, Frank. Untitled essay. Summerhill Society *Bulletin*, December 1967.
———. "Easy Come, Easy Go: Growth and Turnover of Free Schools in North America." Teacher Drop Out Center Newsletter (Amherst, MA), August 1975. (Reprinted from an unspecified issue of *New Schools Exchange Newsletter*.)
Marin, Peter. "The Open Truth and Fiery Vehemence of Youth: A Sort of Soliloquy." *The Center Magazine* Vol. 2, No.1 (January 1969), 61–74.
———. Untitled letter, *New Schools Exchange Newsletter* #49, 1970, 7.
———. Review of *Freedom and Beyond* by John Holt. *Learning*, November 1972, 90.
Matusow, Allen J. *The Unraveling of America: A History of Liberalism in the 1960s*. New York: Harper and Row, 1984.
McCluskey, Neil G. *Public Schools and Moral Education: The Influence of Mann, Harris, and Dewey*. New York: Columbia University Press, 1958.
McLaren, Peter, with Henry A. Giroux. *Critical Pedagogy and Predatory Culture: Oppositional Politics in a Postmodern Era*. New York: Routledge, 1995.
Mercogliano, Chris. *Making It Up as We Go Along: The Story of the Albany Free School*. Portsmouth, NH: Heinemann, 1998.
Miller, James. "*Democracy is in the Streets*": *From Port Huron to the Siege of Chicago*. New York: Simon and Schuster, 1987.
Miller, Ron. *What Are Schools For? Holistic Education in American Culture* (1990). Brandon, VT: Holistic Education Press, 1997.
———. *Educational Freedom for a Democratic Society: A Critique of National Goals, Standards and Curriculum*. Brandon, VT: Resource Center for Redesigning Education, 1995.

Mintz, Jerry (alternative school activist since 1965; founder of Alternative Education Resource Organization). Interviewed February 9, 1998.

Mumford, Lewis. *The Human Prospect.* Edited by Harry T. Moore and Karl W. Deutsch. Boston: Beacon, 1955.

Nasaw, David. *Schooled to Order: A Social History of Public Schooling in the United States.* New York: Oxford University Press, 1979.

Nathan, Joe. "Let Us Be Extremely Frank—A Concise History of Public Alternative Schools." *New Schools Exchange Newsletter,* #132, March 31, 1976.

National Coalition of Alternative Community Schools (NCACS). *There Ought to Be Free Choice* (1981–82 Directory of Alternative Schools). Ann Arbor, MI: Author, 1981.

National Commission on Excellence in Education (NCEE). *A Nation at Risk: The Imperative for Educational Reform.* Washington, DC: U.S. Government Printing Office, 1983.

Neef, Joseph. *Sketch of a Plan and Method of Education* (1808). New York: Arno/New York Times, 1969.

Neill, A. S. *Summerhill: A Radical Approach to Child Rearing.* New York: Hart, 1960.

New Jersey Student Union. "Resource Catalog for Reforming Change and Survival in the Schools." NJ: Author, n.d. (probably around 1970).

New Schools Exchange (NSE) Papers. Manuscripts and Archives Department, Sterling Memorial Library, Yale University.

Nyquist, Ewald, and Gene R. Hawes. *Open Education: A Sourcebook for Parents and Teachers.* New York: Bantam, 1972.

Parker, Francis W. *Talks on Pedagogics* (1894). New York: Arno/New York Times, 1969.

Perkinson, Henry J. *The Imperfect Panacea: American Faith in Education, 1865–1965.* New York: Random House, 1968.

———. *Two Hundred Years of American Educational Thought.* New York: David McKay, 1976.

Perron, Jack. "Alternative Publishing and Education." *Phi Delta Kappan* Vol. 54, No. 7 (March 1973), 461–64.

Postman, Neil, and Charles Weingartner. *The School Book: For People Who Want to Know What All the Hollering is About.* New York: Delacorte, 1973.

Purpel, David. *The Moral and Spiritual Crisis in Education: A Curriculum for Justice and Compassion in Education.* Granby, MA: Bergin & Garvey, 1989.

Rasberry, Salli, and Robert Greenway. *Rasberry Exercises: How to Start Your Own School and Make a Book.* Albion, CA: Freestone, 1970.

Ravitch, Diane. *The Troubled Crusade: American Education 1945–1980.* New York: Basic, 1983.

Reitman, Sanford W. *The Educational Messiah Complex: American Faith in the Culturally Redemptive Power of Schooling.* Sacramento: Caddo Gap, 1992.

Resnik, Henry S. *Turning On the System: War in the Philadelphia Public Schools.* New York: Pantheon, 1970.

Rogers, Carl. *Freedom to Learn.* Columbus, OH: Merrill, 1969.

Rosenfeld, Stuart. "Reflections on the Legacy of the Free Schools Movement." *Phi Delta Kappan* Vol. 59, No. 7 (March 1978), 486–489.

Rossinow, Doug. *The Politics of Authenticity: Liberalism, Christianity, and the New Left in America*. New York: Columbia University Press, 1998.

Rossman, Michael. *The Wedding Within the War*. Garden City, NY: Doubleday, 1971.

Roszak, Theodore. *The Making of a Counter Culture*. Garden City, NY: Anchor/Doubleday, 1969.

Roszak, Theodore (editor). *The Dissenting Academy*. New York: Random House, 1967.

Rousseau, Jean Jacques. *Emile* (1762). London: Dent, 1911.

Satin, Mark. *New Age Politics: Healing Self and Society*. New York: Delta, 1979.

Schulman, Bruce J. "Out of the Streets and into the Classroom?: The New Left and the Counterculture in U.S. History Textbooks," prepublication manuscript, 1998.

Sehr, David T. *Education for Public Democracy*. Albany: State University of New York Press, 1997.

Sheffer, Susannah (editor of John Holt's papers and of *Growing Without Schooling*). Interviewed December 8, 1997.

Shields, Jim. "Education for Liberation." *New Schools Exchange Newsletter* #104, October 31, 1973.

Shields, William A. "J. Lloyd Trump: An Historical Perspective of an Innovator in American Education." Unpublished Ed.D. dissertation, Loyola University (Chicago), 1998.

Shor, Ira. *Culture Wars: School and Society in the Conservative Restoration 1969–1984*. London: Routledge & Kegan Paul, 1986.

Silberman, Charles. *Crisis in the Classroom*. New York: Random House, 1970.

Sizer, Theodore R. *Places for Learning, Places for Joy: Speculations on American School Reform*. Cambridge, MA: Harvard University Press, 1973.

Snitzer, Herb. "At the Heart of the Matter—It's a Matter of Heart." *New Schools Exchange Newsletter* #92, February 15, 1973.

Snitzer, Herb, and Doris Ransohoff. *Today is for Children—Numbers Can Wait*. New York: Macmillan, 1972.

Soder, Roger (editor). *Democracy, Education, and the Schools*. San Francisco: Jossey Bass, 1996.

Solo, Len. "Some of our Children May Live: A Study of Students in Alternative and Innovative Schools." Unpublished Ed.D. dissertation, University of Massachusetts, 1972.

———. *Alternative, Innovative, and Traditional Schools: Some Personal Views*. Lanham, MD: University Press of America, 1980.

———. (co-founder of the Teacher Drop Out Center in 1969; public alternative school principal since 1974). Interviewed December 8, 1997.

Solomon, Norman. "Alternatives and Liberation." *Edcentric* #37. February–March 1976.

Spicer, Jack (teacher at Pacific High School, 1968–70). Interviewed January 22, 1998.

Spring, Joel. *Wheels in the Head: Educational Philosophies of Authority, Freedom, and Culture from Socrates to Paulo Freire*. New York: McGraw Hill, 1994.

Stevens, William K. "Bright Milwaukee Students Find School Dull and Form their Own." *New York Times*, February 13, 1970.

Stretch, Bonnie Barrett. "The Rise of the 'Free School,'" in Martin Carnoy, ed., *Schooling in a Corporate Society*. New York: David McKay, 1972. (Originally published in *Saturday Review*, June 20, 1970.)

Swidler, Ann. *Organization Without Authority: Dilemmas of Social Control in Free Schools*. Cambridge, MA: Harvard University Press, 1979.

Theobald, Robert. *An Alternative Future for America*. Chicago: Swallow, 1968/1970.

Tyack, David. *The One Best System: A History of American Urban Education*. Cambridge, MA: Harvard University Press, 1974.

Tyack, David, and Elisabeth Hansot. "Conflict and Consensus in American Public Education." *Daedalus* Vol. 110, No. 3 (1981), 1–25.

Wallerstein, Immanuel, and Paul Starr. *The University Crisis Reader*, Volume II: *Confrontation and Counterattack*. New York: Random House, 1971.

Welter, Rush. *Popular Education and Democratic Thought in America*. New York: Columbia University Press, 1962.

Westbrook, Robert B. *John Dewey and American Democracy*. Ithaca, NY: Cornell University Press, 1991.

———. "Public Schooling and American Democracy," in Roger Soder, ed., *Democracy, Education, and the Schools*. San Francisco: Jossey Bass, 1996.

Williams, Mike. "Rancho Mariposa: Something New and Different in Education." *Ukiah Daily Journal*, January 27, 1971, 8, TDOC papers.

Young, Timothy W. *Public Alternative Education: Options and Choice for Today's Schools*. New York: Teachers College Press, 1990.

INDEX